Critics and Poets
on Marianne Moore

Critics and Poets
on Marianne Moore

"A Right Good Salvo of Barks"

Edited by

Linda Leavell, Cristanne Miller, and Robin G. Schulze

Lewisburg
Bucknell University Press

Associated University Presses
2010 Eastpark Boulevard
Cranbury, NJ 08512

The paper used in this publication meets the requirements of the American National Standard for Permanence of Paper for Printed Library Materials Z39.48-1984.

Library of Congress Cataloging-in-Publication Data

Critics and poets on Marianne Moore : "A right good salvo of barks" / edited
    by Linda Leavell, Cristanne Miller, and Robin G. Schulze.
       p.   cm.
    Includes bibliographical references and index.
    ISBN 0-8387-5616-6 (alk. paper)
    1. Moore, Marianne, 1887–1972—Criticism and interpretation.   2. Women
and literature—United States—History—20th century.   I. Leavell, Linda, 1954–
II. Miller, Cristanne.   III. Schulze, Robin G., 1961–   IV. Title.
    PS3525.O5616Z64   2005
    811′.52—dc22

                                                                              2005000637

PRINTED IN THE UNITED STATES OF AMERICA

Contents

Preface

Small dog, going over the lawn nipping the linen and saying
that you have a badger—remember Xenophon;
only rudimentary behavior is necessary to put us on the scent.
"A right good salvo of barks," a few strong wrinkles puckering the
       skin between the ears, is all we ask.
           —("Picking and Choosing," *CPo* 45)

For MARIANNE MOORE THE TASK OF THE CRITIC AND THE TASK OF THE poet were never far apart. Both must engage in "picking and choosing." Like the advertiser, both must "educat[e] visualization" (*CPr* 215); like Xenophon's hunting dog, both must "put us on the scent." The essays and poems collected here attempt to show that the trails to understanding Marianne Moore and her place in literary history are as redolent as ever.

Moore's poems, moreover, "put us on the scent" to understanding the pressing issues of the twenty-first century, just as they did those of the early twentieth century when she began writing. The continuing relevance of Moore's poetry was brought most dramatically to public consciousness following September 11, 2001, when Robert Pinsky chose to read "What Are Years" on public television, presenting Moore's rumination on personal responsibility and the horrors of World War II as a poetic call to courage.[1] Several of the essays in this volume address Moore's responsiveness to national and international cultural and political crises or controversies, as reviewed below. In other areas as well, her engagement at multiple levels with multiple issues remains instructive. In "The Labours of Hercules," first published in the *Dial* in 1921, Moore concludes with emphatic insistence that despite "controversialists" "one keeps on knowing / 'that the negro is not brutal, / that the Jew is not greedy, / that the Oriental is not immoral, / that the German is not a Hun'" (*BMM* 265). While her vocabulary ("negro" "Oriental") and the reference to American prejudices during World War I (Germans as "Huns") now sound dated, the conviction that it requires constant "labor" to resist prejudices exacerbated by international conflict strikes us with new timeliness today, in light of the anti-Arab sentiment that threatens to overtake reasonable response to the dangers of terrorism. Moore's life and poems also prove useful in relation to current reconsiderations of the identity politics of sexuality. As late twentieth- and twenty-first-century critical theory comes to recognize the limitations in easily definable categorizations of sexuality ("gay," "straight," "bisexual"), Moore's resistance to restrictive sexological definitions of the early twentieth century seems germane: through characteristic indirection, she encourages thorniness in the feminine rose, praises maternal qualities in the "hero," and relishes the sensuality of physical detail through what might be considered an open erotics of observation rather than the narrower lines of narrative erotic encounter. Moore's poems have also found a contemporary audience with those who study literature and the environment. Her ethical explorations of the human relationship to the natural world and her appreciation of biodiversity speak to present ecological concerns. These are exciting directions for Moore studies, and for the study of American poetic modernism, that reassert Moore's centrality to a critical and poetic field in which she has been surprisingly marginalized.

This is the first collection of essays about Marianne Moore to appear in well over a decade. In 1948 the *Quarterly Review of Literature* created the first such collection with a special issue devoted to her work. It includes such notable poets and critics as Elizabeth Bishop, Louise Bogan, Cleanth Brooks, Wallace Stevens, and William Carlos Williams. Two collections appeared in the 1960s. *Festschrift for Marianne Moore's Seventy Seventh Birthday* (1964), edited by Tambimuttu, contains tributes, reminiscences, poems and drawings by her friends and admirers. The latter include many prominent poets of the day—John Ciardi, Stanley Kunitz, May Swenson, Robert Penn Warren, Richard Wilbur—with voices as unlikely as Louis Untermeyer at one extreme and Allen Ginsberg at another. Still invaluable as an introduction to Moore's work is Charles Tomlinson's *Marianne Moore: A Collection of Critical Essays* (1969), which attests to the high esteem Moore earned early from her peers—Eliot, Pound, Stevens, and Williams—and from the critics who defined modernism for the next generation—R. P. Blackmur, Kenneth Burke, Denis Donoghue, Randall Jarrell, Hugh Kenner, Roy Harvey Pearce, and John Crowe Ransom.[2]

Fifteen years would elapse before the next collection of essays, *Twentieth-Century Literature*'s special issue on Moore (1984), edited by Andrew J. Kappel. Kappel brought together the first group of scholars who (along with Laurence Stapleton) made use of the Moore archive at the Rosenbach Museum & Library: Bonnie Costello, Celeste Goodridge, Margaret Holley, Taffy Martin, Grace Schulman, John M. Slatin, Lisa M. Steinman, and Patricia C. Willis.[3] These would be the most influential scholars and critics of Moore to emerge in the 1980s.

The centennial of Moore's birth, 1987, precipitated several important gatherings in her honor. A month-long celebration in Chicago, sponsored by the Modern Poetry Association, resulted in *Marianne Moore: The Art of a Modernist* (1990), edited by Joseph Parisi. This volume of essays includes poet-critics David Bromwich, Sandra M. Gilbert, John Hollander, Richard Howard, Maxine Kumin, Alicia Ostriker, and Robert Pinsky. The centennial conference hosted by the National Poetry Foundation at Orono, Maine, attracted a great number of scholars, including those just making a name for themselves in the field of Moore studies and many of those soon to do so. The conference spawned two collections of essays: *Marianne Moore: Woman and Poet* (1990), edited by Patricia C. Willis; and a special issue of *Sagetrieb* (1987), guest edited by Celeste Goodridge. Also that year Harold Bloom added *Marianne Moore* to his Modern Critical Views series. *Helicon Nine, Poesis,* and the *William Carlos Williams Review* honored the centennial with special issues.[4]

The emergence of feminist criticism in the 1970s at first seemed to elide Moore, but by her centennial it was becoming evident not only that Moore championed woman suffrage in her youth but also that her poetry—in form as well as content—subverted patriarchal authority well after she earned the right to vote. Subsequent years have seen the publication of important feminist studies of Moore—by Joanne Feit Diehl, Betsy Erkkila, Sandra M. Gilbert and Susan Gubar, Jeanne Heuving, Cynthia Hogue, Kathryn R. Kent, Jayne E. Marek, Jeredith Merrin, Cristanne Miller, Sabine Sielke, Lesley Wheeler, and Kirstin Hotelling Zona.[5] Moore has long been considered a modernist, but recent work by George Bornstein, Darlene Williams Erickson, James Fenton, Elizabeth Gregory, Elisabeth W. Joyce, David Kadlec, Christopher J. Knight, Andrew M. Lakritz, Linda Leavell, Catherine Paul, Zhaoming Qian, Robin G. Schulze, and Cynthia Stamy has enhanced our understanding of the interpersonal, interdisciplinary, and intercultural dimensions of that movement.[6] Moore has also figured prominently in recent studies by Bonnie Costello, Randy Malamud, Timothy Morris, Elisa New, Richard Poirier, Guy L. Rotella, and John Vincent that define ecocritical, "queer," or other (mostly) American literary traditions.[7] Marianne Moore's engagement with cultural and political history is by now irrefutable. It is no longer possible to dismiss this poet as a demure eccentric.

In 1986 Patricia C. Willis collected the remarkable oeuvre of Moore's criticism in *The Complete Prose of Marianne Moore*. Craig S. Abbott's *Marianne Moore: A Descriptive Bibliography* had been available since 1977 and Gary Lane's *A Concordance to the Poems of Marianne Moore* since 1972. Otherwise, scholarship on Moore has been slow to catch up with that of her modernist peers. There was no full-length biography until Charles Molesworth's *Marianne Moore: A Literary Life* in 1990. *The Selected Letters of Marianne Moore* (1997), edited by Bonnie Costello with Celeste Goodridge and Cristanne Miller, now allows readers to glimpse Moore's voluminous correspondence without a pilgrimage to the Rosenbach. And *The Critical Response to Marianne Moore* (2003), edited by

Elizabeth Gregory, provides a much needed reception history of Moore's work.[8]

Although Moore proclaimed that "omissions are not accidents" in her misnamed *Complete Poems* (1967; revised 1981), it has frustrated scholars and general readers alike that more than a third of the poems published in Moore's lifetime had to be tracked down in special collections and rare book rooms. This situation is at last remedied with the publication of two important collections. *Becoming Marianne Moore: The Early Poems, 1907–1924* (2002), edited by Robin G. Schulze, reproduces in facsimile Moore's complete oeuvre of published poems through 1924 and includes varioum information about each one. It also makes available a facsimile of *Observations,* the long-out-of-print collection that earned Moore the *Dial* award in 1925 and established her reputation as a modernist. Serving a broader readership, *The Poems of Marianne Moore* (2003), edited by Grace Schulman, arranges in chronological order all of Moore's poems that appeared in print and many that remained in typescript.[9] Both of these volumes allow readers to examine for themselves the chronological development of Moore's poetry.

Given the greater accessibility to Moore's work provided by these new editions and the fifteen years since the centennial conference at Orono, the editors of this volume decided it was time for a reassessment of Moore's work. We organized a conference in March 2003 on the campus of Pennsylvania State University. The present volume grew out of that conference. Marianne Moore is coming into sharper focus, we find, because of changes in the critical lenses scholars are using to examine her work. The restoration of religion, for example, as a category of literary analysis equivalent to race, class, and gender opens up long neglected aspects of Moore's ethics and politics. The emerging field of ecocriticism brings new insights into Moore's poems about plants and animals. Reception theory prompts a reexamination of Moore's public persona. The concept of "hybridity" from border theory and postcolonial theory grants new perspectives upon Moore's complex notions of nationhood. And the restoration of sex and gender as historical rather than psychoanalytic categories allows critics to reread Moore's notions of personal identity.

Some of the essays collected here analyze Moore's poems as products of their particular times and places. In "'What Is War For?': Moore's Development of an Ethical Poetry," Cristanne Miller argues that World War I prompted Moore to undertake a search for models of ethical speech in wartime that led her to the Hebrew poet-prophets of the Bible. Miller's readings of Moore's numerous "poet-prophet" poems make clear the importance of the war to both Moore's early verse and her lifelong conception of poetry as a necessarily ethical activity vital to the creation of human community. In her essay "'The magnitude of their root systems': 'An Octopus' and National Character," Fiona Green places Moore's great poem of the 1920s in the context of early twentieth-century discourses about eugenics and race. "An Octopus," Green argues, responds directly to a variety of contemporary arguments about how to best maintain America's national vigor, and racial purity, in the face of massive immigration. Charles Berger, in turn, reads a group of Moore's poems from the 1930s in the context of her growing concerns about the rise of destructive ideologies of nationalism and hero-worship both at home and abroad. Berger's essay, "The 'Not-Native' Moore: Hybridity and Heroism in the Thirties," suggests that Moore's poetry of the 1930s constructs a vision of hybrid citizenship that challenges fascist conceptions of authentic national identity. Moore's poems of the period, Berger argues, explore the dangers that arise when "native moves in the direction of nativism" and claims to propriety become the means to oppress others.

Other essays offered here reconsider Moore's verse in the context of sex and gender. In her essay, "'Injudicious Gardening': Marianne Moore, Gender, and the Hazards of Domestication," Robin Schulze restores the context of early twentieth-century biodeterministic notions of maleness and femaleness in order to explore the ways in which Moore's poems about plants and animals frequently address issues of gender. Moore's plant and animal poems, Schulze contends, often focus on the domestication of such creatures in ways that invoke the human relationship to the domestic sphere. In Schulze's view, the human and the biotic worlds merge in Moore's poetic considerations of the hazards of domestication. Elizabeth Wilson turns to Moore's late career and offers readings of her two "valentine" poems, "For February 14th" and "Saint Valentine," in the context of Moore's own life choices with regard to sex, marriage, and family. Drawing a relationship between Moore's poems and conversation diaries, Wilson contends that Moore never stopped exploring the pleasures and pains of her own human relationships. The "valentine" texts, Wilson argues, demonstrate, even in the context of the so-called sentimental late career, the complexity of Moore's attempts to assess her literary vocation in the context of her personal desires. Even Moore's late works, Wilson points out, express her profound awareness of the flesh.

Essays in this volume also offer new readings about the evolution and character of Moore's aesthetics. In her essay "'Combat Cultural': Marianne Moore and the Mixed Brow," Elizabeth Gregory takes on the issue of what scholars have long read as a shift in Moore's poetic sensibility. The poetry of the first half of Moore's career seems, to many, unflinchingly highbrow—a poetry consciously designed to bespeak its own status as a cultured product. The poetry of her late career abandons the highbrow in favor of a middle brow stance of sentiment and celebration. In Gregory's view, however, the story of Moore's cultural positioning of her poetry is far more complex. Drawing on a range of scholarship, Gregory argues that

Moore consciously manipulated her brow position in the context of her poems and her persona, creating mixed brow positions throughout her career that express the mutual embeddedness of high and low culture. In her essay "Marianne Moore and the Seventeenth Century," Patricia Willis sheds new light on Moore's verse by reading her poetry against a genre vital to her moral and aesthetic upbringing: the Protestant sermon. Tracing Moore's family roots in seventeenth-century writing, as well as her adult engagement with the works of Browne, Milton, Baxter, and Bunyan, Willis fashions a compelling link between the content and structure of Moore's poems and the substance and shape of the sermons that informed her intellectual and family life. Laura O'Connor's essay "Flamboyant Reticence: An Irish Incognita" also approaches Moore's poetry in the context of an important family genre, the Irish bull. O'Connor interprets "Spenser's Ireland" in light of Moore's fascination with Irish culture and her manipulations of her own claims to ethnic Irishness. Moore's uses of the genre of the Irish bull, O'Connor contends, reveal her subtle knowledge of how such speech acts may function as claims to power or coded acts of community resistance. Heather Cass White reconsiders Moore's poetic practice in the context of the works and aesthetics of Gertrude Stein. Both Moore and Stein, White argues, were keenly interested in the association between identity and the public act of authorship and negotiated their relationships with the reading audience in surprisingly similar ways. White's essay makes a compelling argument in support of Moore's position among the ranks of the modernist avant-garde.

Essays in this volume also suggest new ways of reading Moore's aesthetic practice in relation to the other arts. Stacy Hubbard adds a new dimension to the ongoing conversation about the relationship between Moore's poetry and the visual arts. In her essay "Mannerist Moore: Poetry, Painting, Photography," Hubbard contends that the many photographic portraits taken of Moore throughout her career reveal much about Moore's aesthetic attitudes and poetic procedures. Moore's physical attitudes in these portraits, Hubbard points out, constitute visual quotations that invoke the art of the Renaissance and reflect directly upon Moore's senses of art and artistry. Linda Leavell's essay "Kirkwood and Kindergarten: A Modernist's Childhood," in turn, offers a new portrait of Moore's early life in Kirkwood, Missouri. Leavell considers Moore's poetics in relation to various childhood influences and, in particular, to the late nineteenth-century kindergarten movement. Moore's first educational experience beyond her family home occurred in a kindergarten classroom. Leavell argues that Moore's aesthetics, and those of many of her modernist peers, were shaped by kindergarten's revolutionary pedagogical practices.

Poets have always figured prominently among Moore's advocates. So high is their regard for her in proportion to the breadth of her readership that she has sometimes been dubbed a poet's poet. Her earliest reviewers included H.D., Eliot, Pound, Williams, and Yvor Winters. Leading poets of the next generation—Auden, Bishop, Lowell, Ginsberg, Plath, Merrill, and Ashbery—unequivocally acknowledged her importance, if not her direct influence.[10] And poets Jean Garrigue, Donald Hall, Grace Schulman, and Pamela White Hadas were among the first to provide extended critical analyses of Moore's work.[11] Although Moore maintained a strong legacy among poets throughout the twentieth century, what kind of legacy will she carry into the twenty-first? Has her importance been obscured by the growing enthusiasm for Elizabeth Bishop and Gertrude Stein, even Laura Riding? Ben Friedlander, himself a poet, addresses these questions directly in "Marianne Moore Today." He queried fifteen poets about the degree to which Moore serves as a model for today's experimental poetry. In response to the variety of answers he received, he offers some philosophical reflections on the differences between the poetry of "sensibility" exemplified by Stein and the poetry of "intelligibility" exemplified by Moore. The appeal of the former, he contends, has overshadowed the latter in recent years.

"If tributes cannot be implicit," Moore wrote, "give me diatribes and the fragrance of iodine" (*CPo* 151). To acknowledge that Moore's highest tributes often are implicit, the editors of this volume have chosen to include poetry here as well as prose. Readers familiar with Moore criticism will recognize the names of most of the poets included as authors of essays or books on Moore as well as of multiple volumes of poetry of their own. Grace Schulman, a close friend of the elderly Marianne Moore, recounts some of her memories in "In the Country of Urgency, There is a Language" and reveals the continued presence of her mentor in two more recent poems. Cynthia Hogue sent us three poems that demonstrate "Moore's foremothering (as it were)." Jeredith Merrin told us that she wrote "Parasailing in Cancún" at a conference in Cancún after hearing a paper on "The Steeple-Jack" that did not, in her view, take into account Moore's "many-angled vision of a *place*." The poems Joanie Mackowski chose for us "probe that junction [in Moore] between visual clarity and distortion" and "work with tropes of self-effacement, and with paradox." Jeanne Heuving relates directly to Moore through what she describes as "poems of flora and fauna and intermingled human life for the shifting relations, ever finer." It is not difficult to determine why Lisa M. Steinman told us that a volume devoted to Marianne Moore would be "the best possible setting" for her poem "Marriage—."[12]

The editors present this "right good salvo of barks" in hopes of prolonging the discussion of Marianne Moore well into the new century.

Linda Leavell
Cristanne Miller
Robin G. Schulze

NOTES

1. Robert Pinsky, "Poetic Response: Robert Pinsky Responds to the Tragedy Through Poetry," *A NewsHour with Jim Lehrer Transcript,* Online NewsHour, PBS, September 18, 2001, *http://www.pbs.org/newshour/bb/terrorism/july-dec01/poem_9-18.html* (accessed July 10, 2004). Pinsky has also put this poem on a Rutgers University alumni Web site (along with three poems by other poets) noting that "many people have sought poetry in response to the death, terror, courage, and disruption following the recent attack and massacre." See Robert Pinsky, "Compiled by Robert Pinsky," http://www.alumni.rutgers.edu/attack/poems/ (accessed July 10, 2004).

2. See José Garcia Villa, ed., *Marianne Moore Issue,* special issue, *Quarterly Review of Literature* 4, no. 2 (1948); Tambimuttu, ed., *Festschrift for Marianne Moore's Seventy Seventh Birthday* (New York: Tambimuttu and Mass, 1964); Charles Tomlinson, ed., *Marianne Moore: A Collection of Critical Essays* (Englewood Cliffs, NJ: Prentice-Hall, 1969).

3. Andrew J. Kappel, ed., *Marianne Moore Issue,* special issue, *Twentieth Century Literature* 30 (Summer/Fall 1984). Also, see Laurence Stapleton, *Marianne Moore: The Poet's Advance* (Princeton, NJ: Princeton University Press, 1978); Bonnie Costello, *Marianne Moore: Imaginary Possessions* (Cambridge, MA: Harvard University Press, 1981); Celeste Goodridge, *Hints and Disguises: Marianne Moore and Her Contemporaries* (Iowa City: University of Iowa Press, 1989); Margaret Holley, *The Poetry of Marianne Moore: A Study in Voice and Value* (Cambridge: Cambridge University Press, 1987); Taffy Martin, *Marianne Moore: Subversive Modernist* (Austin: University of Texas Press, 1986); Grace Schulman, *Marianne Moore: The Poetry of Engagement* (Urbana: University of Illinois Press, 1986); John M. Slatin, *The Savage's Romance: The Poetry of Marianne Moore* (University Park: Pennsylvania State University Press, 1986); Lisa M. Steinman, *Made in America: Science, Technology, and American Modernist Poets* (New Haven, CT: Yale University Press, 1987); Patricia C. Willis, *Marianne Moore: Vision into Verse* (Philadelphia: Rosenbach Museum and Library, 1987); and Patricia C. Willis, ed., *Marianne Moore Newsletter* 1–7 (1977–1983).

4. See Joseph Parisi, ed., *Marianne Moore: The Art of a Modernist* (Ann Arbor, MI: UMI Research Press, 1990); Patricia C. Willis, ed., *Marianne Moore: Woman and Poet* (Orono, ME: National Poetry Foundation, 1990); Celeste Goodridge, ed., *Marianne Moore,* special issue, *Sagetrieb* 6 (Winter 1987); Harold Bloom, ed., *Marianne Moore,* Modern Critical Views Series (Broomall, PA: Chelsea House, 1987); Gloria Vando Hickok, ed., *Marianne Moore,* special issue, *Helicon Nine* (Summer 1988); Thomas H. Jackson, ed., *A Celebration of H.D. and Marianne Moore,* special issue, *Poesis* 6, nos. 3/4 (1985); Theodora Rapp Graham, ed., *Marianne Moore,* special issue, *William Carlos Williams Review* 14 (Spring 1988).

5. Following are books published since 1989 that devote at least a chapter to Moore and that focus on gender: Joanne Feit Diehl, *Elizabeth Bishop and Marianne Moore: The Psychodynamics of Creativity* (Princeton, NJ: Princeton University Press, 1993); Betsy Erkkila, *The Wicked Sisters: Women Poets, Literary History, and Discord* (New York: Oxford University Press, 1992); Sandra M. Gilbert and Susan Gubar, *No Man's Land: The Place of the Woman Writer in the Twentieth Century,* Vol. 3: *Letters from the Front* (New Haven, CT: Yale University Press, 1994); Jeanne Heuving, *Omissions Are Not Accidents: Gender in the Art of Marianne Moore* (Detroit: Wayne State University Press, 1992); Cynthia Hogue, *Scheming Women: Poetry, Privilege, and the Politics of Subjectivity* (Albany: State University of New York Press, 1995); Kathryn R. Kent, *Making Girls into Women: American Women's Writing and the Rise of Lesbian Identity* (Durham, NC: Duke University Press, 2003); Jayne E. Marek, *Women Editing Modernism: "Little" Magazines and Literary History* (Lexington: University Press of Kentucky, 1995); Jeredith Merrin, *An Enabling Humility: Marianne*

Moore, Elizabeth Bishop, and the Uses of Tradition (New Brunswick, NJ: Rutgers University Press, 1990); Cristanne Miller, *Marianne Moore: Questions of Authority* (Cambridge, MA: Harvard University Press, 1995); Sabine Sielke, *Fashioning the Female Subject: The Intertextual Networking of Dickinson, Moore, and Rich* (Ann Arbor: University of Michigan Press, 1997); Lesley Wheeler, *The Poetics of Enclosure: American Women Poets from Dickinson to Dove* (Knoxville: University of Tennessee Press, 2002); Kirstin Hotelling Zona, *Marianne Moore, Elizabeth Bishop, and May Swenson: The Feminist Poetics of Self-Restraint* (Ann Arbor: University of Michigan Press, 2002).

6. The following books, all published since 1989, devote at least a chapter to Moore: George Bornstein, *Material Modernism: The Politics of the Page* (Cambridge: Cambridge University Press, 2001); Darlene Williams Erickson, *Illusion Is More Precise than Precision: The Poetry of Marianne Moore* (Tuscaloosa: University of Alabama Press, 1992); James Fenton, *The Strength of Poetry: Oxford Lectures* (New York: Farrar, Straus and Giroux, 2001); Elizabeth Gregory, *Quotation and Modern American Poetry: "Imaginary Gardens with Real Toads"* (Houston, TX: Rice University Press, 1996); Elisabeth W. Joyce, *Cultural Critique and Abstraction: Marianne Moore and the Avant-garde* (Lewisburg, PA: Bucknell University Press, 1998); David Kadlec, *Mosaic Modernism: Anarchism, Pragmatism, Culture* (Baltimore: Johns Hopkins University Press, 2000); Christopher J. Knight, *The Patient Particulars: American Modernism and the Technique of Originality* (Lewisburg, PA: Bucknell University Press, 1995); Andrew M. Lakritz, *Modernism and the Other in Stevens, Frost, and Moore* (Gainesville: University Press of Florida, 1996); Linda Leavell, *Marianne Moore and the Visual Arts: Prismatic Color* (Baton Rouge: Louisiana State University Press, 1995); Catherine Paul, *Poetry in the Museums of Modernism: Yeats, Pound, Moore, Stein* (Ann Arbor: University of Michigan Press, 2002); Robin G. Schulze, *The Web of Friendship: Marianne Moore and Wallace Stevens* (Ann Arbor: University of Michigan Press, 1995); Cynthia Stamy, *Marianne Moore and China: Orientalism and a Writing of America* (Oxford: Oxford University Press, 2000).

7. These recent books likewise devote at least a chapter to Moore: Bonnie Costello, *Shifting Ground: Reinventing Landscape in Modern American Poetry* (Cambridge, MA: Harvard University Press, 2003); Randy Malamud, *Poetic Animals and Animal Souls* (New York: Palgrave, 2003); Timothy Morris, *Becoming Canonical in American Poetry* (Urbana: University of Illinois Press, 1995); Elisa New, *The Line's Eye: Poetic Experience, American Sight* (Cambridge, MA: Harvard University Press, 1999); Richard Poirier, *Trying It Out in America: Literary and Other Performances* (New York: Farrar, Straus and Giroux, 1999); Guy L. Rotella, *Reading and Writing Nature: The Poetry of Robert Frost, Wallace Stevens, Marianne Moore, and Elizabeth Bishop* (Boston: Northeastern University Press, 1997); John Emil Vincent, *Queer Lyrics: Difficulty and Closure in American Poetry* (New York: Palgrave, 2002). The three broad divisions in this paragraph are obviously somewhat arbitrary since many of the studies could be multiply classified. Also somewhat arbitrary is the omission here of the many Moore critics whose recent work appears in dissertations, journal articles, and chapters of multiauthor books. For a descriptive bibliography of Moore criticism prior to 1990, see Bonnie Honigsblum, "An Annotated Bibliography of Works about Marianne Moore, 1977–1990," in Willis, *Woman and Poet,* 443-620.

8. See Marianne Moore, *The Complete Prose of Marianne Moore,* ed. Patricia C. Willis (New York: Viking, 1986); Craig S. Abbott, *Marianne Moore: A Descriptive Bibliography* (Pittsburgh, PA: University of Pittsburgh Press, 1977); Gary Lane, *A Concordance to the Poems of Marianne Moore* (New York: Haskell House, 1972); Charles Molesworth, *Marianne Moore: A Literary Life* (New York: Atheneum, 1990); Marianne Moore, *The Selected Letters of Marianne Moore,* ed. Bonnie Costello, Celeste Goodridge, and Cristanne Miller (New York: Knopf, 1997); Elizabeth Gregory, ed., *The Critical Response to Marianne Moore* (Westport, CT: Praeger, 2003).

9. Marianne Moore, *The Complete Poems of Marianne Moore* (New York: Macmillan/Viking, 1981); Marianne Moore, *Becoming Marianne Moore: The Early Poems, 1907–1924,* ed. Robin G. Schulze (Berkeley and Los Angeles: University of California Press, 2002); Marianne Moore, *The Poems of Marianne Moore,* ed. Grace Schulman (New York: Viking, 2003).

10. Reviews by a number of these poets are collected in Gregory, *Critical Response.*

11. See Jean Garrigue, *Marianne Moore* (Minneapolis: University of Minnesota Press, 1965); Donald Hall, *Marianne Moore: The Cage and the Animal* (New York: Pegasus, 1970); Grace Schulman, "Marianne Moore: The Poetry of Engagement" (Ph.D. dissertation, New York University, 1971); Pamela White Hadas, *Marianne Moore: Poet of Affection* (Syracuse, NY: Syracuse University Press, 1977).

12. Cynthia Hogue via e-mail, 11 October 2003; Jeredith Merrin via e-mail, 6 October 2003; Joanie Mackowski via e-mails, 21 October and 1 November 2003; Jeanne Heuving via e-mail, 17 June 2004; Lisa Steinman via e-mail, 5 October 2003.

Acknowledgments

Grateful acknowledgment is made to the following publishers and individuals for permission to reprint materials from copyrighted sources.

Permission for quotations from Marianne Moore's unpublished works granted by Marianne Craig Moore, Literary Executor for the Estate of Marianne Moore. All rights reserved.

Unpublished letters and materials by Marianne Moore and others from the Marianne Moore Collection, reproduced by permission of the Rosenbach Museum and Library, Philadelphia, Pennsylvania.

"Isaiah, Jeremiah, Ezekiel, Daniel," by Marianne Moore. Reprinted with permission of Faber and Faber Limited.

From *Observations* by Marianne Moore, copyright © by the Dial Press: "To Military Progress," "To Statecraft Embalmed," "Reinforcements," "To Be Liked By You Would be a Calamity," "In This Age of Hard Trying, Nonchalance Is Good and," "To a Steam Roller," "The Labors of Hercules," "Sojourn in the Whale," "Is Your Town Nineveh?" "The Past Is the Present," "Silence," "When I Buy Pictures," "An Octopus," "To a Prize Bird," "Injudicious Gardening," "England," "Picking and Choosing." Reprinted with permission of Faber and Faber Limited.

From *Selected Poems* by Marianne Moore, copyright ©1935 by Marianne Moore; renewed ©1963 by Marianne Moore and T. S. Eliot. Reprinted with the permission of Scribner, an imprint of Simon & Schuster Adult Publishing Group, and Faber and Faber Limited.

From *Nevertheless* by Marianne Moore, copyright © 1944, renewed ©1972 by Marianne Moore. Reprinted with the permission of Scribner, an imprint of Simon & Schuster Adult Publishing Group, and Faber and Faber Limited.

"He 'Digesteth Harde Yron,'" reprinted with the permission of Scribner, an imprint of Simon & Schuster Adult Publishing Group, from *The Collected Poems of Marianne Moore* by Marianne Moore. Copyright © by Marianne Moore; copyright renewed © 1969 by Marianne Moore. Used also by permission of Faber and Faber Limited.

"The Plumet Basilisk" and "The Frigate Pelican," reprinted with the permission of Scribner, an imprint of Simon & Schuster Adult Publishing Group, from *The Collected Poems of Marianne Moore* by Marianne Moore. Copyright © 1935 by Marianne Moore; copyright renewed © 1963 by Marianne Moore and T. S. Eliot. Used also by permission of Faber and Faber Limited.

"The Mind is an Enchanting Thing," reprinted with the permission of Scribner, an imprint of Simon & Schuster Adult Publishing Group, from *The Collected Poems of Marianne Moore* by Marianne Moore. Copyright © 1944 by Marianne Moore; copyright renewed © 1972 by Marianne Moore. Used also by permission of Faber and Faber Limited.

From *The Complete Poems of Marianne Moore* by Marianne Moore, copyright © 1981 by Clive E. Driver, Literary Executor of the Estate of Marianne Moore. Used by permission of Viking Penquin, a division of Penguin Group (USA) Inc. and Faber and Faber Limited.

"The Steeple-Jack," copyright 1951 © 1970 by Marianne Moore, © renewed 1979 by Lawrence E. Brinn and Louise Crane, Executors of the Estate of Marianne Moore, from *The Complete Poems of Marianne Moore* by Marianne Moore. Used by permission of Viking Penguin Group (USA) Inc. and Faber and Faber Limited.

"Combat Cultural," copyright © 1959 by Marianne C. Moore, renewed, from *The Complete Poems of Marianne Moore* by Marianne Moore. Used by permission of Viking Penguin, a division of Penguin Group (USA) Inc. and Faber and Faber Limited.

"For February 14th," copyright © 1959 by Marianne Moore, © renewed 1980 by Lawrence E. Brinn and Louise Crane, Executors of the Estate of Marianne Moore, "Saint Valentine," copyright © 1960 by Marianne Moore, renewed, from *The Complete Poems of Marianne Moore* by Marianne Moore. Used by permission of Viking Penguin, a division of Penguin Group (USA) Inc. and Faber and Faber Limited.

"Spenser's Ireland," copyright © 1941 by Marianne Moore, © 1969 by Marianne Moore, from *The Complete Poems of Marianne Moore* by Marianne Moore. Used by permission of Viking Penguin, a division of Penguin Group (USA) Inc. and Faber and Faber Limited.

From *The Complete Prose of Marianne Moore* by Marianne Moore, edited by Patricia C. Willis, copyright © 1986 by Clive E. Driver, Literary Executor of the Estate of Marianne Moore. Used by permission of Viking Penguin, a division of Penguin Group (USA) Inc.

"The Animals Sick of the Plague," from *The Poems of Marianne Moore* by Marianne Moore, edited by Grace Schulman, copyright © 2003 by Marianne Craig Moore, Executor of the Estate of Marianne Moore. Used by permission of Viking Penguin, a division of Penguin Group (USA) Inc.

"The Artic Ox (Or Goat)," from *The Poems of Marianne Moore,* by Marianne Moore, edited by Grace Schulman, copyright © 2003 by Marianne Craig Moore, Executor of the Estate of Marianne Moore. Used by permission of Viking Penguin, a division of Penguin Group (USA) Inc. and Faber and Faber Limited.

From *Stanzas in Meditation* by Gertrude Stein. Used by permission of Standford G. Gann, Jr., Literary Executor of the Estate of Gertrude Stein. All rights reserved.

"In Distrust of Good" by Cynthia Hogue was first published in the *Electronic Poetry Review* (special Marianne Moore issue, 2004), copyright © Cynthia Hogue. Used by permission.

"Hope Is an Orientation of the Spirit" and "What Matters Today Is the Spirit of the Modern" from *The Never Wife* by Cynthia Hogue, copyright © by Cynthia Hogue. Used by permission of MAMMOTH books.

"Marriage," by Lisa M. Steinman, first appeared in *Epoch Magazine* and then in *Carslaw's Sequences* (Tampa, FL: University of Tampa Press, 2003). Reprinted by permission of the University of Tampa Press.

"American Solitude" and "Eve's Unnaming" from *Paintings of Our Lives: Poems by Grace Schulman.* Copyright © 2001 by Grace Schulman. Reproduced by permission of Houghton Mifflin Company. All rights reserved.

"In the Country of Urgency, There Is a Language," from *Days of Wonder: New and Selected Poems by Grace Schulman.* Copyright © 2002 by Grace Schulman. Reproduced by permission of Houghton Mifflin Company. All rights reserved.

"Fortunate Torsos," "Fine Reticule," "Grays," and "Drowse" by Jeanne Heuving, copyright © 2003 by Jeanne Heuving, first appeared in *26: a Journal of Poetry and Poetics*, no. 2 (2003); "Furrow" by Jeanne Heuving, copyright © Jeanne Heuving, first appeared in *Titanic Operas: An Electronic Journal of Poetry and Poetics Sponsored by the Dickinson Electronic Archives:* http://www.emilydickinson.org/titanic/material/heuving7.html. All poems used by permission of Jeanne Heuving.

"Parasailing in Cancún" by Jeredith Merrin, copyright © Jeredith Merrin, appeared in *Poetry International,* no. 6 (2002): 168–70. Used by permission of Jeredith Merrin.

"Bat Ode" by Jeredith Merrin appeared in *Bat Ode* (Chicago: University of Chicago Press, 2001). Reprinted by permission of the University of Chicago Press.

"View from the Bluff," "Wild," and "Zeros, Veers" are from *The Zoo,* by Joanie Mackowski, © 2002. Reprinted by permission of the University of Pittsburgh Press.

Abbreviations

BMM   *Becoming Marianne Moore: The Early Poems, 1907–1924.* Edited by Robin G. Schulze. Berkeley: University of California Press, 2002.

CollP   *The Collected Poems of Marianne Moore.* New York: Macmillan, 1951.

CPo   *The Complete Poems of Marianne Moore.* Revised edition, New York: Macmillan/Viking, 1981.

CPr   *The Complete Prose of Marianne Moore.* Edited by Patricia C. Willis. New York: Viking, 1986.

O   *Observations.* New York: Dial Press, 1924.

P   *Poems.* London: Egoist Press, 1921.

PMM   *The Poems of Marianne Moore.* Edited by Grace Schulman. New York: Viking, 2003.

SL   *The Selected Letters of Marianne Moore.* Edited by Bonnie Costello, Celeste Goodridge, and Cristanne Miller. New York: Knopf, 1997.

SP   *The Selected Poems of Marianne Moore.* London: Faber and Faber, 1935.

RML   *Marianne Moore Collection, Rosenbach Museum and Library, Philadelphia, Pennsylvania.*

Critics and Poets
on Marianne Moore

Kirkwood and Kindergarten:
A Modernist's Childhood

Linda Leavell

J AMES DICKEY ONCE WROTE THAT IF HE COULD CHOOSE A POET TO DESIGN heaven, he would choose Marianne Moore.[1] It is perhaps appropriate then that she began life in a town that was itself almost an "imaginary garden." She remembered Kirkwood, Missouri, as a place of picturesque estates, with "round beds of purple, pale blue, maroon and velvet black or purple pansies."[2] One estate had a vineyard, and Moore recalled small bags tied around each bunch of white grapes to protect them from bees and flies. Another contained a lake, and at its edge, amid masses of shrubbery, stood a lighthouse. On the same estate, in a sunroom overlooking the grounds, a glass case held two chameleons—probably responsible, she thought, for her "extreme interest in lizards."[3]

Marianne Moore was born in Kirkwood at the home of her maternal grandfather, the Reverend John Riddle Warner, on 15 November 1887. When her parents married in 1885, they moved to Newton, Massachusetts. But John Milton Moore failed to find employment there and eventually fell into such an irrational state that the Reverend Warner feared for his daughter's safety and that of his infant grandson. After supporting the couple for almost two years, Reverend Warner persuaded Mary to leave her husband and return to Kirkwood.[4] Mary refused her husband's pleas for reconciliation and soon severed all ties with him and his family. Neither she nor her children ever saw him again. For seven years Mary found solace in Kirkwood with her beloved "Pa," her aunt Mary Craig Eyster, and her two children. "And what is the *home,*" she asked, "but a nest, where the young are cherished, & where the old again grow young, beholding childish joy?"[5] She called their home the Wren's Nest.

When Reverend Warner first learned of the open pulpit at Kirkwood's Presbyterian Church in 1867, a fellow minister described the town as "the most pleasant place in Missouri." "Kirkwood is a beautiful suburban town," wrote another, "and is growing with great rapidity. The church there is not large in its membership at present but is strong in faith and good work and pecuniary ability. . . . The congregation is united, harmonious, and intelligent. I am sure the situation would be a pleasant one to any faithful minister."[6] By the middle of the nineteenth century, the ills of industrialization had already reached St. Louis, the nation's westernmost city. Yet, while some of its residents longed for the fresh air and woodland streams of their agrarian past, they were unwilling to forgo urban prosperity. The opening of a fifteen-mile stretch of Pacific Railroad in 1853 made it possible to have both. Kirkwood became the first planned community west of the Mississippi. Men could work in the city and yet protect their families from urban dangers, such as the cholera epidemic and fire that devastated St. Louis in 1849. The planners of Kirkwood laid out broad streets and in the 1870s planted thousands of elms and maples alongside them to complement the native groves of oaks and cottonwoods. By the end of the century, trees arched nearly every street, and the town boasted of a "high location, excellent drainage, freedom from smoke, clear, sparkling water, and high standards of morals."[7]

Social diversity did not appear to threaten those standards. One of the earliest churches in Kirkwood was African Methodist Episcopal, and the suburb attracted European immigrants of all social classes.[8] Among those who owned the estates, the Mermods, close family friends, were Swiss, and a number of Germans came to the area because it resembled the wine country of their homeland. One could witness Kirkwood's diverse population even within Reverend Warner's own home. Though middle class, the household of five employed four servants: an Irish-Catholic nursemaid, a Danish cook, a white country "girl," and a black manservant (who had charge of, among other things, the fastidious reverend's clothes). John Warner's own parents were Irish immigrants; the family considered itself Scotch Irish.

The Presbyterian manse occupied a central location in Kirkwood. Green shutters adorned the white frame house, and gingerbread trimmed its porches. On the side opposite the church, a galvanized fence supported jacqueminot roses and a sprawling vine of tiny white clematis—the product of Mary Eyster's green thumb. In the back a potted oleander once broke the fall of a three-year-old Marianne from out of a second-story window. And in front of the house a path led to the picket fence that separated the house from the street. "Oaks and acorns and blue jays, persimmons about the size of a small plum" impressed themselves upon the memory of the future poet. Warner, she recalled, "could imitate a blue jay perfectly."[9]

That was not all he could imitate. Even before he could talk, he named his sister the "yah-yah" after the sounds that emanated from his mother's room. "The solemnest baby mortal ever looked at" is how Mary remembered the early weeks of her daughter's life. And then, when the baby was first brought downstairs, Warner danced around the baby carriage beating two sticks together. To the astonishment of the adults, the baby "burst into

Marianne Moore (in white) and John Warner Moore (seated) in front of their home in Kirkwood, ca. 1894. Rosenbach Museum and Library.

a ha-ha-ha; a regular person's haw-haw of laughter."[10] "Yah-yah" may, in fact, have been Marianne's earliest name, and it remained in the family vocabulary for years to come. Sometime within the first few days or weeks of her life, she was given the name Marian. Mary always pronounced her name this way, even after changing the spelling a year later to Marianne.[11] The name joined those of Mary's two aunts: Mary Craig Eyster and Anne Warner Armstrong. Marianne's middle name, Craig, honored her maternal grandmother's family. But the practice of "home names," as Mary called it, started early, if unimaginatively. Warner was called Buddy and Marianne, Sissy—a name her mother never altogether relinquished in the six decades they lived together.

As the children grew into adolescence, they took the practice of "home names" to elaborate heights of fancy and developed a private vocabulary that would preserve their childhood intimacy until the end of their lives. Much of their "home language" drew on the baby-talk of their Kirkwood years: "vey" for "very," "kam" for "calm," "yah-yah" for "baby." Mary, who had no siblings of her own, began early to reinforce the bond between her children, and she, especially, preserved their childish expressions in her conversation and letters. But the children's mutual devotion needed little encouragement. "One day Warner & [Marianne] were playing they were birds," Mary wrote shortly after Marianne's sixth birthday, "now robins, then thrushes, & again 'chippies': when Warner said 'When I'm a chippy, *you* have to be a *frush!*' 'O no Buddie,' she replied in a dear little coaxing voice—'*You know we are just almost the same;* and when you are a chippy, I *have* to be a chippy too; & when you are a fwush, *I* have to be a fwush!'"[12]

Warner and Marianne never outgrew this game. Although they assumed many different personae over the years, the one constant past childhood was Marianne's insistence that she be Warner's *brother* and hence "he" in the home language—perhaps so that she and Warner would be "just almost the same." One of Marianne's most vivid memories from these years was a neighborhood birthday party at which boys were divided from girls for a game of London Bridge. Even this separation from Warner terrified her. As late as 1945 she wrote: "Every time I go to a party, let alone speak in public, I feel *away* with it. I could just run home the way I did from the children's party in Kirkwood."[13]

The little girl, whose childhood games made precocious distinctions between species of birds, had little tolerance for individuation herself. But her adult relatives enjoyed watching the children's unique personalities emerge. Their great aunt Annie observed when Marianne was not yet a year and a half that, unlike Warner, "sorrow and grievances sit lightly upon the heart of that 'Pitty Lady' Marian. It will do her good all her life." Annie admonished her brother, "Try to watch yourself that you will not get down under every rolling wave. Take Marian for example, just see her constant little sweet grin."[14] His granddaughter's disposition did cheer Reverend Warner, who wrote a few months later: "Marianne is very well—bright & happy, and one of the most charming companions you ever saw. I could not begin to tell you of her sweet winning ways. She has a quick temper, a real little 'spitfire,' but is soon over it & will kiss & caress you two minutes after she has been scolding you severely."[15]

Marianne's "temper" often amused her elders. Her grandfather wrote that he wished he had "the genius of a painting" when Marianne lost a quarrel to Warner: "She'll stand like a little spoiled beauty—with head down, little pouting lips stuck out—and looking at you sideways—will exclaim with all the earnestness she can express, 'I veye much displeesed' repeating it over & over."[16] A few years later her mother reported an incident revealing Marianne's "funny mixture of dignity & impatience." The servant girl was filling glasses before dinner and asked each person, "Will you have some water?" According to her custom, she would not pour a drop until receiving an answer. When she reached Marianne and slowly asked her if she would have water, Marianne sat "straight as a ramrod" to conceal her irritation and answered calmly, "I *always* take *water.*"[17] Persons who knew

**Marianne Moore at seventeen months. Photograph by F. W. Guerin, St. Louis, 1889.
Rosenbach Museum and Library.**

Moore later in life recognized her quick—and quickly suppressed—temper by a flash of red in her cheeks.[18]

Many of Mary's letters from these years tell of Warner's naughtiness and
especially his proclivity for biting and evading the truth. "My brother and
I were by no means exemplary children," recalled Marianne. It was a
source of pride that they never told on one another and took joint responsibility for any misdeed.[19] Their mother regarded Marianne as the more
malleable of the two, at least more responsive to scolding. But the little sister was often her brother's accomplice.

"One beautiful Sunday morning," Warner recalled years later, "during
eleven o'clock preaching service, my grandfather was disturbed by the fact
that few of the congregation on the left side of the church seemed able to pay
attention to what he was saying. The day was warm, the windows were open
in the auditorium, and also the door between the auditorium and what was
called 'the lecture-room,' was wide open. Through this door, Marianne and
I, aged perhaps five and six, were seen turning somersaults over the pews—
pew after pew, in succession—while our high Irish nurse-maid, afraid to enter a Protestant place of worship, stood at another door, one which opened
into the yard, imploring the two acrobats, to 'come out of there.'"[20]

Concepts of childhood changed rapidly during the nineteenth century,
and Mary reared her children under different assumptions from those under which she herself was reared, especially in the decade she lived in Pittsburgh with her Warner grandparents. Although her grandparents and aunts
and uncles doted upon her, they considered whipping and scolding essential to her upbringing. Good was instilled through memorizing the cate-
chism. Mary recalled that her elders "demanded perfect righteousness of
everybody, of me more than of all the rest," that they "filled my life with
Don't."[21] There were no birthday presents, no parties. Her most vivid
memory of childhood was playing with her shadow on the wall while her
grandparents read the Bible by candlelight. She longed for the company of
other children and especially for her absent Pa.

By the time her own children were born, Mary subscribed to a Victorian
understanding of childhood that was, according to some scholars, "one of
the most important inventions of the industrial era."[22] As in Wordsworth's
"Ode: Intimations of Immortality," children were seen as conduits of spir-
ituality and their innocence required protection against the corrupting influence of industrialization. (Thus the appeal of suburbs such as Kirkwood.) But at the same time adults sought their own spiritual renewal by
observing childish antics, they preserved Enlightenment notions of childhood as a blank slate, where the future could be carefully inscribed. While
Mary's training methods were no doubt gentler than her grandmother's, it
never occurred to her that children could get too much parenting or ever

"We children attended a kindergarten and carried a small market basket holding an orange and butter-thin biscuits" (*CPr* 662). Marianne Moore and John Warner Moore. Photograph by J. F. Phillips, St. Louis, ca. 1893. Rosenbach Museum and Library.

outgrow the need for it. Overindulgence, or "spoiling," was considered a real threat, and no imperfection was trivial enough to pass without correction. When Mary was in her seventies, she admitted to Warner, "I wasn't a wise caretaker . . . I was too direct & did not ease fault finding" but even then could not shake the idea that "there's *nothing* so useful as getting hold of an error; *any way;* by hook or by crook."[23]

As her children entered adulthood in the new century, Mary's attachment to the concept of childhood became central to her moral and religious vision. She often advised Marianne in college to "be a little child again" and wrote to Warner as a young man: "Remember how well Peter Pan flew, till he began to consider the manner of his flying. Oh! don't be introspective! We are bidden to be like little children that we may enter the kingdom of heaven."[24] The child as a model for Christian faith is a frequent theme in Mary's letters to her adult son, as when she wrote him in 1919 "that we are not nowadays the children of a simple faith; we have our subways and our taxis—when as children of a simple faith we could only fly to our true Home as hydrogen when let loose flies to oxygen."[25] J. M. Barrie's ever youthful Peter Pan captured the public imagination in the first decade of the twentieth century, as it did Mary's, and she remained a devoted admirer of Barrie long after the public lost interest in him. All three adult Moores read children's books and shared them with one another. Most notably, in 1914 they read Kenneth Grahame's *The Wind in the Willows* and adopted its woodland personae for themselves.

Perhaps the thing that most distinguished Mary's view of childhood from that of her grandmother was the concept of play. Before the nineteenth century, children, like adults, were valued for their ability to work, to be useful. But as public sympathy moved to exclude children from the industrial workforce, play came to be seen as the child's equivalent of work, as a necessary stage in one's educational development. Mary encouraged her children to play and fantasize but had lingering doubts that she should have directed their play more than she did toward "ennobling purpose."[26] Capitalism also contributed to the valuation of play by marketing toys and child-size furniture to parents entranced by the world of childhood. Although Marianne later described dolls as "abhorrent and meaningless" to her, she owned at least two, one china and one wax. Not surprisingly, she preferred toy animals and recalled "a sheep with wool and green glass eyes that could baa, a horse with real skin, [and] a rubber elephant."[27] Warner had a cast-iron train and a cast-iron fire wagon, from which his sister extracted the horses. There were real animals, too: a baby alligator Tibby, brought by Mary Eyster from Florida, and Toby, the pug dog of a friend in St. Louis. Both would survive as family personae: Toby for Warner and Tibby for Marianne.

The phenomenon most responsible for widespread changes in the attitude toward play is the international kindergarten movement of the late nineteenth century. By 1893, when Warner and Marianne entered kindergarten in Kirkwood, the movement had gained considerable momentum in the United States, and nowhere was that momentum greater than in St. Louis, the site of the nation's first public kindergarten.[28] Kindergarten's German inventor, Friedrich Froebel, viewed the years from three to seven as an opportunity to direct a child's natural impulse to play toward developing his social and familial life, his relationship with an invisible spirit, and his appreciation for the natural world. "Play is the purest, the most spiritual activity of man at this stage," he wrote, "and, at the same time, typical of human life as a whole—of the inner hidden natural life in man and all things."[29] Following Rousseau, Froebel was one of the earliest educators to promote self-directed learning, where, in contrast to the prevailing method of teaching through recitation, children were encouraged to develop their own imaginations and follow their own natural curiosity.

In the late nineteenth century a typical kindergarten day lasted about three hours. The day began with a song and morning chat and might move from there to an object lesson, during which the children would sit in a circle while the teacher presented for their scrutiny a natural object such as a seashell, quartz crystal, or cotton flower. A teacher well trained in Froebelian methods would encourage them to observe the object's harmonious, geometrical design and especially its inner connection to other natural forms. Following an object lesson about, for example, a bird's nest, the

A kindergarten object lesson about seashells. Illustration by Irving R. Wiles for Williams, "The Kindergarten Movement," 372.

Children playing "Birdies in the Greenwood." Illustration by Irving R. Wiles for Williams, "The Kindergarten Movement," 371.

children might sing a song about birds, play a game pretending they were birds, or hear a story about birds. Unlike the typical children's stories of the time that ended in a moral lesson, kindergarten stories allowed children to draw their own conclusions. All of these activities, and alternative ones such as gardening and nature walks, directed the child toward close observation of the natural world and toward a sense of connection with its forces.

Froebel's training as a crystallographer—and particularly his belief that growth occurs according to geometric principles—informed his whole concept of kindergarten. He invented a series of twenty toys, or "gifts," to develop children's imaginations through manipulation of abstract geometrical forms. A kindergarten day included one or two sessions of play with the gifts. Each session lasted thirty to forty minutes and took place at long tables etched with a one-inch grid to give their play an underlying geometric structure. Some of the gifts, such as wooden blocks and modeling clay, were used to make shapes that resembled man-made or natural structures. Other gifts, designed to develop a sense of beauty, allowed children to create their own abstract designs through paper weaving or paper folding, and these they could take home. Referring to two of the gifts, Marianne recalled that in kindergarten she "made mats from glazed color paper or constructed geometric forms by running sharp toothpicks into dried peas."[30]

The purpose of kindergarten was not to produce artists. Nevertheless, the artists who emerged from kindergarten's early decades revolutionized the arts. By the 1880s the kindergarten movement had spread through most of Europe, the United States, and even Japan. Calling kindergarten "the seed pearl of the modern era," cultural historian Norman Brosterman has shown that early twentieth-century paintings by artists such as Kandinsky, Braque, Klee, and Mondrian bear an astonishing resemblance to abstract designs created with kindergarten gifts. In most cases, the influence occurred so early that artists could hardly be conscious of it. But a few, such as Frank Lloyd Wright, whose mother introduced him to the gifts when he was eight or nine, acknowledged their impact. Buckminster Fuller likewise credited kindergarten, and in particular the toothpicks and dried peas, with inspiring the invention of his geodesic dome.[31] An artist not mentioned by Brosterman but important to Moore is Joseph Cornell, whose mother was trained as a kindergarten teacher. Cornell's wooden boxes, which he sometimes called "gifts," resemble those in which the Milton Bradley Company

Making cylinders in clay. Illustration by Otto H. Bacher for Williams, "The Kindergarten Movement," 372.

packaged the kindergarten gifts. Many of Cornell's boxes contain toys and images evoking childhood as well as small natural objects such as feathers and butterflies. Cornell and Moore became acquainted in the 1940s and, according to their mutual friend Monroe Wheeler, were "kindred artists."[32]

Marianne Moore entered kindergarten in May 1893, at the age of five, and attended less than a year. Kindergarten is at least minimally significant for being her first educational experience outside her own family. At most, it can be credited with giving shape to her modernist sensibility. One of the hallmarks of this sensibility is close observation of nature and especially of its geometric forms: the jerboa's leaps "by fifths and sevenths," the crape myrtle blossom's "pyramids of mathematic circularity," a seashell's "close-laid Ionic chiton-folds" (PMM 194, 222, 238–39). "The Icosas-phere" is an especially Froebelian poem comparing birds' nests, "little bits of string and moths and feathers and thistledown, / [woven] in parabolic concentric curves," to the icosahedron, a feat of engineering that antici-pates Fuller's geodesic dome. Like other Moore poems, "The Icosasphere" equates geometric perfection with moral perfection. The "spherical feats of rare efficiency" contrast sharply with the self-destructiveness of humans "avid for someone's fortune" (PMM 277).

More than one reader of Moore's poetry has noted the gridlike structures of her stanzas. She herself used "pattern," "symmetry," and "architecture" to describe her inaudible pattern of syllables and barely audible rhyme scheme. "The Fish," for example, has a pattern of 1–3–9–6–8 syllables per line with an aabbx rhyme scheme. Against this geometrical pattern she places her ir-regularly cadenced sentences, what she calls the "tune." When the stanzaic pattern requires surprising breaks in the flow of the sentence, it is not hard to imagine the poet "playing" against a self-imposed "grid," especially with lines such as "ac- / cident—lack" in "The Fish" (PMM 127–28).

Perhaps the most significant legacy of Moore's kindergarten experience is her almost instant affinity, when she encountered it in the early twenti-eth century, for the work of other moderns. For example, the paintings and especially the theories of Kandinsky had enormous appeal for American painters and poets in Moore's circle. Just after Moore visited 291 and other New York galleries for the first time in December 1915, she bought a copy of Kandinsky's Der Blaue Reiter, in which he and other artists assert their theories about the spiritual origins of art. Kandinsky believed in a spiritual "inner necessity" that connects artists across geographical and historical boundaries and that manifests itself, as it does in nature, in abstract pattern. Kandinsky's "inner necessity" anticipates Moore's notion of the "gen-uine," which can take surprising but expedient forms in art and nature. Kandinsky's introduction to the German Romanticism that informed his ideas may well have occurred—symbolically at least—in kindergarten, which he attended at the age of three.[33]

Mary Eyster died in February 1893, and in February 1894 the Reverend Warner died suddenly of pneumonia. Just after his funeral Warner and Mary came down with scarlet fever, and in May the family threesome left Kirkwood. It was a desperate time for them both financially and emotionally. They lived with cousins near Pittsburgh for two and a half years before Mary could summon enough courage to establish her own home two hundred miles away in Carlisle. Never again would the family enjoy the standard of living they had in Kirkwood. Never again would they feel quite so innocent or so armored against the outside world.

Like that of other kindergarten alumni such as Kandinsky, Paul Klee, Mondrian, and Frank Lloyd Wright, Moore's modernism might well be described as "utopian." William Carlos Williams praised her poetry as "a brittle, highly set-off porcelain garden," where each word can stand "crystal clear with no attachments; not even an aroma."[34] But critics now regard Moore, especially in comparison with other poets, as much more a realist and pragmatist than a romantic. To call her utopian, one must imagine a utopia firmly rooted in the observable world and ready to adapt, like science, to the instability of that world.[35] The threats to this utopia are not change and diversity but human depravity. Moore was never squeamish about urban life. She lived for years in a Brooklyn neighborhood that shocked her visitors and their cab drivers. Yet the fiction of Sherwood Anderson, Faulkner, Dos Passos, Hemingway, Katherine Anne Porter, and most other modern realists disgusted her. This distaste was usually taken to be prudery, but Moore insisted otherwise. "All my stinging legs stand out like the fretful porpentine," she said after a row with Matthew Josephson, "when I am told that if I were cosmopolitan I'd like lewdness too."[36] If the heaven Moore would design admits no lewdness, it nevertheless would resemble a Cornell box more than it would the pure abstraction of a Mondrian painting. The aroma of organic fertilizer may not waft through her "imaginary garden," but one must be wary of toads. Their unstable presence brings confusion to the garden as well as playful surprise.

NOTES

A few passages from this essay have appeared in a different context in my article, "Marianne Moore, Her Family, and Their Language," *Proceedings of the American Philosophical Society* 147, no. 2 (2003): 141–43.

1. James Dickey, "What the Angels Missed," review of *Tell Me, Tell Me: Granite, Steel, and Other Topics* by Marianne Moore, *New York Times Book Review,* December 25, 1966, 1.

2. Marianne Moore to Mrs. F. H. Morgan, 15 May 1961, quoted in June Wilkinson Dahl, *A History of Kirkwood Missouri: 1851–65* (Kirkwood, MO: Kirkwood Historical Society, 1965), 158. I am indebted to Dahl's careful history for much of my information about

Kirkwood, and also to John Lindenbusch, *Four Walking Tours of Historic Kirkwood Missouri* (1981), http://www.kirkwoodarea.com/tourism/walking_tours.htm (accessed July 24, 2003).

3. Marianne Moore, "Coming About" (unfinished memoir, Moore Family Collection, West Hartford, CT), 7. The first of these estates belonged to A. S. Mermod, one of John Warner's closest friends. The second belonged to a prominent horticulturist, Charles W. Murtfeldt, and his family. The elaborate gardens were used both for social events and horticultural experiments. Mermod and Murtfeldt were elders in Warner's church.

4. Mary was indeed miserable in the second year of her marriage, but there is no indication that she feared for her own or her child's safety. She described her husband as irrationally obsessed with his own salvation but nevertheless kind and affectionate. I am grateful to the Moore family for making available to me letters that chronicle the years in Newton.

5. Mary Warner Moore to Anne Warner Armstrong, 25 August 1893, *RML.*

6. D. A. Wilson to John Riddle Warner, 23 February 1867 and Samuel J. Niccolls to John Riddle Warner, 26 January 1867, *RML.*

7. *Suburban Leader,* December 4, 1896, quoted in Dahl, *History of Kirkwood,* 67.

8. In 1900, about a fifth of Kirkwood's 3,000 residents were black. Some citizens fought to keep saloons out of the community but not, so far as I can tell, racial or ethnic groups.

9. Marianne Moore to Mrs. F. H. Morgan, 15 May 1961, quoted in Dahl, *History of Kirkwood,* 158; Moore, "Coming About," 1.

10. Mary Warner Moore to John Warner Moore, 5 May 1921, *RML.* Mary Warner Moore often told this story as evidence of her children's devotion to one another.

11. This spelling more fully indicated the Mary and Anne than did Marian, and yet was distinct in spelling and pronunciation from the name of the children's nursemaid, Mary Anne.

12. Mary Warner Moore to Anne Warner Armstrong, 24 November 1893, *RML.*

13. Marianne Moore to John Warner Moore, 25 January 1945, *RML.*

14. Anne Warner Armstrong to John Riddle Warner, 1 April 1889, *RML.*

15. John Riddle Warner to Henry Warner Armstrong, 8 July 1889, *RML.*

16. John Riddle Warner to Henry Warner, 28 May 1890, *RML.*

17. Mary Warner Moore to Anne Warner Armstrong, 18 October 1892, *RML.*

18. Marianne Craig Moore and Sarah Eustis Moore, in conversation with the author, 25 August 1999.

19. Moore, "Coming About," 3.

20. John Warner Moore, untitled carbon typescript, 30 December 1954, *RML.*

21. Mary Warner Moore to John Warner Moore, 8 April 1924 and 25 September 1921, *RML.* The births of Mary Warner Moore's four grandchildren from 1919 to 1926 prompted many reflections on the subject of child rearing.

22. Stephen Kline, "The Making of Children's Culture," in *The Children's Culture Reader,* ed. Henry Jenkins (New York: New York University Press, 1998), 96. This essay and others in this volume inform much of my thinking about late nineteenth-century childhood. The seminal study of the social construction of childhood is Philippe Ariès, *Centuries of Childhood: A Social History of Family Life* (New York: Knopf, 1962).

23. Mary Warner Moore to John Warner Moore, 4 January 1937, *RML.*

24. Mary Warner Moore to Marianne Moore, 14 January 1907 and Mary Warner Moore to John Warner Moore, 17 March 1909, *RML.*

25. Mary Warner Moore to John Warner Moore, 6 July 1919, *RML.*

26. Mary Warner Moore to John Warner Moore, 10 January 1924, *RML.*

27. Moore, "Coming About," 3–4.

28. Talcott Williams, "The Kindergarten Movement," *Century Magazine,* January 1893, 378. Susan E. Blow, one of America's strongest kindergarten advocates, opened the first public kindergarten in this country in St. Louis in 1873. Because of her sustained influence and close adherence to Froebel's theories, kindergarten in St. Louis evolved away from his methods more slowly than in other cities.

29. Friedrich Froebel, *The Education of Man,* trans. W. N. Hailmann (New York: D. Appleton, 1895), 53–54.

30. Moore, "Coming About," 3.

31. Norman Brosterman, *Inventing Kindergarten* (New York: Harry N. Abrams, 1997), 7, 84. This provocative, liberally illustrated book informs most of my remarks about kindergarten.

32. Monroe Wheeler, interviewed in *Marianne Moore: In Her Own Image,* Program 8 of *Voices & Visions* television series produced by the New York Center for Visual History, Santa Barbara, CA: Intellimation [distributor], 1988, video recording.

33. Brosterman, *Inventing Kindergarten,* 131–32. For further analysis of Moore's affinities with modern architects, painters, photographers, and sculptors, see my *Marianne Moore and the Visual Arts: Prismatic Color* (Baton Rouge: Louisiana State University Press, 1995). Of particular relevance to my points in this essay are the sections on functionalism (184–94), on Moore's architectural stanza (56–85), and on "inner necessity" (135–68).

34. William Carlos Williams, "Marianne Moore (1925)," in *Marianne Moore: A Collection of Critical Essays,* ed. Charles Tomlinson (Englewood Cliffs, NJ: Prentice-Hall, 1969), 54, 57.

35. Although she does not describe Moore as utopian, Chiaki Sekiguchi ("In Touch with the World: Marianne Moore, Objects, Fantasy, and Fashion" [Ph.D. dissertation, State University of New York at Buffalo, 2003]) makes an excellent case for the interplay of fantasy and fact in Moore's poetry.

36. Marianne Moore, quoted in Mary Warner Moore to John Warner Moore, 8 May 1923, *RML.*

Marianne Moore
and the Seventeenth Century

Patricia C. Willis

Marianne Moore had roots in the seventeenth century. Her literary lineage drew on the great writers of that era while her religious orientation stemmed from Protestant Reformation practices. As an educated woman, she knew her Milton, and as a Presbyterian, her Calvin. Earlier treatment of this topic by Jeredith Merrin and Andrew Kappel has laid important groundwork. Merrin discussed Moore's interest in Thomas Browne with special attention to his "literary menagerie" in *Pseudodoxia Epidemica* and to aspects of his diction.[1] Kappel examined Richard Baxter's *The Saints' Everlasting Rest* and Moore's extensive borrowing of his language in "An Octopus" and other poems.[2] Turning to Moore's Protestant roots, Kappel looked for the many "connections between her old fashioned religion and her modern poetry."[3] And Merrin further established the presence of American Calvinism in Moore's world with regard to issues of individuality and subjectivity and the importance of the "struggle" to lead the Christian life as an animator of the poems.[4]

With these points in mind, I turn to the seventeenth-century writing that Moore wrapped up in the Protestant sermon. She chose the sermon form during the 1930s, the period some critics would call her second wave of poetry, one marked by important differences in method from the poetry that preceded her going to the *Dial* in 1925 and its subsequent seven-year poetry hiatus.[5] "The Frigate Pelican" serves as the illustration of the way she developed the sermon to contain her modernist verse. As background, I will examine two of Moore's early experiences which I identify as familial and social, her first orientation to seventeenth-century writing and to Protestant sermons. Then I will examine her adult engagement with the work of four writers, Browne, Milton, Baxter, and Bunyan and, finally, explore her development of her sermon form in "The Frigate Pelican."

THE WELL OF RESERVES FOR POETRY

It is only when we reach back beyond the finished, adult poetry to Moore's early experiences that we find her earliest resources for her later development. At this level lie what I call the familial and social reserves that develop during childhood and youth. Yeats describes this level:

> When a man writes any work of genius, or invents some creative action, is it not because some knowledge or power has come into his mind from beyond his mind? . . . [O]ur images must be given to us, we cannot choose them deliberately.
>
> I know now that revelation is from the self, but from that age-long memoried self, that shapes the elaborate shell of the mollusk and the child in the womb. . . .[6]

This "memoried self" dyes the poet's imagination with the colors she will find most congenial as she learns her craft.

Among the familial reserves, I place books read at home and enjoyed from earliest days. Moore repeatedly cites Bunyan's *Pilgrim's Progress* as a highly influential work familiar from childhood (*CPr* 670, 672). "Manner-without-manner's true model," she called it later, an allegorical adventure story in straightforward prose. The work played such a significant role in her imagination that Moore refers playfully in her letters to "Worldly Wiseman" or "Fair Countenance." This seventeenth-century masterpiece epitomized the approved Protestant text suitable for children in the Moore household. That is not to say that Jacob Abbott's Rollo books or Andrew Lang's fairy books were not welcome—for they were great favorites—but the long arc of religious literature worked its way, through this book, into Moore's imagination and consciousness.

To turn to social resources, I submit that the Protestant sermon has a function similar to that of *Pilgrim's Progress* in preparing the future poet. Moore spent her first six years in the Manse of her grandfather, John Riddle Warner, in Kirkwood, Missouri. The Reverend Warner, following his training at the Theological Seminary of the Associate Reformed Church at Allegheny, Pennsylvania, and several years in Gettysburg, Pennsylvania, during the Civil War, received a call to the Presbyterian Church in Kirkwood.[7] At what age Marianne began to attend sermons is unclear but the fact of the weekly exercise had to be inescapable. In later years, she heard sermons in Carlisle, Pennsylvania, by the Rev. George Norcross. Upon the ordination of her brother, John Warner, as a Presbyterian minister, she read his sermon outlines, sent home in letters, as well as her mother's commentaries on them. Sermons played the major role in this Presbyterian family for conveying Scripture, its meaning and its application to life. That those sermons also generated poetic patterns for the adult writer will emerge later in a discussion of her poetry.

These two sources, familial and social, literary allegory and the Protestant sermon, were already at work in the young poet when she began consciously to develop the formal literary aspects of her education at Bryn Mawr. An intellectual poet, like her Handel in "A Frigate Pelican," a clandestine creator who was "never known to have fallen in love,"[8] Marianne Moore made poetry from what came to hand. For this Modernist enterprise, she relied on the sources available to her as an educated woman, which meant her Bryn Mawr curriculum of humanities and sciences. Where the two parts of the curriculum intersected—in writing about the natural world—Moore found her chief interest.

GOD'S SECOND BOOK: BROWNE, MILTON, AND BAXTER

What Moore garnered through formal education was not only traditional academic content but process: the opening of a window, the opportunity to apply the mind to new matter and to go in search of new ideas. Moore learned to read seventeenth-century writers for her own purposes. What she gathered from them—or what she chose to find—was to her consistent with her broadest interests. It yielded a poem like "The Frigate Pelican" furnished with not only Audubon's exquisite rendering of *Fregata aquila* and his scientific notes about the bird but also Grimm's Hansel and Gretel, Handel, Artemis, Erasmus, and the wild life of the Caribbean jungles. In short, she absorbed what in her youth was called "natural philosophy," the quasi-scientific, layman's study of nature—creation—and how it worked. The writings of Browne, Milton, Baxter, and Bunyan, products of the age of discovery and scientific inquiry, explore this territory relentlessly with the understanding that to know the natural is to appreciate the divine.

Moore's path to the first of these writers came through an elective, "Imitative Writing," offered in her senior year at Bryn Mawr by Georgianna Goddard King.

> I had an interview with Miss King this afternoon after Christian Doctrine. She is most critical, but most encouraging. She says if I absolutely relinquish my own notions of things and immerse my self in style pure and simple as found in the classics (17th century) I'll come out A number one—She said my paper was interesting but she took it head from body. She said (it was on Sir T. Browne, imitation) "you use fashion"—she said "fashion you couldn't possibly use— You would not find it—a bit earlier, than Addison." That illustrates her exactness. She likes me I think. I don't think she could possibly fail me.[9]

This first scrape with Browne during "Imitative Writing" was no doubt made poignant by its emotional association with Moore's ongoing trouble with teachers who found her writing unclear. It has echoes in subsequent years, beginning in her days at the *Dial*. In an editor's "Comment" in the *Dial* Moore turns to Browne, reminded of him by his biographer Samuel Johnson (*CPr* 164). She salutes his "verbal effectiveness" and "effortless compactness which precludes ornateness" (*CPr* 165). In the next "Comment," dated May 1926, she continues to laud felicity of language and technique while turning to larger issues. Here, "imagination seems to provide its own propulsiveness . . . in Browne's 'Bees, Ants, and Spiders'": "'In these narrow Engines there is more curious Mathematicks'—than in whales, elephants, dromedaries, and camels—'and the civility of these little Citizens more neatly sets forth the Wisdom of their Maker'" (*CPr* 165). The last phrase is key. Browne writes: "[T]here are two books from whence I collect my divinity. Besides that written one of God, another of his servant, nature, that universal and publick manuscript, that lies expansed unto the eyes of all."[10] God's "second book" became a common trope for the book of nature, Scripture's companion in divine tutelage; the concept helps to reinforce Moore's intense observation of and writing about nature and her pursuit of a weighty second-scriptural understanding. *"Vir amplissimus,"* Moore called Browne, an exceptional man, an inspiration, not least for keeping his eyes on God and nature together (*CPr* 502). God's "second book" confronted Moore at every turn, from her earliest interests through her college courses in biology and zoology and beyond.[11] As Jeredith Merrin points out, the table of contents in Browne's *Pseudodoxia Epidemica*—"Of Snayles," "Of the Chameleon," "Of the Oestridge," or "Of the picture of the Pelecan"—is a roster of Moore's poetic subjects.[12] In fact, "The Frigate Pelican" is based on Audubon's picture of that bird.

If Browne was a discovery made in college, a kind of revelation of both style and matter for poetry, Milton was a companion of her adolescence, and his work a *vade mecum* of her college years. Two incidents attest to this notion. First, a sophomore assignment, sixty-five lines of Milton to be memorized, became a task lightened when Professor Lucy Donnelly pointed to the "charming Miltonian flower" Moore was using to bookmark her copy (*SL* 27). The next year, with literature classes safely over, she confesses to her mother that writing is her only desire and that for a moment's leisure when "the weather is cold but fine as silk . . . I think I shall take Milton and go out" (*SL* 47). In the midst of her ongoing struggle to achieve grades high enough to graduate, she turned to Milton for refreshment.

She also turned to Milton for his reimagining of Scripture. Moore said she admired Milton's "'harmonious world,'" "'passionate temperament,'" and "'ardor for religion and art considered as one'" (*CPr* 232–33). Most telling is the last phrase for it is Milton, not Genesis, that Moore uses for the several occasions when she considers Adam and Eve in the Garden in her poems. From Book IV of *Paradise Lost* she draws images for her earthly paradise in "An Octopus." In "Marriage" she quotes directly from

Book IV in her description of Adam and she paraphrases Book IX where Eve suggests that she and Adam work apart in the garden (Satan's opportunity with Eve). She draws on Book III for the image of Paradise before Eve for "In the Days of Prismatic Color" and on Book XII for the image of Michael taking Adam by the hand in "When I Buy Pictures." She reflects *Paradise Lost* again in "The Frigate Pelican" where her huge bird, whose name is or is not "pelican," rides the thermals. Milton's Raphael tells Adam about the flight of the good angels:

> for high above the ground
> Thir march was, and the passive Air upbore
> Thir nimble tread; as when the total kind
> Of Birds in orderly array on wing
> Came summon'd over Eden to receive
> Thir names of thee.[13]

And as he continues the story of creation, Raphael says that on the fifth day, the birds

> soaring th' air sublime
> With clang despis'd the ground, under a cloud
> In prospect; there the Eagle and the Stork
> On Cliffs and Cedar tops their Eyries build
>
> . . . .
>
>   so steers the prudent Crane
> Her annual Voyage, born on Winds; the Air
> Floats as they pass, fann'd with unnumber'd plumes.[14]

Here the birds fly so high that the earth appears cloud-covered while even the air itself seems to float. Moore's bird and its companions

> aimlessly soar
> as he does; separating, until
>   not flapping they rise once more
>
> . . . . .
>
> and blow back, allowing the wind to reverse their direction.

(*SP* 39)

As in Scripture, as expressed by Milton, Adam named the birds, Moore too struggles with the identity of her frigate pelican: "unless swift is the proper word / for him . . . a kind of superlative / swallow . . . he is not a pelican" and shows him seemingly afloat in the passive air (*SP* 38).

A third major seventeenth-century writer in Moore's stable is Richard Baxter, the Nonconformist preacher and author whose longest work, *The Saints' Everlasting Rest* (1650), was one of the most popular devotional books ever published.[15] Moore chose to read this "great master of English prose" in the early 1910s when she wrote "Pedantic Literalist."[16] She took it up again in 1923, making notes from it in the workbook she used for "Marriage" and "An Octopus." She quotes directly from passages she found attractive, using them to buttress a description of married people: "seldom and cold, up and down / mixed and malarial / with a good day and a bad."[17] She quotes Baxter on the source of spiritual life, turning his words into a Greek argument for a philosophy of happiness as "an accident or a quality, / a spiritual substance or the soul itself, / an act, a disposition, or a habit" (*CPo* 75). These choices are what Andrew Kappel refers to as her own "*verba ardentia*"[18] which pulled Moore into their orbit and which she adopted (sometimes in quotation marks, sometimes not) as her language.

Moore also relished Baxter's associations with "those inferior works of God"—Christ being the superior work—"this great house which here we dwell in." From his last chapter on contemplation, in which is found one passage Moore chose for "Marriage," he rhapsodizes about the earth: "The floor so dressed with various herbs and flowers and trees, and watered with springs and rivers and seas; the roof so wide expanded, so admirably adorned; such astonishing workmanship on every part.[19] Baxter saw God's workmanship in the godliness of nature; it is "workmanship" that appeals to Moore and that she finds in every aspect of creation, whether in "the dove-neck's iridescence" (*CPo* 135) or / in the frigate pelican's "toe / with slight web, air-boned body, and very long wings / . . . [and] the changing V-shaped scissor swallow- / tail" (*SP* 38). Always, the design of the creature, the way it is put together and functions, reveals for Moore the Creation.

BUNYAN AND NATURE POWERED BY THE INVISIBLE

Browne, Milton, and Baxter influenced both Moore's poetry and prose through the 1930s. They provided intellectual animation, turns of thought that enriched the poet's field of literary vision, moral clarity, and what we might call artistic weavings together of their work and hers. They suggest enthusiasms chosen early in her career as she strove to identify herself as poet. These influences we might call external—selected from among the panoply of literary works discovered in early adulthood. Alongside them, two other aspects of seventeenth-century literature that stand as arguably more central still to Moore's poetic enterprise are those that are more internal, referred to above as the early familial and social matter of her imagination that the poet made her own without conscious effort.

We have seen how Bunyan's *Pilgrim's Progress* lay hold of a very young Moore and sustained her interest—without obvious homage but present nonetheless—for many years. Here I address the importance of Bunyan to the mature poet whose work so constantly emphasized and engaged with nature. Like Browne and Milton, Bunyan championed the beauty of God's second book. At the beginning of the story, he reports Christian's vision of his goal:

> [A]nd then, said they, we will, if the day be clear, show you the Delectable Mountains; which, they said, would yet farther add to his comfort, because they were nearer the desired haven than the place where at present he was; so he consented and stayed. When the morning was up, they had him to the top of the house, and bid him look south. So he did, and behold, at a great distance, he saw a most pleasant mountainous country, beautified with woods, vineyards, fruits of all sorts, flowers also, with springs and fountains, very delectable to behold.[20]

One sees here the mountain of "An Octopus" where the text from Isaiah plays out as well. In addition to this association with God's book of nature, Bunyan's allegory provides another ongoing thread that is essential to Moore's poetry. Pilgrim is given an embroidered coat for his journey and whenever he thinks of it, he finds renewed power to overcome the obstacles in his path to the delectable mountains. As editor N. H. Keeble points out, "It is this sensitivity to the interpenetration of the visible by the invisible, this consciousness of the immanence of ultimate realities" that informs Bunyan's story and gives its emblems life.[21] One hardly need elaborate on Moore's concern for the invisible behind the visible, an enduring theme from "A Jellyfish" (1909) to "O to Be a Dragon" (1959) and elsewhere in her work. "The Plumet Basilisk," for example, salutes its Costa Rican lizard:

> He runs, he flies, he swims, to get to
> his basilica—"the ruler of Rivers, Lakes, and Seas,
>   invisible or visible," with clouds to do
> as bid—and can be "long or short, and also coarse or fine at pleasure."
>
> *(SP 32)*

And the ostrich:

> The power of the visible
> is the invisible; as even where
> no tree of freedom grows,
> so-called brute courage knows.[22]

Even when not made explicit in the poems, Moore repeatedly conceals, hides, camouflages or otherwise challenges the visible natural signs of invisible power. The jerboa "honors the sand by assuming its color," the glacier in "An Octopus" lies "deceptively reserved and flat"; and the frigate pelican "hides / in the height and in the majestic / display of his art" (*CPo* 14, 71, 25–26). Moore's genius was to seize on the device of hidden, emblematic meanings and to apply it to lizards, mountains, rodents, and birds.

Moore found much to admire in Bunyan and surely none more than his expressed purpose for his work, its metaphors and emblematic meanings as he states in his verse prologue. There his critic takes on *Pilgrim's Progress:*

> "Well, yet I am not fully satisfied
> That this your book will stand, when soundly tried."
> Why, what's the matter? "It is dark." What though?
> "But it is feigned." What of that? I trow
> Some men by feigned words, as dark as mine,
> Make truth to spangle, and its rays to shine.
> "But they want solidness." Speak, man, thy mind.
> "They drown the weak; metaphors make us blind."
> Solidity, indeed, becomes the pen
> Of him that writeth things divine to men:
> But must I needs want solidness, because
> By metaphors I speak? Were not God's laws,
> His gospel laws, in olden time held forth
> By types, shadows, and metaphors? Yet loth
> Will any sober man be to find fault
> With them, lest he be found for to assault
> The highest wisdom! No, he rather stoops,
> And seeks to find out what, by pins and loops,
> By calves and sheep, by heifers, and by rams,
> By birds and herbs, and by the blood of lambs,
> God speaketh to him; and happy is he
> That finds the light and grace that in them be.[23]

Bunyan here promotes his evangelical Protestant approach to his work, suggesting that God speaks to man through the commonest elements of nature and that he has written his story with God's second book in mind.

While Bunyan's posthumous fame rests on his allegorical tale, his notoriety in life derived from his Protestant preaching, the cause of his twelve-year imprisonment during which he wrote *Pilgrim's Progress.* His writing made him a success but his preaching made him a hero, two reasons for the esteem in which the Moore family held him.

A SERMON ON NATURE

If Moore derived important aspects of her poetry from Browne, Milton, Baxter, and Bunyan, it is not unlikely that she sought a vehicle with seventeenth-century connections to contain her observations. The Protestant sermon, experienced from childhood and understood and appreciated as an adult, lay close at hand. Perry Miller serves as the best mediator to convey the tradition of the sermon, developed in England and brought to America with the first Puritan colonists, to the modern reader.[24] With his help, I will examine the nature of the sermon in its origins, in its transmission to Moore through the legacy of her grandfather, preacher extraordinary, and in its application in one representative poem, "The Frigate Pelican," 1934. Seen through this long lens, the sermon is a natural resource for Moore; her affinity for it should come as no surprise.

The Protestant sermon arose as evangelical reformists sought to bring to bear in the pulpit issues of sin and regeneration "'after the plain and profitable way'" as the Reformation took hold in England in the seventeenth century.[25] This sermon in the "plain style" evolved in contrast to those of University or Anglican preachers who would "'stuffe and fill their Sermons with as much Quotation and citing of Authors as might possibly be.'" In practice, the distinction between styles was one of concentration on Scripture "by raysing of Doctrine, with prepounding the Reasons and Uses" stemming from the sacred text, in contrast to learned discourses that ranged across secular history, arts, and letters as sources of rhetorical flourish and intellectual delight. Hence the "plain style," not only one embracing Professor Georgianna Goddard King's straightforward sentence structure but also one eschewing embellishment by extended metaphor and high flown references. The goal of the exercise was to call listeners to salvation by dint of reasonable argument evolved from the word of God.

The structure of this sermon became so recognizable as to serve as a party badge: Protestant not Anglican. It consisted of text, doctrines, reasons and uses presented without quotations from Church fathers and classical writers but with elaborate documentation from Scripture, its sources referenced in the body of the work. Following the statement of text taken from a brief biblical passage, the preacher "opens" the text slightly by explicating its grammar, moves to the theological points or doctrines deduced from it, speaks next of the intellectual persuasions or reasons why the doctrines are essential for consideration, and finally addresses the uses or applications of these points to the hearers' behaviors as they strive for salvation. Where the Anglican sermon indulged in purple patches in describing, for example, the joys of heaven, the Protestant one "reduces even the rapture of resurrection to a numerical method" and merely lists the spiritual aspects of heaven as points one through three.[26] Miller gives a telling example of a "rolling and sonorous accumulation of iterative phrases and modulated clauses" from a Donne (Anglican) sermon:

A new earth, where all their waters are milk and all their milk, honey; where all their grass is corn, and all their corn manna; where all their glebe, and all their clods of earth are gold, and all their gold of innumerable carats; where all their minutes are ages, and all their ages, eternity, . . . every minute, infinitely better than it ever was before.[27]

Miller goes on to say that

> Puritan piety was no less intense . . . but in Puritan sermons intensity of piety was balanced by the precision and restraint of a highly methodical form, a rigid dialectical structure and the ecstasy was severely confined within the framework of doctrine, reasons, and uses."[28]

It is hard not to see in these contrasting sermon styles where Moore's poetry falls if we recast the Puritan version as "intensity of emotion" subject to "highly methodical poetic structure" in a "framework of principles, evidence, and moral applications."

A sermon of John Cotton demonstrates the Protestant sermon in early America. Formerly a preacher of the most florid Anglican sermons, upon conversion Cotton bored his audience to the point that they drew their hats over their eyes, with the exception of one auditor who realized that his salvation depended on what he was hearing and bolted upright, hat restored to head. It is hard to see this effect from the dryness of what follows but Cotton's success is everywhere attested. Preaching in Massachusetts Bay in 1641 on "Now when they heard this, they were pricked in their hearts" (Acts 2:37), Cotton "opens" his text by explaining that Peter's audience were struck to realize that they had crucified Jesus.[29] The doctrine evolved: "The very first work of living and saving grace gives a deadly stroke to the life of sinful nature." The reason: "We must die with Christ before we can have fellowship in his Resurrection" (Rom. 6:3–11). The use: "Dost thou find . . . thou hast no delight in sin? . . . Then I say, thy heart is pierced and wounded." The sermon stops with the last use—there is no peroration, no final appeal to the senses, merely "Consider it therefore, so much as God had pricked thy heart, so much it sits loose from the world . . . let your hearts run freely to all good office in the behalf of your brethren." The summary moral closes the work.

While this distillation belies the much more fluid prose of the sermon, it emphasizes that the subject of the sermon is less important here than its style and organization. The subject is as straightforward as its biblical opacity and complexity will allow and its writer's skill can elucidate with clarity. The style and organization derive from an agreed-upon logic, namely, that the text from divine revelation will, of itself, and through the minister's mediation, yield relevant, theologically correct doctrines, or tenets to be believed, with intellectually supported rationalizations for those tenets—their conformity to man's understanding—and finally, lead to applications of this teaching to the conduct of daily life in pursuit of salvation. Text, doctrine, reason use—tightly woven, gracefully written.

The tradition of the Protestant sermon, in which Cotton stands near the beginning, continued to mark the preaching of Protestant ministers in the succeeding centuries. Not least among those inheritors, John Riddle Warner learned to organize his sermons after the fashion of Cotton and others, with allowances for natural shifts in language and education over three centuries.

In his "Sermon VI"[30] Warner follows the traditional order. His text, from Hos 6:4, is "O Ephraim, what shall I do unto thee? O Judah, what shall I do unto thee? for your goodness is as a morning cloud and as the early dew it goeth away." He opens the text to explain that God addresses all men whose weak efforts at profession of faith soon evaporate—a condition recognized by the Lord's desert-dwelling audience. As a doctrine, he educes that men called to conversion can be distracted from their goal by their trouble in perfectly understanding revelation. As a reason in support of this doctrine, he appeals to God's second book (if not by name), quoting Jeremiah: "The stork in the heaven knoweth her appointed times; and the turtle and the crane and the swallow observe the time of their coming; but my people know [understand] not the judgment of the Lord."[31] Warner expands on this reason with the example of the migrating instinct of birds from Central America who know when northern ice has broken up: "And who, by unerring guidance, has taught them the course they never mistake? How often do we find God's irrational creatures performing feats to which the most accomplished sons of science have never attained!"[32] At the end, he cites the use or moral: You know that many Christians overcome their doubts and "live a life derived from the Invisible." To get rid of doubts, attend to the practical duties toward God and man. "Consecrate your life in all things to the service of Him who loved you and gave Himself up for you. Let it be a protest against that superficial profession . . . which was 'like the morning cloud and the early dew which goeth away.'"[33]

Most notable in this sermon are its organization and several of its ideas. The structure follows that of the traditional Protestant sermon—more flowingly written than Cotton's, to be sure, yet in the plain style without rhetorical flourishes. The content, while in service of a text commending belief to overcome lack of understanding, draws on examples from nature and invokes a "life derived from the Invisible." When Moore takes her turn, she produces a poem with enough characteristics of the Protestant sermon to qualify her as a practitioner in this tradition.

Nowhere, of course, has Moore called herself a preacher. Her poems point a moral, comment on right behavior and disparage wrongdoing. They are her vehicles of moral vision just as sermons are the preacher's. Moore steps across that divide, at least in "The Frigate Pelican," to create a poem-as-sermon.

The poem takes its text from Samuel Johnson:[34]

The Frigate Pelican

Rapidly cruising or lying on the air there is a bird
that realizes Rasselas's friend's project
of wings uniting levity with strength.

(*SP* 38)

Moore "opens" her text with attention to the meaning of "bird":

This
hell-diver, frigate-bird, hurricane-
bird; unless swift is the proper word
for him, the storm omen. . . .

(*SP* 38)

There follows the doctrine or statement of principle: this magnificently built pirate naturally flies superbly and feeds, without ever touching water, on fish caught by less agile birds. Reasons in support follow: he is not truly a pelican but *Fregata aquila,* like an eagle (speed and sight); he has the wingspread of a swan and the tail shape of a swallow (power and feeding aloft); he outflies airplanes with wings that flap and quills that bend (ailerons of flexibility for riding thermals).

While Moore does not footnote Johnson, since she expects her readers to know *Rasselas* as well as she does, she supplies four notes to the poem to document obscure sources. Her pattern of notes is much like that of the sermon writer who might feel condescending in supplying "John I:1" for "In the beginning was the word" while knowing that "O Ephraim . . . O Judah" may not strike his readers as a verse from a minor prophet, the equivalent of Moore's notes in this poem to a Linnenean name, a photograph, a Peruvian legend, and a Hindoo saying. The poet next contrasts each of the bird's attributes with characteristics of other animals, all exhibiting flawed or unnatural behavior induced by humans, until she proclaims "*Festina lente*" (*SP* 40, line 82). Erasmus's gloss on this adage is "the right timing and the right degree, governed alike by vigilance and patience, so that nothing regrettable is done through haste, and nothing left undone through sloth."[35] Thus begins the "use" or moral application. The bird follows this adage as it

rise[s] from the bough [at dawn], and though flying [is] able to foil the tired
moment of danger, that lays on heart and lungs the
weight of the python that crushes to powder

(*SP* 41)

avoiding death that would have resulted from flying too high, too fast. This is nature's answer to Rasselas's friend's project, and, drawn from "God's

second book," it is also the divine answer: the frigate pelican, while a pirate, nonetheless fulfils its mission and its divine plan.

The poem concludes:

> The reticent lugubrious ragged immense minuet
> descending to leeward, ascending to windward
> again without flapping, in what seems to be
> a way of resting, are now nearer,
> but as seemingly bodiless yet
> as they were. Theirs are sombre
> quills for so wide and lightboned a bird
> as the frigate pelican
> of the Caribbean.
>
> (*SP* 41)

The moral rests on contradictions: the unturbulent bird uses turbulence to
fly; it fixes its flexible wings; it seems to rest as it glides; its huge wings
dwarf its powerful body; and, lastly, the "wide and lightboned" bird has
such "somber" quills. The bird can "alter any quill-tip," the source of its
flexibility that distinguishes this nature-made creature from the man-made
airplane of 1934. But for all its impressive power, the frigate pelican has
dark characteristics—"lugubrious," "somber," "reticent": in fulfilling its
role in nature, it steals, has victims, is dishonest, soars aimlessly. Moore
brings us to the human application. While the bird never strays from the requirements of his nature, he is part of a poem in which he "realizes Rasselas's friend's project." The Prince's friend created "many ingenious con-
trivances to facilitate motion and unite levity and strength" but his wings
failed utterly and landed him in the lake. Herein lies the final moral and this
sermon's last "use": just as no device could lift the Prince out of the Happy
Valley, where he would finally have to spend his life, so too the frigate pelican does not veer from his prescribed path. Yet the poem's reader, only human, learns that on either path, his own en route to his destiny, presumably
salvation, or the bird's to his in conformity to his fixed nature, passes
through darkness. Here we see the working out of the visible powered by
the invisible in a poem written to persuade us of that power.

Moore's sermon in verse proclaims her experience of God's second book
just as Browne's *Religio Medici* and *Pseudodoxia Epidemica,* Milton's
Paradise Lost, Baxter's *The Saints' Everlasting Rest,* and Bunyan's *Pilgrim's Progress* proclaimed theirs. Moore, however, always disguised at
least part of her intention through the intricacies of her articulation, the obscurity of her sources, and her unconventional approach to emblems, sym-
bols, or typology. Concerning the last, she leads us to assume that her rational approach to her natural subjects forebears our seeking symbolic

meaning. But if she has rendered a sermon of her own design in "The Frigate Pelican," it is hard not to allow her bird to share the emblematic features of the scriptural pelican, a figure of the redemptive Christ.

Moore's interest in seventeenth-century writers and the Protestant sermon, fostered in early youth and developed in maturity, marks her poetry, particularly that of the 1930s. The appreciation of nature as God's "second book" by evangelical Protestants along with the heightened inquiry into the workings of the world by such writers as Browne fed both her fondness for the natural world and her ongoing quest for understanding its inhabitants. The rich poetry of Milton and the complex expressiveness of Baxter offered passages for direct quotation in her Modernist verse, part of the amalgam she mixed with her own words to express her moral vision. Bunyan portrayed for her the invisible as the power behind the visible, the hidden spiritual forces that the Christian identifies with redemption through Christ. When Moore chose the form of the sermon to envelop her frigate pelican, she reconstituted a seventeenth-century model as a Modernist poem.

A helpful next step in the process of understanding Moore's use of these and related subjects would be the attention of an expert in seventeenth-century literature and of a historian of the Reformation to her work.[36] As Jeredith Merrin points out, in the Modernists' struggle to "make it new," they had to be aware of their inheritance: the poets "must have some idea of what the 'it' is."[37] Even as we seek further elucidation of the work of this difficult poet, however, we come face to face with Eliot's remark about the connection of a poet to her subject matter. "We all," he said in his essay on Moore, "have to choose whatever subject-matter allows us the most powerful and most secret release; and that is a personal affair."[38]

NOTES

1. Jeredith Merrin, *An Enabling Humility: Marianne Moore, Elizabeth Bishop, and the Uses of Tradition* (New Brunswick, NJ: Rutgers University Press, 1990). See chapter 1, "'To Explain Grace Requires a Curious Hand': Marianne Moore and Seventeenth-Century Prose.'"

2. Andrew Kappel, "The *Verba Ardentia* of Richard Baxter in the Poems of Marianne Moore," *Christianity and Literature* 41 (Summer 1992): 421–44.

3. Andrew Kappel, "Notes on the Presbyterian Poetry of Marianne Moore," in *Woman and Poet,* ed. Patricia Willis (Orono, ME: National Poetry Foundation, 1990), 39–51.

4. Jeredith Merrin, "Sites of Struggle: Marianne Moore and American Calvinism," in *The Calvinist Roots of the Modern Era,* ed. Aliki Barnstone et al. (Hanover, NH: University Press of New England, 1997), 91–106.

5. In her first poems published after the *Dial* closed, those in *Poetry* in 1932, Moore returned to her stanzaic syllabic meter. I would argue that at that time she also concluded most of her poems with a "moral" of the Aesopian kind, an explicit statement far less cryptic than the endings of many of her earlier poems.

6. W. B. Yeats, *The Autobiography of William Butler Yeats, Consisting of Reveries Over Childhood and Youth, The Trembling of the Veil, and Dramatis Personae* (Garden City, NY: Doubleday & Company, 1958), 182.

7. John Riddle Warner, *Sermons of the Rev. John R. Warner, D.D., with a Sketch of His Life,* ed. Mary Warner Moore (Philadelphia: J .B. Lippincott, 1895), 2ff.

8. *SP* 38–41. This text of the poem will be used throughout. It includes many lines cut in later editions.

9. Marianne Moore to Mary Warner Moore and John Warner Moore, 9 February 1909, *RML.*

10. Sir Thomas Browne, *Religio Medici,* in *The Major Works,* ed. C. A. Patrides (Harmondsworth, UK and New York: Penguin, 1977), par. 16, 78–79. I would not argue that Browne is the only source for Moore on this subject; the notion of the second book was widespread in the seventeenth century and persists today. See Kappel, "Notes," for his association of Moore and nature as God's second book.

11. See, for example, the first letter in *SL* 9, written to her brother Warner on his nineteenth birthday, where she draws a very elaborate conceit comparing him to a toad, an ongoing game between them.

12. Merrin, *Enabling Humility,* 29.

13. John Milton, *Paradise Lost,* in *John Milton: Complete Poems and Major Prose,* ed. Merritt Y. Hughes (New York: Macmillan, 1985), Book 6, lines 71–76, 325.

14. Ibid., Book 7, lines 421–32, 356–57.

15. Richard Baxter, *The Saints' Everlasting Rest,* ed. William Young (London: Religious Tract Society, 1907), xv. Published in the tens of thousands in 1650 and subsequently in other editions, the work was pirated and reedited over the centuries.

16. See Kappel, *"Verba,"* 422.

17. Marianne Moore, "Marriage," *CPo* 66; Baxter, *Saints' Everlasting,* 50.

18. Kappel, *"Verba,"* passim.

19. Baxter, *Saints' Everlasting,* 427. The "Marriage" quotation is in the previous paragraph.

20. John Bunyan, *The Pilgrim's Progress,* ed. N. H. Keeble (Oxford: Oxford University Press, 1998), 41.

21. Ibid., xxii.

22. Marianne Moore, "He 'Digesteth Harde Yron,'" *CPo* 100.

23. Bunyan, *Pilgrim's Progress,* 1.

24. I owe the suggestion of Perry Miller's work to Rev. Ross Luderman, a Presbyterian pastor and graduate of Princeton Theological Seminary.

25. Perry Miller, *The New England Mind in the Seventeenth Century* (Cambridge, MA: Harvard University Press, 1939), 331. Miller's chapter on "The Plain Style" details the development of the sermon as it came to be practiced in America. In his acknowledgments, Miller explains that many of his quotations are given without notes (which can be found deposited in a library) so Miller's pages alone will be cited here.

26. Ibid., 334.

27. Ibid.

28. Ibid.

29. John Cotton, *The Way of Life, Or, Gods Way and Course, in Bringing the Soule into, keeping it in, and carrying it on, in the wayes of life and peace. Laide downe in foure severall Treatises in foure Texts of Scripture* (1641), excerpted in *Colonial and Federal American Writing,* ed. George F. Horner and Robin A. Bain (New York: Odyssey, 1966), 92–98.

30. Warner, *Sermons,* 76–86.

31. Ibid., 80.

32. Warner continues this "reason" with the example of carrier pigeons used during the

Franco-German war to communicate with cut-off Paris. Moore's poem "Pigeons," 1935, addresses this phenomenon at length during World War I.

33. Warner, *Sermons,* 86.

34. Samuel Johnson, *The History of Rasselas, Prince of Abyssinia,* ed. Gwin J. Kolb (New York: Appleton Century Crofts, 1962), 15. A fuller reading of the poem against this text would be a fruitful exercise but one beyond the scope of this essay.

35. Erasmus, *Collected Works of Erasmus,* vol. 33: *Adages* II i 1–II vi 100, trans. Margaret Mann Phillips and R. A. B. Mynors (Toronto, Canada: University of Toronto Press, 1992), 3.

36. See Robert Babcock, "Verses, Translations, and Reflections from 'The Anthology': H.D., Ezra Pound, and the Greek Anthology," *Sagetrieb* 14, nos. 1–2 (Spring/Fall 1995): 202–16, for an example of a classicist's expertise brought to bear on H.D.

37. Merrin, *Enabling Humility,* 37.

38. T. S. Eliot, Introduction to *SP,* 9.

"What Is War For?"
Moore's Development of an Ethical Poetry

Cristanne Miller

Eᴀʀʟʏ ɪɴ ꜰᴇʙʀᴜᴀʀʏ 2003, ʟᴀᴜʀᴀ ʙᴜꜱʜ ᴘʀᴏɴᴏᴜɴᴄᴇᴅ ɪɴ ᴇꜰꜰᴇᴄᴛ ᴛʜᴀᴛ poetry should have nothing to do with politics. This position was articulated in relation to a White House symposium she had just cancelled celebrating the poetry of Walt Whitman, Emily Dickinson, and Langston Hughes—three poets keenly interested in the politics of their respective eras.[1] Moreover, the cancellation occurred when the First Lady got wind of the fact that Sam Hamill was encouraging poets to send him poems or statements "against the [impending] war" against Iraq. Within a few weeks, by March 3, over 13,000 poets—including Carolyn Kizer, Adrienne Rich, Philip Levine, Galway Kinnell, and Rita Dove—had contributed to Hamill's anthology.[2] To explain his decision not to contribute, John Hollander wrote, "I don't feel poetry should be merely an expression of opinion. . . . When asked to make a political statement, I say, 'As a citizen, I will; as a poet, I will not.'"[3]

Marianne Moore would have agreed with Hollander that poetry should not express mere opinion; on the other hand, Moore, I believe, did not distinguish her role as citizen from her role as poet, and she saw both as ethical. Whether she would have contributed to Hamill's anthology is a moot point, given the very different circumstances of the Bush administration's war against Iraq from those of World War I. Although Moore was a pacifist, she felt strong ambivalence about whether the U.S. should enter the war, eventually tipping toward support—no doubt in part because of her brother Warner's enlistment as a navy chaplain in 1917. It is, however, a matter of simple fact that Moore's earliest publications established her simultaneously as a formally innovative poet and as a poet speaking out on issues of national concern, in particular in relation to World War I. Although Moore had been writing poems with some seriousness since 1907, she first turned to writing poetry as her primary occupation in the summer of 1914. Moore took the summer off from teaching at the Carlisle Indian School, and then the department in which she taught closed in September. Because her mother and brother felt that Moore had been overworked at the school, she decided not to look immediately for another job.[4] During these months of intensive writing, Moore also turned to ancient Hebrew poet-prophecy as a model for ethical speech to a national community in time of war—partly spurred by a Bible study class she was participating in with the family's minister, Edwin H. Kellogg. Biblical prophets frequently spoke as a voice of conscience to their communities, and Moore read the prophets through the interpretive lens of liberal Protestant theologians who stressed the ethical positioning of the prophets in relation to Israelite history. Ancient Hebrew poet-prophets, as she understood them through her Bible class and reading, provided a respected tradition of personal speech about public issues that did not foreground the self either as privileged speaker or as spouter of opinion.

The years 1914 and 1915 saw a general shift in Moore's poetic, from the typically short and relatively simple, playful, or referentially obscure poems of her early years to the longer, formally more innovative, and thematically more complex poems that were to make her one of the most widely admired Modernist poets by the mid-1920s. Many of her war and poet-prophet poems remained unpublished; others were published only once, or not again after *Observations*. These poems, however, seem to have served almost as a workshop. Dealing with issues of war, ethical self-positioning through poetic voice, relation to audience, and construction of what Moore called a clarity "as clear as our natural reticence allows us to be" but with "a sort of contempt for hard and fast definitions," these poems led Moore to her mature style.[5] Moreover, the body of her early published and unpublished work reveals the extent to which Moore saw politics, ethics, religion, and art as virtually indistinguishable in some respects. Her listing of multiple titles for several early poems, for example, shows that the same group of lines resonated for her politically, spiritually, and aesthetically.

According to Tobin Siebers, "The heart of ethics is the desire for community."[6] Moore's experimentation with address and tone in her early poems displays her attempt to forge a desired community through dramatic monologues of opposition and a broaching of aesthetic, social, and political issues that goes beyond private or partisan expression. If the heart of ethics is community, then the heart of Moore's poetic was ethical. This has not been the primary reading of Moore's poetry, for a number of reasons— of which I will mention three.[7] First, ethics was not a popular topic of literary criticism during the periods of either New Critical or Structuralist/Deconstructive dominance, when Moore criticism received its initial academic impetus and directions. Second, the 1970s and 1980s replacement of New Criticism with various theoretical and cultural approaches to literary study initially promoted a widespread assumption that the formal surface difficulty of Modernist poetry was allied with an apolitical, elitist, or even fascist poetics, thereby discouraging attention to the politics of

Moore's poems. Even within early feminist criticism, Moore's work was of little interest to the feminist agendas of the 1970s and early eighties.[8]

Third, even some of Moore's greatest early admirers contributed to the tendency to see her work in terms of old-fashioned moralism rather than ethics. At the end of her posthumously published essay on Moore, "Efforts of Affection," Elizabeth Bishop muses: "manners; morals . . . manners and morals; manners *as* morals? Or is it morals *as* manners?"[9] Similarly, Randall Jarrell famously wrote that in reading Moore's poems "one is often conscious . . . of the cool precise untouchedness, untouchableness, of fastidious rectitude . . . Some of her poems have the manners or manner of ladies who learned a little before birth not to mention money, who neither point nor touch, and who scrupulously abstain from the mixed, live vulgarity of life."[10] These voices carried great authority and continue to affect readings of Moore. Betsy Erkkila, for example, reads Moore largely from the perspective suggested by Bishop's remarks in her 1992 *The Wicked Sisters: Women Poets, Literary History, and Discord* and Cynthia Stamy quotes Jarrell more than any other Moore critic in her 2001 *Marianne Moore in China.* Such positioning identified Moore as one whose manneredness was moralistic, based on strict preconceived beliefs about right and wrong or propriety, rather than as one who attempts to address questions of what it means to live in a principled way in a complex world.

Since the mid-1990s, several critics *have* turned to questions of ethical agency in literature. In particular, Charles Altieri proposes that even poets wary of universal judgments may take ethical positions through grammatical structures and forms of address that imply interdependence.[11] As I've argued in *Questions of Authority,* Moore's verse indeed develops an implied interdependency through its repeated quotations, negations, questions, direct address to a reader, and generally unemphatic first-person presence. In this structural foregrounding of multiple sources and voices, Moore even goes so far in "A Note on the Notes" as to describe her "method of composition" as "hybrid"; "the chief interest" of many lines, she writes, "is borrowed" (*CPo* 262). Such a claim directly contradicts any assumption of authorial inspiration or elevation, defining a poetic based on hearing and reading the words of others. While no written text in fact interacts with an audience, hers asserts structures of interaction. As Tess Gallagher suggests, Moore "preferred the responsibility of conversation to the responsibility of the orator."[12] Yet here is the key point: at the same time, she is also comfortable with a stance of judgment as such. Judgment, this poetic implies, is the result of such listening, talking, and reading; it occurs in relation to the multiple voices of the poet's world, not in independence from them or reliance on any privileged source. Judging, it further implies, is a duty, especially when the historical context demands the weighing of apparently opposed values. Moore's poetry, then, is ethical not just through its grammatical, implicitly interactive or conversational structures but also in its posing of questions about individual and "conversational" responsibilities and behavior. Moreover, her poems pose such questions without providing easy answers for readers, hence function not to prescribe but to goad readers to further thought.

According to Moore, this was also the function of Hebrew prophecy. In an essay titled "Marianne Moore and a Poetry of Hebrew (Protestant) Prophecy," I argue that Moore's reading of liberal Protestant theologians and her Bible class with Kellogg led her to see Hebrew prophetic poetry as "an ancient and revered justification for the mixture of ethical, public, and aesthetic principles important to her."[13] Moore understood prophecy not as prediction or the literal speech of God but as an act of community engagement, in which the speaker addressed immediate political and social issues in spiritual terms in order to encourage reflection. As theologian George A. Smith wrote, Hebrew prophets were not philosophers or soothsayers but men who declared "the character and the will of God" by addressing current "political and ethical" issues; prophets stressed "justice and equity"; they emphasized religious observance "most frequently for social ends" and attempted to "liberate" individuals from "a *merely* national religion."[14] In her extensive notes on Smith's *The Book of the Twelve Prophets,* Moore includes: "these (Hebrew) men . . . worshipped God neither out of sheer physical sympathy w. nature . . . nor out of a selfish passion for their own salvation like so many modern Christian fanatics; but in symp. w. their nation's aspirations for freedom and her whole political life."[15]

Moore found in Hebrew prophecy not only a general ethical stance as speaker to a community, but also a model for the repeated necessity to grapple with issues of warfare and violence. The prophets she cites in her early verse take significant stances against violence as justified or mandated by God. Isaiah declares that the people "shall beat their swords into plowshares, and their spears into pruninghooks: nation shall not lift up sword against nation, neither shall they learn war any more" (Isa. 2:4); Jeremiah twice commands, "do no violence to the stranger, the fatherless, nor the widow, neither shed innocent blood in this place" (22:3 and 7:6); according to Ezekiel, the "just" man "hath not oppressed any . . . hath spoiled none by violence, hath given his bread to the hungry, and hath covered the naked with a garment" (18:7); and Daniel instructs a king: "Break off your sins by practicing righteousness, and your iniquities by showing mercy to the oppressed" (4:27). Daniel is also famous for responding to threatened violence peacefully, as in the lion's den. These poets use their verbal gifts to guide and teach. In less direct ways, Moore attempts the same. Such a stance of authority is particularly surprising at the beginning of a female poet's career in an age when women were rarely taken seriously as public political or moral guides, let alone as poets.

Moore writes about the war in her letters of 1914. By August 5, Austria-Hungary had declared war on Serbia, Germany had declared war on Russia and France and had invaded Belgium, Britain had declared war on Germany, and President Wilson had declared U.S. neutrality. On September 13, she writes her brother that she is writing a "war poem" to compete in a contest;[16] on October 4, in another letter to Warner, she assumes that he will have spoken about the war in his sermon, adding that in the service she attended "Kel [Reverend Kellogg] harrangued a long time to great point and said that peace is not the only alternative in the case of loyalty to God"—an interesting comment in its apparent assumption that peace would be the obvious route to such loyalty (*SL* 96). Ten days later, she writes: "Poor Europe!! I cannot imagine the state of my mind if we were at the front (in person I mean though it is every bit as bad as it is, now)."[17] For the next few months, she frequently mentions the war in letters to Warner and in a mock-newspaper she sent him, called *The File*. The November 29 *File* is titled "Common Sense on The War" and concludes that "the war is an outrage" (VI.20.12).

Drafts of poems written during Moore's Carlisle years show the extent to which both the European war and ethical issues of aggression and response were on her mind. Most of these poems are undated, typed on small greenish-blue stationery, and labeled with the poet's Carlisle address, indicating that she had probably submitted them to publishers.[18] Letters and notebooks provide little assistance in assigning dates to individual poems, but most were probably written in the first two years of the war, after she had ceased to work at the Carlisle Indian School and before she and her mother moved to Chatham in the fall of 1916. Three address the "Kaiser," criticizing his squandering of wealth on military goals and suggesting that the Kaiser's "consuls" leave "Heaven" or divine guidance behind them "when they go to war" even while fighting in the name of God.[19] A 1915 poem entitled "To a Stiffwinged Grasshopper" includes the opening lines: "As I unfolded its wings / In examining it for the first time, / I forgot the war"—as though this is something she rarely did.[20] "To Pharoah's Baker Plucking up Courage to ask the Interpretation of his Dream, when a Favorable Interpretation had been Accorded the Dream of Pharoah's Butler" comments, "Free men fare worst / when . . . doomed men perish on the plain."[21]

Other poems deal indirectly with issues of conflict and engagement, perhaps posed by the spreading European conflict. A poem titled "To an Enemy Sharpening His Eyes upon Me" worries about "Dissension" and "Prevention" through reference to a broken "Crock."[22] "The Candle-Stick Maker" presents a monologue which begins: "Have I extinguishers to snuff out my benighted fellow men!"[23] The title "To a Cantankerous Poet Ignoring his Compeers—Thomas Hardy, Bernard Shaw, Joseph Conrad, Henry James" (all favorite authors of Moore's during this period) suggests the competitive jockeying of modern writers for status. The opposition of a "cantankerous poet" to these "compeers" allied with her own aesthetics hardly constitutes warfare, but it does condemn a stance of bad-tempered competition and ignorance. "Am I a Brother to Dragons and a Companion to Owls?" addresses not the war but why a poet might feel obliged to write about such public issues. The entire poem reads: "I am exactly that: brusque, blind—/ Unsocialized in deed, convinced in mind, / Of my strict duty to mankind," suggesting that only extinct or unsociable beings (dragons, owls, and poets?) take seriously a "duty to mankind."[24] Moore may also here humorously mock passions or "blind[ness]" of her own that could make her sense of duty appear like an owl's or dragon's attack. The poem's asserted sense of duty without any claim to effectiveness may also be self-mocking.

Another early poem titled "Man's Feet are a Sensational Device" plays in one line with the idea that "ethics" or, as originally typed, "the clear field of moral choice" enables movement:

> The clear field of moral choice affords men's
> Feet, crackling ice
> To tread, and feet are
> A sensational device.[25]

People may proceed across the thin ice of a sense of moral responsibility when reason alone gives them no ground at all to place their feet on: ethical choice enables action but involves risk. Other early drafts are suggestively titled: "To Pacifists in War Time" (also titled "To a Public Servant in War Time" and "To the Faithfully Weary"), "The Assassins," and "Patriotic Sentiment and the Maker."[26] In an early 1920s notebook containing drafts of "Marriage," "An Octopus," and other poems, Moore writes, "When you get what you fought for it is not what you fought for but diminished. Ethics is here mixed with art," making explicit what she elsewhere implies: art involves a battle of values, and means can defeat ends. Any self-positioning that structures an argument along the lines of victory and defeat necessarily taints the victory. In the same notebook, Moore similarly queries "Is to admit defeat to ack[nowledge] that an argument has two sides."[27] In art, in a principled life, and in international contexts involving war, it is crucial to consider both whether overcoming an opponent constitutes victory and whether negotiation, compromise, or any other strategy acknowledging the value of differing positions constitutes defeat.

Moore sees personal, national, and international duty as equally implicated by the ethics of choice, as she indicates in her religion class notebook, where she writes that the "nation [is] good by the same moral principle as [the] individual."[28] In a more specific conjunction of individual and national behaviors, Moore types out a poem already published in the *Lantern* (1910) as "Qui S'Excuse, S'Accuse" and now called "Looking at It," adding an epigraph. The epigraph reads: "Henry James: Explanation is self accusation / F. G. Cooper: Lemme out. / Max Eastman: Take off your blinders. / The Pre-Evolutionist: I won't take 'em off, I like 'em."[29] The James quotation gives the source for the poem's title; the lines ascribed to political cartoonist Cooper and socialist pacifist Eastman, however, come from a May 16, 1914 *Colliers* cartoon called "The Standpatter," which Moore copied into a reading notebook.[30] In the cartoon, a speaker resembling Uncle Sam and wearing huge blinders says "No! I *won't* take 'em off! I LIKE 'EM!!," while a tiny figure in the corner, also wearing blinders, cries "lemme out." This cartoon was published, and Moore may have revised her poem, before European fighting began. Its representation of willfully ignorant authority, however, anticipates the critique of specifically antiwar poems and, if written after August 1914, may share their reference to national blindness.

"Piningly" deals with similar issues of ends and means, introducing a more pointed critique of tunnel-vision in figures of authority. In this poem, an unidentified "they" "manufactured" "extravagant freedom" "out of wealth" and "discussed 'commerce / and the national destiny'—averse / To the nightmare of anything like a fact."[31] With her science training and interest in pragmatics, Moore was enormously concerned with attention to what could be known.[32] The "stuff of experience," Moore notes in reading Horace Kallen's *Value and Existence* in 1917, "is not the spirit but stones and railway wrecks and volcanoes and Mexico and submarines, and trenches and frightfulness, and Germany and disease, and waters, and trees and stars and mud."[33] One understands the world and the ethics of choice by attention to news of all kinds—from railway accidents to muddy trench warfare in Europe to the scientific study of disease and stars. Just as her own faith was not dimmed by historical scholarship on the Bible, her sense of responsibility to the world included a responsibility to remain open to new "facts" and ways that they might affect one's thinking. Hence, to discuss "national destiny" while ignoring facts could only be wrong-headed. John Dewey's *Essays in Experimental Logic,* quoted on the same page of her notebook as Kallen's work, articulates an opinion Moore shared about human fallibility, and hence the need for vigilance in acquiring "facts": "There is something humorous about the discussion of the problem of error—as if it were a rare or exceptional thing—an anomaly—when the barest glance at human history shows that mistakes have been the rule, and that truth lies at the bottom of a well." While her sense of moral contingency grows stronger after the poems of 1914 and '15, even in the early poems Moore wants not to assert truths but to pose problems by framing opposed behaviors, with repeated critique of the "standpatter," eager to fight to promote his or her own values rather than attempt to see multiple sides of a question.

Moore's early published poems are as emphatic as the unpublished about the ethics of violence and about the war. The speaker of these poems is frequently positioned as beleaguered or bemused—in relation to the war and generally. Published in spring 1915 and almost certainly the "war poem" referred to the previous October, "Isaiah, Jeremiah, Ezekiel, Daniel" constitutes Moore's clearest and earliest statement that war is not mandated by God and that the poet has a duty to speak out against it.[34] The poem's title and epigraph indicate that the four named prophets share a common stance: "Isaiah, Jeremiah, Ezekiel, Daniel, / *Bloodshed and Strife are not of God*"

> What is war
> For;
> Is it not a sore
>   On this life's body?
> Yes? Although
> So
> Long as men will go
>   To battle fighting
> With gun-shot,
> What
> Argument will not
>   Fail of a hearing!
>
> (*BMM* 360)

This poem calls both the prophets of the title and the reader to confirm the speaker's claim, thereby giving it a kind of authority secondary but parallel to theirs. The poet's position is clear: she agrees that God does not approve violence, claims that war is "a sore / on this life's body," and then bemoans the powerlessness of the human voice to overcome gunshot, presenting the voice as an analogue for the even more vulnerable human body. War has always been terrible, but in the modern age of "gunshot" it is both louder and more destructive than ever. This does not, however, reduce the poet's responsibility to speak out against it.

Published on April 1, 1915 but probably written later than "Isaiah, Jeremiah, Ezekiel, Daniel," "To the Soul of 'Progress'" (retitled "To Military Progress" for *Observations*) repeats Moore's horror at the destructiveness of battle that continues "till the evening sky's / red" (*BMM* 188). An earlier version's title, "To Art Wishing for a Fortress into Which she may Flee from her Persecutors, Instead of Looking for a Jail in Which to Confine Them," further articulates Moore's conviction that industrial, military, and artistic behaviors share features of aggressiveness, defensiveness, and responsibility (I:04:57). While neither art nor economic and social institutions of

"progress" order men onto a battlefield, the attitudes they embody or articulate may support hierarchies of power and command. Art that is itself aggressive in attacking "persecutors" may be complicit with attitudes validat-
ing the righteousness of military aggression. With its change of title to "To
Military Progress," Moore beyond all question targets the institution of militarism, although even with its early title the poem's war reference is clear:
a personified "you" "use[s] your mind / like a millstone to grind / chaff" then
with its "warped wit / laugh[s]" at its "torso," or supporting body, cut off
from the controlling and unharmed "head." "The crow . . . calls . . . till the
tumult brings / more / black minute-men / to revive again, / war // at little
cost"—little cost, that is, to the master-"mind" that calls out the men who
turn the sky a bloody "red" with their killing and deaths (*BMM* 61).

Similarly, "To Statecraft Embalmed" (December 1915) went through a
series of titles to reach its caustic critique of any statesman who imagines
that "discreet behavior" is "the sum / of statesmanlike good sense" in a time
of crisis. Such a "necromancer" realizes too slowly that the elitism of power
(the "strict proportion / of your throne") corrupts judgment; it produces a
"wrenched distortion / of suicidal dreams" that will eventually "go / stag-
gering toward itself and with its bill, / attack its own identity, until / foe
seems friend and friend seems / foe." Secrecy, silence, power-hungry display lead to confused violence, in which the state (or statesman) destroys itself. Moore, with her typical indirection, challenges such elitist distortion
through an exclamation of imperfect but vital liveliness: "As if a death mask
ever could replace / life's faulty excellence!" (*BMM* 203). One early title for
this poem links the speaker to the prophet Micah. In her notes on Smith's
Book of the Twelve, Moore writes that the rich in Micah's day "cut up the
people like meat," continuing: "It is extremely difficult for us to fear ourselves in a state of society in w[hich] the fingers both of justice and religion
are gilded by their suitors."[35] The title "To the Bird, Whose Wings—'Both
of Religion and of Politics—are Gilded by her Suitors'" conflates the power
of the wealthy with that of corrupt statecraft, bribed or lobbied by "suitors."
Other titles—"To a System of Politics Purporting to be Immortal" and "To
Formalism, Aesthetic, Religious"—suggest that any reification of attitudes
or self-empowerment that bases its authority on flattery and established patterns will lead to stagnation—again conflating art, religion, and politics.[36]
Truths are contextual and historical. They cannot be understood through
"the incarnation of dead grace," and gilding destroys them by making intellectual movement and flight impossible. Only death enables perfection.
And only active reflection, free of the false shine of flattery, enables one to
distinguish friend from foe and decide on the best approaches to both.

In a 1926 *Dial* essay, Moore explicitly compares art to war, concluding,
"In making works of art, the only legitimate warfare is the inevitable war-

fare between imagination and medium." Although artists are "in some sense always in revolt" and may have violent dislikes to each other's work, "in so far as a thing is really a work of art it confirms other works of art" (*CPr* 177, 176). Moore's early poems about discord or enemies may have a personal basis in her own feelings of aesthetic revolt or embattlement. As Jeredith Merrin and Andrew Kappel have shown, the discourse of armor and battle in Moore's work also resembles that of her mother and brother's Christian militance—a discourse popular among late nineteenth-century Protestants.[37] Yet the discourse of conflict in these early poems would also have had immediate resonance for her audience with the escalating European war; given Moore's repeatedly expressed concern with this war, it is highly likely that it contained the same resonance for her.

Other poems bearing little or no apparent relation to the war in their published form go through drafts linking them to such conflict. An early version of "Pedantic Literalist" (published June 1, 1916) bears the title "To Civilization in its most Violent Form"—surely a reference to war.[38] Moreover, the poem's published text echoes "To Statecraft Embalmed" in its reference to the Literalist's "perfunctory" duty and heart, self-delusion, and "withered" ethical sense, inviting "destruction" (*BMM* 211). "The Pedantic Literalist" appears to be another form of deluded statesman or standpatter. Drafted in Chatham between the fall of 1916 and early 1918, "The Fish" at one point also includes lines pointing to the war: in the sea, "we / Find flowers entwined / With bodies." In the margin, alternate wording indicates that these bodies have met violent ends: "Find beauty intertwined with tragedy."[39] The 1918 "Reinforcements" suggests through its title that the men it describes are soldiers. "Moral machinery is not labeled," Moore warns in this brief poem; she admires those who go "to their work" or approach "experience" without exalting it "into epic grandeur" (*BMM* 232). Yet "the future of time is determined by the power of volition," including the will both to fight and to resist conflict. This poem perhaps reflects Moore's sense of how to make the best of a bad situation: if the U.S. must send "Reinforcements" to Europe, soldiers should not regard their "work" as morally righteous.

That recognizing a "foe" must not entail battle is the lesson of "To Be Liked By You Would Be a Calamity" (July 1916), titled "To the Stand Patter" in an early version—a title again linking national policymakers and scientific ignoramuses with a personal attitude of aggression through Moore's previous uses of this idiom: none will budge from their assumed positions. In this poem, Moore's speaker wittily employs gesture to refuse to engage in violence, turning aside her interlocutor's threats while maintaining the principle of her own difference. "To Be Liked By You Would Be a Calamity" reads in its entirety:

"Attack is more piquant than concord," but when
You tell me frankly that you would like to feel
My flesh beneath your feet,
I'm all abroad—I can but put my weapon up and
        Bow you out.
Gesticulation—it is half the language.
Let unsheathed gesticulation be the steel
Your courtesy must meet,
Since in your hearing words are mute, which to my senses
        Are a shout.

                                        (*BMM* 218)

Although this poem refers through its quotation to a man's sharp criticism
of a woman's writing in a Thomas Hardy novel, its concern with hostility
is in line with Moore's deliberations about national aggression. An early
unpublished poem approving its addressee rather than upbraiding him,
"Like Bertram Dobell, You Achieve Distinction by Disclaiming It," echoes
"To Be Liked By You."[40] It describes its subject as "parry[ing] compliment" with "reticence" in "self-protectiveness" and concludes: "the barrier
of the lips is the best defense," perhaps anticipating the later(?) poem's "unsheathed gesticulation." Published in the same 1916 issue of the *Chimaera*
as "To Be Liked By You," "In This Age of Hard Trying" also concerns indirection or "by-play" as a weapon of "self-protectiveness." Such a weapon
is "more terrible in its effectiveness / than the fiercest frontal attack"—a
comparison revealing the power as well as "humility" of resistance to aggressive "certitude" or attack (*BMM* 198–200).

    "To a Steam Roller" (October 1, 1915) presents a similar spirit of nonag-
gressive willingness to acknowledge difference without mastering it. With
its echoes of the opening lines of "To the Soul of 'Progress,'" this poem
suggests that even a "millstone"-like mind that grinds everything into
"chaff"—or, as "To a Steam Roller" puts it, "crush[es] all the particles
down / into close conformity, and then walk[s] back and forth on them"—
may not be an enemy, or have a perspective in every way alien to one's
own. The repetition of the crushing metaphor also suggests that both poems may have the military as subject, to the extent that war presumes assumptions of good and evil, right and wrong, friend and foe—the kind of
thinking characterizing the aggressive dichotomies of a steam roller, which
can discriminate only between rock that is and is not yet crushed "into . . .
conformity." Yet this poem concludes by demonstrating a generous perspective radically contrasting with that of military industrial leadership and
the steam roller: "As for butterflies," the speaker muses, "I can hardly conceive / of one's attending upon you, but to question / the congruence of the
complement is vain, if it exists" (*BMM* 190). Here, as in "To Be Liked By
You," the speaker demonstrates recognition of difference over ideology,

theory, or any other kind of absolutist distinction. The speaker enacts the behavior that she implies she would like to see a steamrolling absolutist adopt as well.

These poems are not about war per se, but they explicitly reject "the haggish, uncompanionable drawl // Of certitude" ("In This Age of Hard Trying") and promote reflection on the links between speech and attitudes of self-righteous or discriminatory aggression and weaponry, repeating Moore's conviction that the "nation [is] good by the same moral principle as [the] individual." By mid-1916, Moore has for the most part ceased to write specifically about World War I perhaps because she has ceased to oppose U.S. entry—although she remained a pacifist by conviction. It could also be that the war enters into her letters and poems less frequently because its horror is no longer new. By 1916, she may articulate that horror by searching for causes at the level of individual behavior rather than critiquing structures of militarism and statecraft. Certainly the middle war years posed an ethical distress of conflicting responsibilities: both to aid one's allies, and to resist all attitudes that lead to or enable warfare.

To the extent that "To a Steam Roller" deals with prejudicial perspectives, "The Labours of Hercules" reaches a similar conclusion, although this 1921 poem refers to specific biases, including one that arose in direct response to World War I. In its list of prejudices that it would be a labor of Hercules to eradicate, Moore includes that one "keeps on knowing" not only "'that the negro is not brutal, / that the Jew is not greedy, / that the Oriental is not immoral,'" but also "'that the German is not a Hun'" (*BMM* 265). In an era when everything German was being shunned and the large German-speaking populations of Central Pennsylvania, where she grew up, were feeling intense pressure to demonstrate loyalty to the U.S., Moore's reminder is simple and pointed: Germans are not all and forever "Huns."[41] One cannot classify "friend" or "foe" by nationality or past conflict any more than by skin pigmentation or religion.

According to other poems, the values of both pacifism and freedom are contingent. The 1917 "Sojourn in the Whale" (first published as "Ireland") concludes with a metaphor implying Moore's strong support for the Irish Easter Uprising of 1916, comparing British imperialists to old-fashioned men who cannot understand the Irish (or women) except as "circumscribed by a / heritage of blindness and native / incompetence." In contrast, Moore asserts that those who have been oppressed will rise, like water, when "obstacles . . . bar / the path." While one should avoid war, a battle fought for national independence is not only justifiable but natural, her metaphor implies. Here revolutionaries seem to be in the position of Jonah, swallowed by a colonial whale. The spring 1916 poem "Is Your Town Nineveh?" may address similar contingency, dealing with personal, not national, issues of freedom. This poem questions the reader: "Is your town Nineveh? . . . And

are you Jonah / in the sweltering east wind of your wishes?" (*BMM* 183).
If so, the poem implies, you should be attempting to save your city, not follow your selfish desire. And yet the poem's questions also identify
"wishes" with "personal upheaval in / the name of freedom," implying that
it would be a severe loss were all such "upheaval . . . to be tabooed."

In the political contexts of World War I and the Easter Rising, the desire
to be "free" is far from selfish—and from Moore's perspective, "upheaval
in / the name of freedom" also included reference to the American Revolution. The reader, then, is asked to weigh the values of duty and desire, restraint and freedom, on personal and international scales. The poem's conclusion leans toward a freedom that is restrained by communal or higher
good, through references to Jonah's liberation from the whale and the
Statue of Liberty—a symbol of national freedom and international coop-
eration, as a gift from France. Some have, quite reasonably, read "Is Your
Town Nineveh?" biographically, as referring to Moore's feelings of re-
striction within her family or aesthetic positioning within Modernism as
she begins to establish a reputation for herself.[42] Given its date of composition, however, this poem also suggests that some sacrifice of individual
freedom is justified by larger communal goals, such as helping France (and
other allies) in the war. A Jonah of early 1916 might need to warn New York
(the Nineveh in which one may see the Statue of Liberty) of the dangers of
self-serving isolationism rather than heathenism or sexual depravity.

Considering what a Jonah or Isaiah might have said to her own period of
international conflict seems to have been a useful way for Moore to pose
questions both to herself and to her audience in these early poems. The poet-
prophets she most admired attempted to guide through metonymy and analogy—tools of language associated with her own verse. By quoting their
words or asking herself and her readers to imagine themselves in the position of one who feels it a duty both to question and to communicate what it
means to behave morally in a particular situation ("the word of" God),
Moore urges readers and writers to make ethical reflection key to their understanding and behavior. Moore's poetic identification with Habakkuk underlines her conviction that the prophetic stance is not one of righteous
grandeur or certainty. According to Smith, Habakkuk was the first prophet
to initiate speculation into the field of Jewish prophecy. Habakkuk "feels
that revelation is baffled by experience, that the facts of life bewilder a man
who believes in the God whom the prophets have declared," but he searches
for greater clarity through questioning, and complaining to, God. He "arrives at a prophetic attitude" through doubt, query, and confusion.[43] In her
December 1915 "So far as the future is concerned . . ." (later published as
"The Past is the Present"), the speaker asserts "I shall revert to you, /
Habakkuk," if patterns of the past are "outmoded" and "effete" (*BMM* 208).
Habakkuk provides a model for a type of poet who attempts to respond to

events pragmatically without falling back on "outmoded" forms but still maintaining some aspect of the tradition of those forms; he uses his bafflement as a tool of prophecy rather than making it an excuse to reject the tradition of prophet altogether. Following Habakkuk, Moore can voice her questions and convictions without the "drawl of certitude."

Although neither of Moore's Jonah poems positions the speaker in direct relation to the prophet, Jonah is another significant model for ethical reflection and speech. In these poems, the most obvious points of resemblance between the poet and speaker are her Irish heritage (in "Sojourn in the Whale"), her residence near and then in New York beginning in the fall of 1916 (home to the Statue of Liberty, in "Is Your Town Nineveh?"), and her reference in a December 1915 family letter to a trip to New York as her "Sojourn in the Whale" (*SL* 107). Moore's notes on Smith again illuminate the grounds for this identification: "Jonah presents to us a vision of the monotonous millions," Moore writes. His significance lies in his lack of zeal, as prophet, but also in his description of "his country's foes," which deemphasizes "everything foreign, everything provocative of envy and hatred, and unfolds them to Israel only in their teeming humanity." Jonah claims that "under every form and character of human life . . . lies the power of the heart to turn"; "hope," according to Smith, is "the primal human right" learned from the prophet Jonah.[44]

Moore's notes suggest that she sees in this story less a tale of religious conversion than an illustration of the fact that people may change. Even the most reluctant speaker may learn a sense of public responsibility; even the most wicked people should be seen as fellow humans, capable of reform. Like Habakkuk, Jonah models prophesy as resistance. In a time of war, Moore would have looked favorably on Jonah's insistence on the primary humanness of those popularly regarded as "beings created for ignorance and hostility to God, elect for destruction" rather than as "men with consciences and hearts."[45] In this reading, Jonah stands not just for hope for himself and his own conversion, but hope for the world. Moore's "The Labours of Hercules" may be her attempt to follow Jonah's lead in insisting on the humanness of all people and in acknowledging that even to hold this conviction steadily requires Herculean effort. Moore's concerns as poet were far more directly for survival and peace of the world than for conversion, personal election, or salvation. As quoted earlier, she deplored those "modern Christian fanatics" consumed with passion for their own righteousness and attempted to articulate alternatives to such aggressive righteousness or defensiveness that might give hope for change at the levels of personal behavior and national policy. As Victoria Bazin argues, "the task of poetry [for Moore] is not to mirror what is already there but to change it."[46]

Looking at this cluster of poems as a group provides an unmistakable map of Moore's concerns in her early years of national publication. In

1915, she publishes two poems condemning warfare ("Isaiah, Jeremiah, Ezekiel, Daniel" and "To the Soul of 'Progress'"), one critique of statesmen, implicitly condemning the war ("To Statecraft Embalmed"), another critique of self-righteous destructiveness ("To a Steam Roller"), and a poem positioning herself as a Habakkuk-like poet, suggesting not just the formal combination of ecstasy and occasion but also the felt responsibility to question what she sees ("So far as the future . . ."). This is a remarkable number of directly or indirectly political poems for her first year of national publication, especially given that at least some of the nineteen poems published in 1915 were written before the war began.[47] In the following year, she publishes no poem of explicit commentary on the war but three poems about discord, each mentioning violence, weapons, or destruction ("To be Liked By You . . .," "In This Age of Hard Trying," and "Pedantic Literalist"), as well as the first of her Jonah poems, "Is Your Town Nineveh?" During these same years, from 1914 to 1916, Moore drafts (or finishes but does not publish) an additional eight poems of response to the war and five on situations of personal discord.

Some of Moore's poems of the next few years implicitly address the war, focusing on human destructiveness and a critique of the attitudes encouraging warfare, especially prejudice—"Sojourn" (1917), "The Fish" and "Reinforcements" (1918), "The Labours of Hercules" (1921), and "The Bricks Are Fallen Down, We Will Build with Hewn Stones . . . ," a poem quoting Isaiah and first published in *Observations* but almost certainly written in Carlisle. "England," "Novices," and "When I Buy Pictures" all hold up the Hebrew prophets as model crafters of art or a vital language but, for the most part, articulate their political concerns through a mosaic of cultural and topical reference or an accumulation of expressive detail rather than stating "war / . . . Is . . . a sore / On this life's body" or addressing "Statecraft" directly.

Some of the vitriol and much of the baldness of the early poems disappears—not because Moore disguises her concerns but because they take more complex and larger forms. Returning to these early poems, however, reveals the extent to which political commentary underlies Moore's poetic also in its later, more embedded forms, with their repeated echoes of her early distinctions and concerns. It further prepares a reader to hear the unemphatic but significant racial protest of her poems of the 1930s and forties and to hear the mourning of her World War II poems as a return to earlier questions of personal and national responsibility from the perspective of longer and bleaker knowledge of international relations, national politics, and human psychology. The basic stance of ethical urgency developed in response to the crisis of World War I remained a significant element of Moore's writing. Poetry, for Moore, was a forum not for opinion or expression of feeling, but for ethical thinking in relation to natural and human, national and international emergency—sometimes couched in the form of natural historical description, sometimes of parable or monologue, and sometimes of situational context. Moore sought in her own work, in personal interaction, and in international relations a "by-play" that was "'more terrible in its effectiveness / than the fiercest frontal attack,'" a linguistic gesture that could be "unsheathed" in its effectiveness without escalating conflict or hurting others.

NOTES

1. "Poetry and the American Voice" was scheduled for February 12, 2003.

2. For information on Sam Hamill's "Poets Against the War" project, see http://www.poetsagainstthewar.org/ (accessed July 10, 2004).

3. See John Hollander's comments in "Seeking Poetic Justice," *Los Angeles Times*, March 3, 2003, A1, 10–11.

4. Family letters of 1914 explain the circumstances of the department's closure and Moore's decision not to seek paying work. See, for example, letters from Marianne Moore to John Warner Moore, 23 May and 24 September 1914, and Mary Warner Moore to John Warner Moore, 24 September 1914, folders VI:20:6 and VI:20:10, *RML*.

5. For the first quote, see *CPr* 396. For the second see Marianne Moore to John Warner Moore and Mary Warner Moore, 29 November 1908, *RML*.

6. Tobin Siebers, *The Ethics of Criticism* (Ithaca, NY: Cornell University Press, 1988), 202.

7. One of the few essays dealing with this topic, Cynthia Hogue's "Another Postmodernism: Towards an Ethical Poetics," *How2* 1, no. 7 (Spring 2002), http://www.scc.rutgers.edu/however/v1_7_200/current/in_conference/msa/hogue.shtm (accessed July 9, 2004), presents Moore's writing as distinctly ethical and similarly relates her development of this poetic to her reading of Hebrew prophecy.

8. Significant early feminist readings of Moore include Adrienne Rich's 1971 "When We Dead Awaken: Writing as Re-Vision," in *On Lies, Secrets, and Silence: Selected Prose 1966–78* (New York: Norton, 1979), 33–49, where she identifies fore-mothers and describes Moore, in contrast, as "sexually at a measured and chiseled distance" and as "maidenly, elegant, intellectual, discreet" (36, 39); and Suzanne Juhasz's chapter on Moore in *Naked and Fiery Forms: Modern American Poetry by Women, A New Tradition* (New York: Harper Colophon, 1976), 33–56, which positions her in feminist terms while also describing her as limited and self-denying. For a discussion of the long antiethical trend in literary criticism, see David Parker's Introduction to *Renegotiating Ethics in Literature, Philosophy, and Theory,* ed. Jane Adamson, Richard Freadman, and David Parker (Cambridge: Cambridge University Press, 1998), 1–20.

9. Elizabeth Bishop, "Efforts of Affection: A Memoir of Marianne Moore," *Vanity Fair,* May 1983, reprinted in *The Collected Prose of Elizabeth Bishop,* ed. Robert Giroux (New York: Farrar, Straus and Giroux, 1984), 156.

10. Randall Jarrell, "Her Shield," in *Marianne Moore: A Collection of Critical Essays,* ed. Charles Tomlinson (Englewood Cliffs, NJ: Prentice-Hall, 1969), 122.

11. Charles Altieri, "What Differences Can Contemporary Poetry Make in Our Moral Thinking?" in Adamson et al., *Renegotiating Ethics in Literature,* 114.

12. Tess Gallagher, "Throwing the Scarecrows from the Garden," *Parnassus* 12, no. 2 / 13, no. 1 (1985): 50.

13. Cristanne Miller, "Marianne Moore and a Poetry of Hebrew (Protestant) Prophecy," in *Twentieth-Century American Women's Poetics of Engagement,* ed. Cristina Giorcelli, Cristanne Miller, and Shira Wolosky, special issue, *Sources: Revue d'etudes Anglophones* 12 (Spring 2002): 43.

14. George Adam Smith, *The Book of the Twelve Prophets Commonly Called the Minor,* 2 vols. (New York: Doubleday, Doran & Company, 1896), 1:13; George Adam Smith, *Modern Criticism and the Preaching of the Old Testament* (London: Hoder and Stoughton, 1901), 217, 267, 273.

15. Abbreviations Moore's, ellipses mine. See Marianne Moore, reading notebook, 1907–1915, folder VII:01:01, *RML.* For original passage, see Smith, *Book of the Twelve,* 1:13.

16. Marianne Moore to John Warner Moore, 13 September 1914, *RML.*

17. Marianne Moore to John Warner Moore, 14 October 1914, *RML.*

18. On February 7, 1914, Moore writes Warner that Erskine MacDonald at *Poetry Review* has invited her to "compete in a book publishing enterprise . . . series of one-man volumes (60 or so poems each)." See Marianne Moore to John Warner Moore, 7 February 1914, *RML.* On February 21, 1915, Moore writes that she has mailed her batch of poems (presumably around sixty) to MacDonald. See Marianne Moore to John Warner Moore, 21 February 1915, *RML.* Many of the poems typed neatly on blue-green paper may have been included in this submission and later returned; others contain "U.S.A." as a part of their address, suggesting that she (also?) submitted them to magazines abroad.

19. See Moore's unpublished poems "The Grass that Perisheth," folder I:02:13, *RML,* "To a Man who Spoke of his Fame as If," folder I:01:06, *RML,* and "Cisar, or / Caesar, or / Kaiser" which suggests that every emperor callously stands "in his glory / On war's promontory," folder I:04:25, *RML.*

20. Marianne Moore, unpublished poem, "To a Stiffwinged Grasshopper," folder I:04:50, *RML.* In a draft, the poem is titled "Our Imported Grasshopper, 'North of Boston.'" Moore mentions just having read Robert Frost's *North of Boston* on February 9, 1915. See Marianne Moore to John Warner Moore, 9 February 1915, *RML.*

21. Marianne Moore, unpublished poem, "To Pharoah's Baker Plucking up Courage to ask the Interpretation of his Dream, when a Favorable Interpretation had been Accorded the Dream of Pharoah's Butler," folder I:04:60, *RML.*

22. Marianne Moore, unpublished poem, "To an Enemy Sharpening His Eyes upon Me," folder I:04:34, *RML.*

23. Marianne Moore, unpublished poem, "The Candle-Stick Maker," folder I:01:27, *RML.*

24. Marianne Moore, unpublished poem, "Am I a Brother to Dragons and a Companion to Owls?" folder I:01:03, *RML.*

25. Marianne Moore, unpublished poem, "Man's Feet are a Sensational Device," folder I:03:02, *RML.*

26. Marianne Moore, unpublished poems, "To Pacifists in War Time," folder I:04:58, *RML;* "The Assassins," folder I:01:13, *RML;* "Patriotic Sentiment and the Maker," folder I:03:26, *RML.*

27. Marianne Moore, poetry notebook, 1922–1930, 1251/07, folder VII:04:04, *RML,* 16, 6.

28. Marianne Moore, religion notebook, 1914, folder VII:08:03, *RML.*

29. Marianne Moore, "Qui S'Excuse, S'Accuse," folder I:02:58, *RML.*

30. Marianne Moore, reading notebook, 1250/01, folder VII:01:01, *RML.*

31. Marianne Moore, unpublished poem, "Piningly," folder I.03.34, *RML.*

32. On Moore and pragmatism, see David Kadlec, *Mosaic Modernism: Anarchism, Pragmatism, Culture* (Baltimore: Johns Hopkins University Press, 2000).

33. Marianne Moore, reading notebook, 1916–1921, 1250/02, folder VII:01:02, 40.

34. I am indebted to conversation with Linda Leavell for the dating of this poem, as for much of my sense of Moore's consecutive responses to events of these years.

35. Moore, folder VII:01:01, *RML*, 127; Smith, *Book of the Twelve*, 1:393, 398.

36. See Moore's drafts of "To Statecraft Embalmed," folder I.04.63, *RML*.

37. See Jackson Lears, *No Place of Grace: Antimodernism and the Transformation of American Culture 1880–1920* (New York: Pantheon Books, 1981), chapters 3–5. Moore's combining of religion and politics may also stem from William Blake, an author she read enthusiastically. Blake asks, "Are not Religion and Politics the Same Thing?" and makes specific links between the two in his Proverbs of Hell; quoted from Alicia Ostriker, *Dancing at the Devil's Party: Essays on Poetry, Politics, and the Erotic* (Ann Arbor: University of Michigan Press, 2000), 2.

38. See Moore's drafts of "Pedantic Literalist," folder I:03:27, *RML*.

39. See Moore's drafts of "The Fish," folder I:02:04, *RML*. George Bornstein reads "The Fish" as an "anti-war poem" in *Material Modernism: The Politics of the Page* (Cambridge: Cambridge University Press, 2001), 93–99, basing his argument primarily on the "material instantiation" of the poem in the *Egoist*. But Moore's reasons for publishing in this magazine may have had little to do with the war: the *Egoist* was the earliest magazine to publish several of her poems, and H.D. (who had reviewed her early work favorably) was literary editor there from June 1916 until June 1917 (although Eliot was the editor who accepted "The Fish"). Moore disliked Dora Marsden, so Marsden's connection with the magazine would not have been a draw, and by 1917 she would not have been particularly sympathetic to "militant opposition to the war," given that her brother had already joined the Maryland Naval Militia. To my mind, "The Fish" mourns the destructiveness of human carelessness and aggression, including but not pointing toward the war.

40. Marianne Moore, unpublished poem, "Like Bertram Dobell, You Achieve Distinction by Disclaiming It," folder I:02:35, *RML*.

41. In 1915, the National German American Alliance attempted such a demonstration by putting up an expensive bronze statue of Major General Friedrich Wilhelm Baron von Steuben in Valley Forge as a revolutionary war hero. A Prussian soldier, Steuben was famous for teaching the Continental Army to fight with the bayonette. Such a gift was likely to have been noted by Moore, given the historical importance of Valley Forge and its location near Bryn Mawr.

42. John M. Slatin, *The Savage's Romance: The Poetry of Marianne Moore* (University Park: Pennsylvania State University Press, 1986), 35–36; Margaret Holley, *The Poetry of Marianne Moore: A Study in Voice and Value* (Cambridge: Cambridge University Press, 1987), 29–30.

43. Smith, *Book of the Twelve*, 2:131.

44. Moore, folder VII:01:01, *RML*, 132; Smith, *Book of the Twelve*, 2:532.

45. Smith, *Book of the Twelve*, 2:533–34.

46. Victoria Bazin, "Marianne Moore, Kenneth Burke, and the Poetics of Literary Labour," *Journal of American Studies* 35, no. 3 (2001): 439.

47. The four poems published in *Poetry* in May 1915 were already accepted for publication in July 1914.

"Injudicious Gardening": Marianne Moore, Gender, and the Hazards of Domestication

Robin G. Schulze

Some time ago, I remember sitting at a session of the H.D. society at the American Literature Association marveling at the number of people in the room. Half way through the session, I leaned over to a colleague of mine and asked why, in her opinion, H.D. attracted so much scholarly attention and Marianne Moore so comparatively little. "H.D. is sexier," she replied. The comment struck me as both metaphorical and literal. Certainly, H.D., as a scholarly topic, is currently "sexier," as in more popular, than Marianne Moore. Of course, H.D.'s sexy status is due, as my colleague's comment implied, to the literal meaning of the word. H.D.'s sexual adventures, her frank discussions of sexuality and gender in her written work, her interest in sexuality and gender as modern topics of investigation in the realms of psychology and sociology—all of these franknesses make H.D. seem, to many scholars, simply more modern than her seemingly repressed friend.

Thanks to many scholars of Moore's verse active in the field today, notions about Moore's approach to the issue of gender have become more sophisticated, sensitive, and historical.[1] One of the most enduring sites of Moore's supposed "repression" or "submersion" of gender issues, however, remains her poems about plants and animals. In part, we can thank Alicia Ostriker for this enduring link, who went so far as to accuse Moore of literally hiding out behind her animal masks, of stealthily deflecting her gender commentary onto a series of "lower mammals" that served as ciphers for her own oppressed female state.[2] Indeed, for many critics, Moore's creatures continue to constitute her own eccentric take on a Modernist poetics of impersonality, an ethos that critics tend to gender MALE with a vengeance.[3]

Such readings, however, do not do justice to Moore's particular interests or her historical context. Moore came of age as a poet in a distinctly biodeterministic age, one in which Darwinian discourses about nature inevitably intersected with those about human nature, or the biological constitution of maleness and femaleness. As several historians have argued, the movement

74

of women into the public sphere during the late nineteenth century resulted in an intensification of scientific research determined to define the proper and true "nature" of women and men.[4] "As bourgeois women began to challenge the preeminence of female domesticity within the pantheon of bourgeois values," Carroll Smith-Rosenberg states, "the male bourgeoisie elaborated, in an increasingly deterministic language, the original medico-scientific insistence that women's biology was women's destiny."[5] "The feminist challenge [of the late nineteenth century] was sweeping," Cynthia Russett agrees:

> [I]t embraced education and occupation, together with legal, political, and social status. It even dared broach the subject of equality in personal, and especially matrimonial relationships. . . . Scientists responded to this unrest with a detailed and sustained examination of the differences between men and women that justified their differing social roles. Anatomy and physiology, evolutionary biology, physical anthropology, psychology, and sociology evolved comprehensive theories of sexual difference. Scientists in all these fields were guided, with few exceptions, by the beacon of evolution. . . . [T]heories were utilized and adapted to explain how and why men and women differed from each other and, often enough, what these differences signified for social policy, and conclusions drawn from them, display such a remarkable degree of uniformity that it is fair to say that a genuine scientific consensus emerged by the turn of the century.[6]

Throughout the late nineteenth century, male scientists labored to construct a scientific vision of biologically determined sex roles that would underwrite their own exclusive professional privileges and reassert the Victorian "faith in sexual polarity"—"the doctrine," as Rosalind Rosenberg puts it, "that women [were] by nature emotional and passive" and "the dogma that [men] were by nature rational and assertive."[7] Underlying almost all of the Darwinian arguments about the proper place of women was the common assumption by scientists of the period that women were driven by their evolutionary function to bear children.[8] Hence, their bodies dictated their behaviors rather than their minds. In the scientific estimation of Moore's early years, nature was gender.

Indeed, far from deep-sixing her notions about gender, it seems to me that Moore's plant and animal poems often bring gender issues front and center. Moore's poems about plant and animal subjects, as I have argued elsewhere, frequently dwell on the conception of creaturely "fitness," on how well a particular plant or animal seems suited, in evolutionary terms, to the challenges of its environment.[9] For Moore, however, the question of a plant or animal's true "fitness" in relation to its environment was complicated by the notion of human intervention. Perhaps Moore's favorite book of Darwin's was the *Variation of Animals and Plants Under Domestication,* Darwin's attempt to ameliorate the shock of *The Origin of Species* by systematically demonstrating the obvious fact of evolution in the context of every barnyard and garden in the civilized world.[10] The human domestication of animals and plants, the imposition of human notions of biotic fitness on plant and animal forms for material benefit had throughout history, Darwin pointed out, radically transformed the nature of supposedly immutable species. In preserving some animals to breed and killing others, farmers had dramatically changed the biotic world for their own purposes.

Which for Moore begged the question of just who was doing the farming. Several of Moore's plant and animal poems address the fact that, as Darwin noted, the demands of "domestication" seldom worked in favor of the true "fitness" of the creature, but catered instead to the whims of the farmer. And the question of the relationship between farmer and farmed was not merely a question of the human relationship to the biotic world in the Progressive Era in America, but a question of the relationship of human beings to each other. By Darwin's account, humans too could be viewed as the products of centuries of domestication. Whatever natures domesticated creatures once had had long since been eradicated by the pressures of artificial selection. Victorian notions of both female and male "fitness," Moore and other women feared, had created domestic women and men who no longer resembled their fit states in nature. Social conformity, the grip of the domestic sphere, had changed them all. In so many of Moore's poems, the human and the biotic worlds merge, notions of nature and gender merge, through her considerations of the hazards of domestication.

And where better to consider questions of nature, gender, and domestication than in a garden? For the remainder of this paper, I will turn my attention to a pair of poems that Moore first published side by side in the *Egoist* in August 1915: "To Browning" and "To Bernard Shaw: A Prize Bird." Each poem makes use of a locale that emblematizes the human domestication of the natural world. The first, "To Browning," which Moore revised and retitled "Injudicious Gardening" in her 1924 book *Observations,* invokes a rose garden that belonged to poet Robert Browning. To quote the 1915 version of the poem in full:

> If yellow betokens infidelity,
>   I am an infidel.
>   I could not plant white roses on a hill
>   Because books said buff petals boded ill,
>   White promised well.
>
> However—your particular possession—
>   The sense of privacy
>   In what you did, deflects from your estate
>   Offending eyes and will not tolerate
>   Effrontery.

> *(BMM* 174)

A poem to an admired artistic precursor, "To Browning" clearly seems of a piece with many of the poems that Moore wrote in the years just prior to the First World War. "To a Man Working His Way Through a Crowd" (her poem to theater designer Gordon Craig), "To William Butler Yeats on Tagore," "To Disraeli on Conservatism," "Blake," "George Moore," and the poem she paired with "To Browning" in its first presentation, "To Bernard Shaw: A Prize Bird," all attempt in their mixture of "praise and blame," to use Jeanne Heuving's phrase, to construct a usable past out of a decidedly male aesthetic tradition.[11] These poems are filled with assertions of the speaker's likes and dislikes, acts of critical appropriation that make it clear that the speaker of these verses has no qualms about telling her subjects both where they shine and where they fall short.

Moore's poem to Browning, however, is unique in that it focuses on a specific event in the life of the writer addressed that involves not only the writer, but his soon-to-be bride, also a poet. As Moore's notes to the poem in *Observations* indicate, she penned the verse in response to an exchange of letters between Browning and his love, Elizabeth Barrett, printed in the 1899 Harper Brothers volume of their correspondence.[12] In February of 1846, six months after the two had begun exchanging letters, Browning sent Barrett a sprig of hawthorn to show, as he explained in his note, "how Spring gets on!" The hawthorn spray set Barrett to thinking about the very first flower that Browning had bestowed upon her in the course of their difficult courtship:

> The first you ever gave me was a yellow rose sent in a letter, and shall I tell you what that means—the yellow rose? "Infidelity," says the dictionary of flowers. You see what an omen, . . . to begin with![13]

Browning responded to Barrett's playful jibes by taking to his garden with his flower dictionary in hand. In April he reported to Barrett that he had dispatched the yellow rose bushes and had "planted a full dozen more rose-trees, all white—to take away the yellow-rose reproach!"[14] Henceforth his garden would signify the "purity" of his affections rather than the "infidelity" of his attentions.

Of all the issues that came up in the love letters between the famous poets—Browning's poetry, Barrett's poetry, philosophy, politics, the mutual attempts of the two poets to throw off various forms of Victorian tyranny—it seems odd that Moore chose to focus her own poem on Browning's attack on his roses. In doing so, however, Moore immediately links questions of Browning's proper relation to nature with those of Browning's relationship to Barrett. Moore's poem takes place within the confines of the Victorian garden, a controlled, domesticated space that she associates with the hazards of a controlled domesticated world. Moore begins the 1915 ver-

sion of her poem with a condemnation of what she, in an early draft of the
poem, deemed Browning's "act of vandalism" in regard to his plants:

> If yellow betokens infidelity,
>   I am an infidel.
>   I could not plant white roses on a hill
>   Because books said buff petals boded ill,
>   White promised well.
>
> (BMM 174)

Before publishing the poem in her 1924 volume *Observations* under the title "Injudicious Gardening," Moore revised the opening stanza to indicate
more directly her sense of the maliciousness of Browning's act. In the 1924
version, Moore emphasizes the fact that Browning did not merely plant
white roses, he bore "ill will" toward the yellow ones:

> If yellow betokens infidelity,
>   I am an infidel.
>   I could not bear a yellow rose ill will
>   Because books said that yellow boded ill,
>   White promised well;
>
> (BMM 56)

Moore's opening lines play with the related meanings of infidelity, a
term most commonly used to describe marital unfaithfulness, and infidel,
a term most commonly applied to one who remains an unbeliever in respect to a specific religion. Her wordplay yokes relations of the domestic
sphere with the issue of the integrity of the plants in Browning's Victorian
garden. Browning, she suggests, errs in that he views his flowers as dis-
posable sentimental "tokens." Imposing his will on the landscape in an effort to make his garden conform to conceptions of virtue outlined in Victorian books, he devalues living things. Moore's use of the word "infidel"
announces her own unwillingness to subscribe to any system of meaning
that values conventional human notions over the well-being of individual
living organisms. In championing organic forms deemed "impure" by the
Victorian dictionaries, Moore's poem openly challenges a hypermasculin-
ized Victorian conception of Man's place in Nature. As Donald Worster defines the prevailing attitudes of the Victorian period:

> The Victorians were concerned of course with the inner dimensions of their war
> for virtue—the struggle of conscience against the selfish instincts. But they were
> at least as intent on carrying the crusade against nature to the actual surface of
> the earth, on making the land over to serve as a kind of visible, external evi-
> dence of their accession of grace. Huxley's favorite metaphor for this ethic of
> ecological transformation was the hoary image of the Garden of Eden, imply-

ing in this case a civilized landscape surrounded by a wall to guard it from the Darwinian jungle. This garden was to be a place of virtue, but also of material productivity; the two ends were mutually reinforcing. It was, however, to be no limited monastic retreat, but an expanding, dynamic kingdom that one day would embrace the entire world. . . . If humans would . . . work for the "corporate whole," they would see this process spread everywhere to create "an earthly paradise, a true Garden of Eden, in which all things should work together towards the well-being of the gardeners."

Civilization then, according to this policy, became a process of pacification by concerted force.[15]

The quintessential Victorian gardener, Browning kills his plants in order to make his garden over into a visible record of the purity of his romantic intentions.

The roses, however, are not the only organisms whose lives are at issue in "To Browning." Browning's roses inevitably recalled for Moore the other living organism that he wished to bring within his domestic orbit—poet Elizabeth Barrett. Throughout the numerous letters that passed between Browning and Barrett in the interval between Browning's gift of the hawthorn sprig and his report on the destruction of his rose trees, the couple engaged in a frank discussion of the risks and rewards that attended their growing passion. Browning's letters ring with eagerness and impulse. Let's be married, he says; let's to Italy. But Barrett responds with reticence. "Do you know that all that time I was frightened of you?" Barrett wrote to Browning in a letter recalling her early courtship with her frequent guest.

> I felt as if you had a power over me and meant to use it, and that I could not breathe or speak very differently from what you chose to make me. As to my thoughts, I had it in my head somehow that you read them as you read the newspaper—examined them, and fastened them down writhing under your long entomological pins—ah, do you remember the entomology of it all?[16]

Those familiar with Moore's verse will recognize the echo of Barrett's words—"I felt as if you had a power over me and meant to use it"—in Moore's own complex accounting of the enterprise of wedlock, her 1923 poem "Marriage": "men have power / and sometimes one is made to feel it" (*BMM* 78). Barrett's letters make explicitly clear that her love for Browning is as strong as his love for her, but while Browning seems comfortable in the torrent, Barrett seems overwhelmed by the rush. Love means happiness, but also a fearful loss of privacy. Like Prufrock, she imagines herself "pinned and wriggling on the wall," collected like a specimen. A loving marriage to even the most enlightened of men, even as an escape from the most repressive of households, might, as Moore's transmutation of Barrett's thoughts on the subject of "power" suggests, hold unbearable risks for the integrity of the self.

Moore's use of Browning's flower beds thus serves as both a statement about the proper human relationship to nature and a comment about the relationship of men and women to Victorian constructions of the domestic sphere generally. The drive to domesticate and control nature is potentially one with the desire to domesticate human beings, to control, define, and direct human nature. As Browning's replacement of his rose bushes reveals, the entire contents of his "estate" are under his complete command. Any man capable of imposing his will in such a way upon flowers might, the courtship context of the poem implies, tend to a woman, his legal property in marriage, in a similar fashion. Browning's desire to turn the domestic space of his garden into a sentimental image of Victorian purity does not bode well for any woman transplanted onto or into any such male estate. Moore's reading diary of the period betrays her particular concern for the fate of the female artist. As she scribbled during her reading of Browning's and Barrett's letters:

On E. B. Browning

> There was a young lady named Liz
> Who made writing poems her biz
> But when she met Bob
> She gave up her job
> It took all her time to read his[17]

The "promise" held by the white rose or the white wedding, the notion that either could create a viable earthly Eden without destroying something valuable in the process, struck Moore as a bad bet. In vowing to remain an "infidel," Moore vows to keep faith with herself and remain outside the powerfully altering space of such promises.

The first stanza of Moore's poem, then, addresses two different but related levels of her sense of the hazards of domestication. In true Mooreish fashion, however, the poem turns upon itself. As several critics have noted, after passing judgment upon Browning in the first stanza, Moore seems to excuse him in the second.[18] To quote the 1924 version of the poem:

> However, your particular possession—
>   The sense of privacy
>   In what you did—deflects from your estate
>   Offending eyes, and will not tolerate
>   Effrontery.

(*BMM* 56)

Beginning the second stanza with a provisionalizing "however," Moore rethinks Browning's act and recoils from her own potentially rash moment of judgment. Where the first stanza of the poem hinges on the multiple meanings of the word "infidelity," the second stanza plays with multiple definitions of the word "possession." In light of the first stanza, Moore's use of the word immediately brings to mind the uncomfortable closeness between love and ownership. Browning's "possession" refers to his act of asserting control over his flower bed and, by extension, his beloved Barrett. ("Oh, to possess and be possessed!" Browning proclaimed when wishing for a perfect love in his poem "Women and Roses.") In qualifying Browning's deed with the adjective "particular," however, Moore suggests that Browning's uprooting of his roses might have been something other than an expression of expansive Victorian male desire to make nature conform to Victorian norms. The phrase "particular possession" implies that Browning's act was unique, born of deep personal feeling rather than a sense of Victorian propriety. During her composition of her poem, Moore copied into her reading notebook a passage from W. L. Phelps's book, *Robert Browning: How to Know Him,* that speaks to Browning's consciously obstinate resistance to public opinion:

> One of the most admirable things about Browning's admirable career as poet and man is that he wrote not to please the critics, as Tennyson often did, not to please the crowd, as the vast horde of ephemeral writers do, but to please himself. The critics and the crowd professed that they could not understand him; but he had no difficulty in understanding them. He knew exactly what they wanted, and declined to supply it. Instead of giving them what he thought they wanted, he gave them what he thought they needed. That illustrates the difference between the literary caterer and the literary master.[19]

"Particular possession," then, may refer not only to Browning's act of possessing the other, but to his own self-possession—the collected self-assurance that attends Browning's unshakeable belief in the rightness of his actions. Moore makes Browning's passion seem profoundly personal. Set apart from the rest of the stanza by dashes, his "private" act resists Moore's attempts to define his motives. His gardening may not have been an aggressive outward show of social power and propriety, she concedes, but a private act only truly intelligible in the context of the whole of a relationship deeply felt.

In her second stanza, then, Moore judges not only Browning's gardening, but her own act of judgment as well. While she specifically rails against Browning's apparent desire to domesticate and control his living property, Liz included, Moore cannot bring herself to become part of the problem of power, especially where living beings are concerned. If Browning's actions are, indeed, the product of his own deepest sense of what it is right for him to do, then how can the prying poet object? Browning too is a living organism in the poem. He too has an organic integrity. Since his acts are potentially sincere expressions of private emotion rather than mindless convention, they will not bear the poet's impudent corrections. Since she cannot be sure of his motives, Moore grants Browning the benefit of the doubt and resists the impulse to impose upon his nature. Like a good gardener faced with a stand of yellow rose trees, Moore decides that it is best not to uproot Browning for the sake of her own priorities.

Moore's unwillingness to completely condemn Browning's "injudicious gardening" speaks to her reluctance to control, and perhaps distort, what might well be a fellow creature's instinctual response to the world. Her poem to Browning, like many of her early poems, draws a parallel between nature and human nature and concludes that both are best left undomesticated by cultural forces that inevitably suppress valuable instincts. Moore's own rules for good poetry are filled with references to the nature of the poet that put a premium on being true to instinct.[20] On the subject of intelligibility, Moore declared that "one should be as clear as one's natural reticence allows one to be" (*CPr* 508). On the topic of originality, she wrote that it was "in any case a by-product of sincerity" (*CPr* 421). An individual poet's true, natural response to a given subject would, Moore concluded, result in an original poem. "With regard to either prose or verse," she stated, "one can put intelligence and a liking for distinction and even prudence out of one's mind if only one is faithful to the interior necessity that drove one to the writing and made it imperative."[21] Using tropes she often reserved for her favorite writers, Moore defended Emily Dickinson against charges of personal and poetic "vanity" by invoking the issue of her true "nature." "A certain buoyancy that creates an effect of inconsequent bravado—a sense of drama with which we may not be quite at home—was for her a part of that expansion of breath necessary to existence," she argued (*CPr* 292). True to herself and her own instincts, Dickinson simply lived and wrote as she must. Her "bravado" was a matter of innate "necessity," a habit as biologically engrained and unconscious as breathing. To illustrate the difference between poetic spontaneity and artistic vanity, Moore punctuated her argument on Dickinson's behalf with a telling comparison: "and unless it is conceited for the hummingbird or the osprey to not behave like a chicken, one does not find her [Dickinson] conceited" (*CPr* 292). Moore's analogy juxtaposes three very different creatures—two wild birds, both skilled and agile fliers, and a common flightless domestic fowl. Like the hummingbird and the osprey, the true artist, Moore suggests, is a unique untamed creature that follows the call of his or her wild nature, soaring despite public charges of eccentricity or egotism. To expect hummingbirds and osprey to hop, cluck, and scratch like chickens, to insist that any creature, human or otherwise, change its ways to suit rigid definitions of domestic and domesticated utility, struck Moore as a violation of a living thing's vital essence. "Poetry, that is to say the poetic," she commented in the *Dial,* "is a primal necessity," a matter of natural, instinctual need that each poet must satisfy in his or her own way (*CPr* 169).

Moore, however, was under no illusions that naturalness was easy either to achieve or to maintain. The domesticating forces of her culture, a dubious inheritance from her Victorian precursors, mitigated against personal and artistic "fitness" at every turn. The lingering Victorian ideals of both "male" and "female" produced by generations of human domestication often seemed to Moore to be a burden that, like marriage, took all of her "criminal ingenuity / to avoid" (*BMM* 115). As she copied into her conversation notebook covering the years 1929 to 1932: "Everybody makes us wild—; no, we *are* wild and everybody makes us tame *and for a wild thing to be made tame!* And in that condition we don't like ourselves and others don't like us either."[22] Indeed, Moore's companion poem to "To Browning," "To Bernard Shaw: A Prize Bird," underlines the fact that "natural" behavior is a difficult thing for even the most free-thinking of artists to achieve. The driving conceit of Moore's poem to Shaw, the image of Shaw as a "prize bird," issues from the language of poultry breeding and refers to a bird bred for show rather than for stock—one created through generations of artificial selection to embody the ideal characteristics deemed "standard" for a particular breed. A feat of barn-yard engineering, a "prize bird" is the ultimate domesticated fowl. Moore implies that, while Shaw, the outspoken Fabian Socialist, may seem outrageous to some, both his ideals and his art are still the products of the Victorian barnyard in the same way that Browning's are the products of the Victorian garden. Unlike Dickinson, Shaw is no osprey or humming-bird. Shaw is a chicken.

The links between nature, gender, and the hazards of domestication that drive Moore's poem to Browning become more pronounced when "To Browning" and "To Bernard Shaw: A Prize Bird," published together throughout Moore's early career, are read as a pair. "You suit me well," she writes in a haughty tone to Shaw, "for you can make me laugh,"

> Nor are you blinded by the chaff
> That every wind sends spinning from the rick.

(BMM 174)

The opening lines ring true to Moore's lifelong appreciation of Shaw's humor, brashness, and perspicacity. Shaw can always, it seems, distinguish intellectual wheat from ideological chaff, truth from bluster. Throughout the rest of the poem, however, Moore balances her approval of Shaw's ability to see the world clearly with a pointed comparison:

> You know to think and what you think, you speak,
> With much of Samson's pride and bleak
>   Finality, and none dare bid you stop.
>
> Pride sits you well, so strut, colossal bird;
> No barnyard makes you look absurd.
>   Your brazen spurs are staunch against defeat.
>
> (BMM 174)

Invoking Milton's *Samson Agonistes,* Moore creates a range of allusions
that applaud Shaw's social courage. The reference to Milton's Samson immediately identifies Shaw as one who, under duress, is not afraid to question authority. Chained to his grindstone and made to work "in Brazen Fetters under task" (line 35), Milton's Samson rails against the abuses of those
in power—the corrupt, profligate, idolatrous Philistines.[23] Moore's mention of Samson in turn conjures his creator, Milton, himself an outspoken
critic of the political and social tyrannies of his time. Milton openly supported Cromwell's Puritan revolution against the English monarchy and
suffered acutely in the political and religious backlash of its failure. Like
Milton and Samson, Shaw, too, was critical of those in power. A Fabian Socialist, Shaw viewed the stage as the perfect forum to attack the blatant in-
equalities and hypocrisies of British society. As he wrote defiantly in the
1911 preface to *The Shewing-Up of Blanco Posnet,* "I regard much current
morality as to economic and sexual relations as disastrously wrong; and I
regard certain doctrines of the Christian religion as understood in England
today with abhorrence. I write plays with the deliberate object of convert-
ing the nation to my opinion in these matters." Moore's link between Samson, Milton, and Shaw highlights Shaw's sense of himself as not merely a
reformer, but a redeemer who can deliver his nation from sin.

Moore's comparison between Samson, Milton, and Shaw, however, also
brings Shaw's ability to "see" into question. The Samson of Milton's play
is, of course, physically blind—a condition that, as many critics note, reflects the tragedy of Milton's own failing eyesight. Moore claims in her first
stanza that Shaw is not "blinded" by the lies of those in power, but then associates him with two of the most recognized blind men in biblical and literary history. Shaw may see some things well, she suggests, but not others.
Indeed, other than his humor, the feature of Shaw's speech that Moore finds
most characteristic is his "pride." Throughout the course of *Samson Agonistes,* Samson remains a prideful classical hero who revels in the memory
of his great physical strength and pitifully bemoans its loss at the hands of
Delilah and her razor. Unable to understand that heroism might not be simply a matter of brute strength, unable to grasp his fallen condition as a matter of God's will rather than his own weakness, Samson remains metaphor-

ically sightless, lost in the darkness of his own hubris. Moore knew well Shaw's tendency to be flatly dismissive of all forms of idealism, including religious faith. His arrogance rests in his self-important desire to have the last word on issues that Moore felt were, at the very least, open to debate.

While Moore's reference to Samson effectively limits Shaw's vision, it is her overall conceit for the poem that questions both his authority and, at some level, his naturalness. In the final stanza of the poem, Moore imagines Shaw as a beautiful barnyard cock who, she admits, warrants his egotism. The image of Shaw as a "prize bird" in full strut, however, makes his puffed-up performance seem a matter of domesticated affect rather than genuine impulse. Moore wrote of Shaw later in her career: "In his 'Advice to a Young Critic,' . . . Bernard Shaw says, 'Never strike an attitude, national, moral, or critical'—an axiom he did not observe too fanatically" (*CPr* 509). A creature of the Victorian barnyard, Shaw has been bred to crow and strut and Moore pokes fun at his expansive, specifically male, ego—the phallic cock-sureness that seems the creation of his age. Moore ultimately envisions Shaw not as Samson, but as a comic Chauntecleer—another creature duped by his own vanity.[24] Moore carefully deflates her rooster within the oxymoronic moniker "colossal bird." His claws may be "brazen," but such is the word that Milton uses to describe Samson's fetters. In many ways, Moore suggests, Shaw cannot think outside the gendered parameters of the Victorian fence.

Indeed, Moore's address to Shaw looks even more complex in terms of the gender issues that attend Victorian domestication when read in the context of Moore's poem to Browning. In the first stanza of "To Browning," Moore declares herself an "infidel" willing to commit a shameless act of "effrontery" rather than participate in the life-denying habits of Victorian farming. The term "infidel" is the very word that Milton uses throughout *Samson Agonistes* to identify the Philistine Delilah, who robs Samson of his masculine locks. Similarly, in picturing Shaw as Samson, Moore inevitably conjures a Delilah, an "infidel" woman, unwilling to believe in Shaw's creeds, who can coax him into giving up the secrets of his power. The "infidel" speaker of "To Browning" who claims impurity as her credo and vows to stay out of the garden mirrors the infidel witness of Shaw's barnyard antics who, outside the rail of the barnyard, can laugh at his pretensions even as she cuts him down to size. The very image of Samson and Delilah, the ultimate example, in Milton's terms, of marriage as destructive power struggle, serves as a further warning from Moore to stay far away from the deformations of the domestic sphere. Both poems contain admonitions against the "estate" of marriage.

Be it roses or chickens or pigeons or carrots or cows, Moore's poems are filled with plants and animals bred to look and behave in certain ways, fashioned to suit cultural notions of utility frequently at odds with their true "fitness" in relation to their environment. In Progressive Era America, sex and gender were not generally conceived of as constructs of discourse, but of the flesh—products of centuries of evolution that could be directed by the human engineering of those in power. And for Moore, where there was power, there could always be abuse of power. Given the widespread conversation throughout the Progressive Era about issues of human domestication and breeding and the fascination with the science of eugenics which equated human beings with stock to be artificially culled and selected, Moore's reflections on the power relationships of the garden and barnyard ultimately, I believe, raise the issue of "injudicious gardening" to the level of a cultural problem that affects all living things, human or otherwise, subject to the domestic sphere. Perhaps this is why Moore's poems about animals and plants seem to slide so easily into being poems about people, about women, about herself. In a time that frankly viewed all people as biologically determined animals, that viewed gender as nature, the gap between species on the evolutionary ladder could often seem small. Moore's poems about the hazards of domestication, then, are perhaps best read as multivalent works that situate gender issues in relation to broader considerations of the relationship between nature and culture.

NOTES

1. Cristanne Miller provides what I consider to be the best historical account of Moore's gender strategies in *Marianne Moore: Questions of Authority* (Cambridge, MA: Harvard University Press, 1995). In her chapter "'Your Thorns Are the Best Part of You': Gender Politics in the Nongendered Poem," 93–127, Miller considers Moore's poems in the context of American Progressive Era attitudes about the changing role of women and relates Moore's approach to the subject of gender to the ideologies of her time. The result is a strong, convincing argument that explains the seeming deliberate unsexiness of Moore's work. Miller goes on to note, however, that Moore does not neglect the issue of gender, but rather transmutes her gender concerns into wider considerations of value and power. Moore's early verse, Miller claims, reveals "an ongoing analysis of ways in which power relationships and various constructions of value are affected by . . . widespread gender constructions" (104–5). Moore thus acknowledges the hierarchies imposed by gender ideologies, but assumes a gender neutral perspective in her verse from which she freely overturns common gender assumptions about both men and women. For another excellent account of Moore's verse that places her poems in the context of Progressive Era concerns about gender, see Rachel Blau DuPlessis's *Genders, Races, and Religious Cultures in Modern American Poetry, 1908–1934* (Cambridge: Cambridge University Press, 2001), 29–51. For a range of readings of Moore's verse grounded in feminist theory, see Cynthia Hogue, *Scheming Women: Poetry, Privilege and the Politics of Subjectivity* (Albany: SUNY Press, 1995); Sabine Sielke, *Fashioning the Female Subject: The Intertextual Networking of Dickinson, Moore, and Rich* (Ann Arbor: University of Michigan Press, 1997); Jeanne Heuving, *Omissions Are Not Accidents: Gender in the Art of Marianne Moore* (Detroit: Wayne State University Press, 1992); Rachel Blau DuPlessis, "No Moore of the Same: The Feminist Poetic of Marianne Moore," *William Carlos Williams Review* 14, no. 1 (Spring 1988): 6–32, and

Kirstin Hotelling, "'The I of each is to the I of each, a kind of fretful speech which sets a limit on itself': Marianne Moore's Strategic Selfhood," *Modernism/Modernity* 5, no. 1 (1998): 75–96. For a discussion of Progressive Era notions of sexuality in relation to Moore's work, see Linda Leavell, "Marianne Moore, the James Family, and the Politics of Celibacy," *Twentieth-Century Literature* 49, no. 2 (Summer 2003): 219–45.

2. In *Stealing the Language: The Emergence of Women's Poetry in America* (Boston: Beacon Press, 1986), Alicia Ostriker claims that "Moore's proliferating bestiary of creatures in protective armor and camouflage are not only personal self-portraits in code, as many critics have observed. They imply over and over the necessary timidities and disguises of a brilliant woman in a world where literary authority is male" (52). Moore's animals serve as deep cover for the thoughts about gender roles that Moore was afraid to state more directly. In her article, "In the Twilight of the Gods: Women Poets and the American Sublime," in *The American Sublime,* ed. Mary Arensberg (Albany: SUNY Press, 1986), Joanne Feit Diehl echoes Ostriker's sense of Moore's animals. "The choice of animal over human as subject," she asserts, "achieves a distancing and provides a necessary disguise through which Moore can articulate her perceptions of self in relation to the world. In this identification with the animal, one discovers unselfconscious sexual identity and a power that evades categories of cultural convention and human stereotypes" (189). In the Freudian terminology that frames Diehl's argument, Moore's animal poems amount to acts of "sublimation" (187). Other critics have noted the possibility of reading Moore's animal poems as commentaries on gender issues, but have given Moore credit for choosing her subjects rather than resorting to them out of fear. In *Omissions Are Not Accidents,* Heuving argues that Moore's animal poems of the 1930s should be read as efforts at specular self-portraiture that seek "to establish coherent forms of identity" in a masculine culture (150–51). In her article "Marianne Moore as Female Female Impersonator" in *Marianne Moore: The Art of a Modernist,* ed. Joseph Parisi (Ann Arbor, MI: UMI Research Press, 1990), Sandra Gilbert reads Moore's forays into natural history as acts of "implicit feminism" in that many of her poems seek to "imagine alternatives to the voracity and ferocity of history" (41). In "No Moore of the Same," DuPlessis notes that "Moore identifies with the nobility and charity of . . . plundered and brutalized species" and finds the "confluence of female poet and animals of otherness" to be "very suggestive" (19).

3. Readings of Moore's plant and animal poems as exercises in "impersonal" poetry have a long tradition in Moore criticism. In his influential introduction to Moore's 1935 *Selected Poems,* T. S. Eliot wrote of Moore's "The Jerboa": "For a mind of such agility, and for a sensibility so reticent, the minor subject, such as the pleasant little sand-colored skipping animal, may be the best release for the major emotions . . . We all have to choose whatever subject-matter allows us the most powerful and most secret release; and that is a personal affair" (*SP* 9). Eliot aligned Moore's animal poems with the modernist aesthetic of the mask and many critics since have followed his lead. Donald Hall, for example, argues in *Marianne Moore: The Cage and the Animal* (New York: Pegasus, 1970) that the "surface perfections" (11) of Moore's poems are designed specifically to hide the depths of Moore's emotions. "It is almost axiomatic," he states, "that in Marianne Moore's poetry the more glittering the surface, the greater the underlying emotion" (13). For a sampling of such readings, see R. P. Blackmur, "The Method of Marianne Moore," in *Marianne Moore: A Collection of Critical Essays,* ed. Charles Tomlinson (Englewood Cliffs, NJ: Prentice-Hall, 1969), 85; Charles Molesworth, *Marianne Moore: A Literary Life* (New York: Atheneum, 1990), 256; Richard Howard, "The Monkey Business of Modernism," in *The Art of a Modernist,* ed. Parisi, 3. For the first-wave feminist critiques of Moore's involvement in the male-dominated aesthetic of impersonal poetry, see Suzanne Juhasz, *Naked and Fiery Forms: Modern American Poetry by Women, A New Tradition* (New York: Harper Colophon, 1976), 33–56; and Adrienne Rich, *On Lies, Secrets, and Silence: Selected Prose 1966–78* (New York: Norton, 1979), 36.

4. See Carroll Smith-Rosenberg, *Disorderly Conduct: Visions of Gender in Victorian America* (Oxford: Oxford University Press, 1986), particularly pages 167–81; Rosalind Rosenberg, *Beyond Separate Spheres: Intellectual Roots of Modern Feminism* (New Haven, CT: Yale University Press, 1982), Cynthia E. Russett, *Sexual Science: The Victorian Construction of Womanhood* (Cambridge, MA: Harvard University Press, 1989); and Carl N. Degler, *In Search of Human Nature: The Decline and Revival of Darwinism in American Social Thought* (New York: Oxford University Press, 1991).

5. Smith-Rosenberg, *Disorderly Conduct,* 178.

6. Russett, *Sexual Science,* 10.

7. Rosenberg, *Beyond Separate Spheres,* xiv.

8. Russett, *Sexual Science,* 104–29.

9. Robin Schulze, "Marianne Moore's 'Imperious Ox, Imperial Peach' and the Poetry of the Natural World," *Twentieth Century Literature* 44, no. 1 (Spring 1998): 1–33.

10. For Moore's notes on Darwin's *Variation of Animals and Plants Under Domestication* (1868), see Marianne Moore, reading notebook, 1916–1921, 1250/2, folder VII:01:02, *RML* 99–102.

11. I agree with Heuving's assessment in *Omissions Are Not Accidents* that "[i]n addressing powerful masculine figures, Moore's poems of praise and blame allow her to confront her own desires and fears for power. By distinguishing good power from bad power—power as 'gusto' and power as force—Moore can begin to define for herself a kind of power which is acceptable and necessary" (65).

12. For Moore's notes to the 1924 *Observations* version of the poem, see *BMM* 137.

13. Robert Browning and Elizabeth Barrett, *The Letters of Robert Browning and Elizabeth Barrett, 1845–1846* (New York: Harper Brothers, 1899), 1:513.

14. Ibid., 2:39.

15. Donald Worster, *Nature's Economy: A History of Ecological Ideas* (San Francisco: Sierra Club Books, 1977; reprint, Cambridge: Cambridge University Press, 1985), 178–79.

16. *Letters of Robert Browning and Elizabeth Barrett,* 1:502.

17. Marianne Moore, reading notebook, 1907–1915, 1250/1, folder VII:01:01, *RML* 30.

18. Critical explanations for Moore's change of heart vary. In *Marianne Moore: Imaginary Possessions* (Cambridge, MA: Harvard University Press, 1981), Bonnie Costello categorizes "Injudicious Gardening" as one of Moore's many poems devoted to challenging the conventional symbolic meaning of a particular object—in this case, the "yellow rose." Costello further argues that the poem remains intentionally ambiguous as to her true position on Browning's gardening. "Moore will not," she states, "create closure around either point of view" (45). In *Omissions Are Not Accidents,* Heuving extends Costello's sense of Moore's ambiguity into the realm of gender. Heuving reads "Injudicious Gardening" as an example of Moore's poetic mode of "contrariety," a doubling of perspective that Heuving sees as evidence of Moore's difficult position as a woman author writing back against a male literary tradition. Moore's "incapacity to take on the authoritative conventions of an earlier masculine literary tradition and her refusal to assume a position of secondariness in writing a poetry of 'plaint' [about her female status]," Heuving argues, "left her with a severe lack of [poetic] resources" (50). As a result, Moore created a poetry of "opposing terms" in which both "are equally true," attempting to avoid the use of a domineering, traditionally male, lyric "I" while at the same time resisting any subject position that would mark her as a less than a universal speaker (50). "Injudicious Gardening" reveals the tensions implicit in her gendered position. Moore both praises Browning's sense of privacy and "exposes him." Her presentation of this obvious "contrariety" shows Moore's "deep need to cross the boundaries between the private realm—which often constrains women—and the public—which often excludes her" (64). Linda Leavell, in *Marianne Moore and the Visual Arts: Prismatic Color* (Baton Rouge: Louisiana State University Press, 1995), relates "Injudicious Gar-

dening" to Moore's penchant for "object portraits," in which she, like cubist artist Arthur Dove, "uses an object or combination of objects to suggest, often cryptically, aspects of the subject's character" (101). In *Cultural Critique and Abstraction: Marianne Moore and the Avant-garde* (Lewisburg, PA: Bucknell University Press, 1995), Elizabeth Joyce reads the contrary positions of "Injudicious Gardening" as evidence of Moore's tactics of "Dada subversion," a poetics of "photomontage" that includes a number of "equally moral statements on how culture ought to be" (107).

19. William Lyon Phelps, *Robert Browning: How to Know Him* (Indianapolis, IN: Bobbs-Merrill Company, 1915), 39. For Moore's record of snippets from Phelps's quote, see Marianne Moore, reading notebook, 1913/14–1916, 1250, folder VII:01:00, *RML* 19.

20. Leavell relates these comments to Moore's interest in Kandinsky's concept of "inner necessity." See *Prismatic Color,* 143–44.

21. Marianne Moore, notes for November 26, 1936 public lecture, Brooklyn Institute, New York City, New York, folder II:09:03, *RML.*

22. Marianne Moore, conversation diary, 1929–1932, 1250/28, folder VII:03:12, *RML* 17.

23. John Milton, *Samson Agonistes,* in *Complete Poems and Major Prose,* ed. Merritt Y. Hughes (New York: Macmillan, 1985), 552.

24. In *Marianne Moore: A Study in Voice and Value* (Cambridge: Cambridge University Press, 1987), Margaret Holley describes "To Bernard Shaw: A Prize Bird" as a poem in which the "complexity" of Moore's picture has "a satiric effect." The composite picture of Samson and barnyard rooster, she claims, is "ridiculous enough to qualify the apparent praise" (27–28).

Poems by Grace Schulman

In the Country of Urgency, There Is a Language

To Marianne Moore

> *"Ezra Pound said never, NEVER to use*
> *any word you would not actually say in*
> *moments of utmost urgency."*

1

"Can you hear me? I talk slowly now,"
you said, months past. "When Ezra Pound
Came, he could not say a word."
When your voice waned, I prodded syllables,
Examined frequencies, listened for cadences,
Demanding clarity. Sounds inconceivable
Have meaning now. Four heavy stresses:
"How is your work?" Light syllables:
"Do I look well?" Fire-forced speech
Caught, wordless. It will suffice.

2

December 22, 1970

In the country of urgency, there is a language
I hear as I follow the fall of your hand
and a blue light from the door of your dark apartment.
Your body vanishes behind bedrails.
Your hand I can't let go flows into me.

Blue eyes burn images in me. Those images,
Those sounds, those necessary gestures
Are a language. They will suffice.

3

September 17, 1969

No note from you. Remembering your leopard,
"Spotted underneath and on its toes,"
And how you'd said, "a leopard isn't spotted
Underneath, but in the tapestries it is,
And I liked the idea," I brought the photograph
Of leopards spotted everywhere. Home from the hospital,
Immobile, in a billowing blue gown,
You stalked those beasts and raised yourself in bed:
"Those are cheetahs, Grace!" and lay down again.

4

Your silence is a terrible fire in me that sings on to be fed,
A musical wind that splits my craft, hail-hard, that lashes me dumb.
It is a strange country. Where are the maps,
The lighthouses, the gyroscope you gave me
That rights itself in motion? I have forgotten my name
As well as the irregular conjugations I memorized.
Occasionally, though, a blue light flashes directions
Over dangerous shale, and I hear you
Over protest shouts, explosions, immolations,
Over unreliable telephone connections, I hear you
Over labels, over a broken air conditioner, a plane;
I hear you over the silences we call conversation.
Your voice rolls in me thunder in a night of invisible stars,
And I wake to the sounds of your silence. They are a language.
They will suffice.

American Solitude

"The cure for loneliness is solitude."
—*Marianne Moore*

Hopper never painted this, but here
on a snaky path his vision lingers:

three white tombs, robots with glassed-in faces
and meters for eyes, grim mouths, flat noses,

lean forward on a platform, like strangers
with identical frowns scanning a blur,

far off, that might be their train.
Gas tanks broken for decades face Parson's

smithy, planked shut now. Both relics must stay.
The pumps have roots in gas pools, and the smithy

stores memories of hammers forging scythes
to cut spartina grass for dry salt hay.

The tanks have the remove of local clammers
who sink buckets and stand, never in pairs,

but one and one and one, blank-eyed, alone,
more serene than lonely. Today a woman

rakes in the shallows, then bends to receive
last rays in shimmering water, her long shadow

knifing the bay. She slides into her truck
to watch the sky flame over sand flats, a hawk's

wind arabesque, an island risen, brown
Atlantis, at low tide; she probes the shoreline

and beyond grassy dunes for where the land
might slope off into night. Hers is no common

emptiness, but a vaster silence filled
with terns' cries, an abundant solitude.

Nearby, the three dry gas pumps, worn
survivors of clam-digging generations,

are luminous, and have an exile's grandeur
that says: In perfect solitude, there's fire.

One day I approached the vessels
and wanted to drive on, the road ablaze

with dogwood in full bloom, but the contraptions
outdazzled the road's white, even outshone

a bleached shirt flapping alone
on a laundry line, arms pointed down.

High noon. Three urns, ironic in their outcast
dignity—as though, like some pine chests,

they might be prized in disuse—cast rays,
spun leaf-covered numbers, clanked, then wheezed

and stopped again. Shadows cut the road
before I drove off into the dark woods.

Eve's Unnaming

Not horses, but roan
against the blue-green bay,

not crocuses, but wings
folded over suns,

not rhododendrons, but fire that wilts
to straw in the rain.

How to tag
stone, shell, gull,

hands enfolding lamb's-ear,
a bee sucking the delphinium,

when the sea writes and revises,
breaks, pours out, recoils,

when the elm's leaves
turn silver at dawn.

To see in the dark
the south window strew flowers

on the chapel floor,
or wind peel a sand rose,

is unnamable,
like joy,

like my love's grin
between a cap and a jacket.

Names are for things
we cannot own.

Poems by Cynthia Hogue

In Distrust of Good

with a line by Wallace Stevens

A mind reasoning the good
in violence isn't a good. Truth
wanders through its waving fields

of untruths, all alike grown tall
in the rich soil. "Who's good?"
"Whose good?" the dead call beneath
gray trees with shorn branches.

An empty street, a dark house,
still, as if raided, and the life within
fled. The mind harboring

vengeance slips out of season,
heart's munificent rule.
The good is evil's last invention.
It casts aspersions like stones.

Hope Is an Orientation of the Spirit

after lines by Vaclev Havel and Marianne Moore

The sun drops scarlet among clouds
into a sea of green hills.
The sky darkens and we do not know,
we cannot, where before nightfall
and near-rape, the burgled
body discarded,
a scar now upon the once
smooth surface of the face—
facing the walk home, alone.
     "We have tried,"
     you say, and I, "If we
     hadn't, we could not
     live with ourselves."
Oh to live
with one
self sometimes
slowly even
the violent
have dreams
of self but how
restore to
whole? Temples
burned. Burning
incense scents
the ruins. At the river,
a prayer: "Either
we have hope
        within us or
        we don't."
Like a suppliant whose gait
has slowed, we're tired,
"hope not being hope
until all ground for hope
has vanished." This is strength:
"not to live without meaning,
without, finally, love
even in conditions
        as hopeless as ours
        that gives us hope
        here and now."

Here. Now.

What Matters Today Is the Spirit of the Modern

When scientists claim truth
it hurts them more than
hermeticism (which sparkles).
Bawdy and vulgar, they'll look a tree in the eye
and spit nails: "I shall die pig-drunk
if you don't save me."
But don't.
     Bitter
memories refresh the moment.
Emptiness becomes us until
our senses are dispossessed by the extraordinary
and "we must jouk and let the jaw gang by."
Acknowledging the inconclusion of all experience,
we think nature bestows
consolation, something richer than habit,
like old valleys of continuous
flow and cultural pieties.
Far from the totalitarian,
one's body "passes authorities,
false bowing to landlords
of dissemblance."
     In the 12th century
pilgrims readied for each season
as if the world meant to cease
its revelations, stuttering,
breathless. "Old spirits like new
woke to bells in the village,
ringing. Silvery, the rosy day."
One was asked, *Didn't you wake up
when they broke in?* and said,
No, I did not wake up yet now see
"the earth is not a building
but a body depending upon
supreme mutability and power to change
the Rule of Things clearly":
a truth inscribed on parchment weathered
beyond recognition by the elements,
       "the ear following
       the stars' path" for one
       miraculous instant.

—Title from Karl Patten, writing of Charles Cros; quotations from Charles Cros (as translated from the French by Karl Patten), Robert Burns, Georg Trakl, D. H. Lawrence, TuFu (all from the Spring 1996 issue of *Kestrel,* the last three quoted as epigraphs to James Brasfield's long poem, "The Winter Pavilion"); and Marilyn Mumford.

Relentless Accuracy and a Capacity for Fact:
Authorship in Marianne Moore
and Gertrude Stein

Heather Cass White

B Y WAY OF INTRODUCING THIS ESSAY ABOUT THE NATURE OF AUTHORSHIP
in Marianne Moore and Gertrude Stein, I would like to focus on one small
difference between two texts of "An Octopus." The first text is the poem
as it appeared in *Observations,* and the second, as it appeared in the *Dial.*[1]
In *Observations* it begins, as in all subsequent printings, with a title that
immediately becomes the subject of the poem's first brief sentence:

AN OCTOPUS

Of ice.

Such an opening challenges the reader's expectations in a number of ways:
it shows that the title is part of the poem, not its prologue or label; it suggests that the poem will not be about an octopus like any we normally imagine; and it warns us that rapid reversals and shifts are likely to be the rule
rather than the exception in the poem's method. In the poem's first printing in the *Dial* all of these challenges obtain, with one significant difference. In the *Dial* version the poem begins like this:

AN OCTOPUS
BY MARIANNE MOORE

of ice.

In this printing, the configuration of title, named author, and first line illustrates in schematic fashion the mechanism left deliberately implicit in
the effects read above: it is the interposition of "Marianne Moore" that cre-

ates an octopus out of ice. What interests me in particular about the juxta-position between the two printings is how it illustrates the difference be-tween a poem as the author conceives it and the poem as the audience re-ceives it. When Moore has a measure of control over presentation, as in the book version, she is invisible; when she is published by others, according to their format, she is not only visible, but visible in a way disruptive to the poem's theme of implicit, internal power. Thus, a set of assumptions in-tentionally disrupted by Moore is, in the *Dial* printing, reinstantiated at the level of typeset. The insertion of Moore's name in the middle of her poem's opening dramatizes the uncomfortable tension between what an author wants—a text that speaks for itself—and what an audience demands: an author.

What I propose here is that this tension, with its attendant questions of identity, authority, originality, and power, is of primary concern to both Moore and Stein, and that despite manifest differences in their work and its explorations, both writers adopt remarkably similar stances from which to address it. By "stance" I mean several qualities: first, the writer's imag-ined relationship between her self and her poem; second, the poet's imag-ined relationship to her audience; and third, the writer's approach to the language at her disposal. In asserting even this much similarity, however, I have already begun to engage pivotal questions. How shall one discuss a similarity between two writers whose reputations are founded on the idea (of which each was keenly aware and proud) that there never was or would be anyone else whose writing was like theirs? Why should one discuss "likeness" between writers whose work is premised on a rejection of "like-ness" and its allied forms, such as influence, coterie, and mimesis? Two reasons: the first is a belief in the value of comparison as such. Especially in the case of writers who craft written worlds that effect so complete a sense of self-sufficiency and uniqueness as do those of Moore and Stein, comparison can be a useful tool in enlarging a reader's perspective, allow-ing one to focus on otherwise latent aspects of the work. Set next to one another Moore's and Stein's work illuminate one another in surprising ways, showing that, despite their differences as stylists, both of these cere-bral and radically original writers address a common set of issues around identity and authorship that each negotiates in ways similar enough to the other to make them seem at times like a trans-Atlantic community of two. Such a pairing runs counter to the contemporary division of Modernist lin-eages, in which Stein is the most important forerunner of American exper-imental and avant-garde poetry, and Moore, to the extent that she is asso-ciated with a group or school at all, is frequently compared to Wallace Stevens and Elizabeth Bishop and identified with a voice-oriented lyric tra-dition.[2] This division seems to me in part a holdover from a time when

Moore's early work was more difficult to come by and thus paid less critical attention than her more available, and more conventional, later work,
and is also related to Bishop's later ascendancy in the modern canon (with
its attendant emphasis on the ways Moore's work is akin to Bishop's). In
suggesting one consequence of these critical affiliations I hope I will not
be taken as disparaging in any way work that compares Moore to Bishop
or Moore to Stevens; my point is not to argue that a comparison to Stein is
more pertinent than others, but rather to correct the unnecessary and im-
poverishing assumption that such a comparison is largely out of the question. One aim of this essay is to suggest by its comparison that the interest
Moore felt in Stein's work (as evidenced by her careful reviews) is not incidental: both poets were working in multifariously experimental modes,
in the service of projects that are in some ways remarkably similar, and it
is a flaw in literary history that they have been judged wholly unlike.[3]

My second reason for this comparison relates primarily to Moore: it is
my understanding that Moore's early work (that written before 1935) has
as one of its presiding geniuses a "fighting spirit," expressed in part as an
aggressive testing of the boundaries of sense and cohesiveness, that is often overlooked in favor of the moralism that, also present in the early work,
becomes dominant in her later poetry.[4] This moralism and the (comparative) simplicity of Moore's later work, along with her affectations of dress
and manner, are responsible for the familiar caricature of Moore as mere
charming eccentric, a caricature amply documented and refuted elsewhere.[5] My concern here is how this latter image has made Moore seem to
be a poet less interested than she actually was in inquiring into the linguistic
and ethical dimensions of the self as it is constructed within a poem. If later
poems such as "A Carriage From Sweden" and "An Arctic Ox (Or Goat)"
confirm Moore's image as a moral enthusiast, an analogue of the feature
writer, as Marie Boroff argues, much of her earlier work, as I shall show,
not only contradicts that enthusiasm but questions the sense of a stable narrative subject position on which it rests.[6] By comparing her work to that of
Gertrude Stein, I would like to illustrate this point about Moore by showing how similar in many respects her early work is to Stein's in just this inquiry: Stein's trope is arrogance while Moore's is humility, but neither
writer took any part of her stance as author for granted, including most especially her relationship to a reading audience.

THE I OF EACH

Once one begins to look there seems to be no end to the similarities between Moore and Stein. One especially suggestive example involves their
attitudes toward commas; in "Poetry and Grammar" Stein writes:

A comma by helping you along holding your coat for you and putting on your shoes keeps you from living your life as actively as you should lead it and to me for many years . . . the use of them was positively degrading.[7]

In "Humility, Concentration, and Gusto" Moore agrees: "As for commas, nothing can be more stultifying than needlessly over accentuated pauses" (*CPr* 421). Both Moore and Stein display in their use of commas what Moore, in writing about Stein, calls a "precisely perplexing verbal exactness" (*CPr* 121). Moore, for example, regularly deploys sentences such as "We are told, if we do wrong that grace may abound, it does not abound" (*CPr* 369), close cousins to Stein's hairpin grammatical turns in such sentences as "Romanticism is then when everything being alike everything is naturally simply different, and romanticism."[8] Is this shared attitude a coincidence? Perhaps, but Stein writes in the "Henry James" section of *Four in America* that "there is no use hesitating before a coincidence,"[9] and Moore reminds us in "To a Steam Roller" that "to question / the congruence of a complement is vain, if it exists" (*BMM* 63). In this case similar attitudes toward a punctuation mark bespeak ramifying similarities in the two writers' stances toward subjectivity and its stylistic counterparts: precision, difficulty, and virtuosity. In each writer's thinking commas constitute an insulting prop, suggesting that the writing is not in itself precise enough to guide the reader's experience of it. Moore thought that it was an author's "tone of voice" that gives her reader pleasure; by "tone of voice" she meant "that intonation in which the accents which are responsible for it are so unequivocal as to persist, no matter under what circumstances the syllables are read or by whom they are read" (*CPr* 32). She specifically admired this quality in Stein's sentences, of which she writes "It is a feat of writing to make the rhythm of a sentence unmistakable without punctuation" (*CPr* 341). Stein's feeling for the power of a well-written sentence is equally strong: "a long complicated sentence should force itself upon you, make you know yourself knowing it."[10] The source of writing's particular and ineradicable emphasis, according to Moore, is the author's voice, not her command of punctuation; this is important because it underscores how much of the author's self is on the line when she writes. As Moore later puts it, "you don't devise a rhythm, the rhythm is the person, and the sentence but a radiograph of personality" (*CPr* 396). Moore's emphasis on the porous boundary between sentence and self suggests another commonality with Stein, who wonders "what is a sentence for if I am I then my little dog knows me,"[11] and whose novel *The Making of Americans* began with a desire to "put down the complete conception that I had of an individual, the complete rhythm of a personality that I had gradually acquired by listening seeing feeling and experience."[12]

Both writers are complex in their attitudes toward having their writing

tied to a *particular* personality. Stein, who reported delightedly that her experiments with automatic writing suggested that she had no unconscious
mind at all, was dismayed when her brother Leo suggested that unless one
knew her personally, her writing was meaningless. She asserts the contrary:
"I am not I any longer when I see. This sentence is at the bottom of all creative activity."[13] In this way she insists that the definition of creative work
is its separation from the author as an observable person, an insistence she
bolstered by claiming that there was nothing in her life that could help a
reader understand her work. At the same time, however, she continually refined her self-definition as "genius," the ineluctable authorizing presence
behind her writing. Stein distinctly has it both ways in her work, adjusting
a balance of personality and impersonality as it suits her. As she herself allows at the end of *The Geographical History of America,* a book dedicated
to distinguishing the impersonal, transcendent human mind from a merely
personal human nature, "I so easily see that identity has nothing to do with
master-pieces although occasionally and very inevitably it does always
more or less come in."[14]

For Moore, the question of the self and its claims is always a moral one,
and under constant scrutiny. I read, for example, in "Humility, Concentration, and Gusto" a thinly veiled comment on the author's own young am-
bitions when Moore writes, "Humility, indeed, is armor, for it realizes that
it is impossible to be original, in the sense of doing something that has
never been thought of before" (*CPr* 420–21). This thought suggests that
the author who expresses it feels herself in need of defense from the desire
for such primary originality, to the extent that to realize its impossibility
implies a time when such a realization became necessary. An underlying
desire to do what no one else has done or could do is everywhere apparent
in Moore's work. Shall we hear humility in Moore's often-repeated claim
that she called her creations poems for lack of a better category in which
to put them, or shall we hear the desire to create a form never before thought
of? Originality is of course a perpetually unsettled question in Moore, who
makes poems out of quotations so as modestly to give credit to others. Or
does she give credit lavishly so as to enjoy and highlight her own originality with a clearer conscience and a more pointed display of the difference between what she has borrowed and what she has invented?[15] For a
poet whose early work is defined by a "reluctance to be unoriginal" quotation necessarily engages questions of the self and its relation to predeces-
sors and peers.[16] Moore's early poetry, particularly those poems that she
chose not to reprint after the 1935 *Selected Poems,* take a certain "pride in
unserviceableness" (*CPr* 93), as she wrote of Wallace Stevens, that is related to their insistence on the integrity of the individual self. For example,
her elephant doppelganger in "Black Earth" says "I do these / things I do,
which please / no one but myself" (*BMM* 87) and the rose in "Roses Only"

is "a symbol of the unit, stiff and sharp," that exemplifies "the fact that spirit creates form" (*BMM* 83).

However, the "self" is often difficult to locate, in a number of senses, in Moore's poems; in the service of elaborating two of those senses I will briefly read "My Apish Cousins," and "Black Earth." As I read these poems my debt to earlier work on Moore's complex representations of subjectivity will be felt; in particular, I am indebted to the work of Cristanne Miller, Sabine Sielke, and Kristin Hotelling, each of whom discusses in great detail the ways that, in Sielke's words, "Moore's [un-self-centered poems] cannot help but revolve around matters of subjectivity while at the same time fragmenting the subject."[17] The network of shifting identifications in Moore's poems makes it difficult to identify a stable center of perspective and authority even in a poem, such as "My Apish Cousins," that uses a first-person voice. The ostensible narrator of this poem is the visitor to the zoo, the "I" who remembers the various animals seen there. This narrator establishes both her difference from and her connectedness to the zoo animals in the title: the monkeys are her "apish cousins." In this way the narrator becomes both the observer of the poem, describing in particular one of the big cats, that "Gilgamesh among / the hairy carnivora," but also the subject of that cat's observation: human, as are the "trembling" art critics he despises, and an insignificant animal next to the cat himself, with the "slate-gray marks on [his] forelegs and [his] resolute tail" (*BMM* 82). Who is the subject in this strange poem, one third of which is spoken by a cat, in lines that sound as if they may have been quoted from some other context but are not? This poem resists even more than a Moore poem usually does the naturalization of its oddities. It is insufficient, for example, to say simply that the human speaker is a kind of framing device and the cat a mouthpiece for the poet's opinion. Instead, this poem is a model of the multifaceted consciousness constructed by many early Moore poems, whether they contain quotations or not; to the extent that "the rhythm [of this poem] is the person," the "person" it reveals is characterized by juxtaposition and dispersal rather than integration. In this way the subjectivity this poem embodies resembles the model posited by Stein when she asks, "What is the use of being a little boy if you are growing up to be a man?"[18] Stein's point is to suggest that selfhood is not an overarching continuity; as Hugh English writes, "'being one' is not about being 'whole'; rather, 'being one,' 'one' human subject or 'one word,' means being one in a series, one and one and one."[19]

The second sense in which the self is elusive in a Moore poem becomes clear in a poem written in a more traditionally integrated voice, where it is impossible for the poet to locate a secure demarcation between the self and the outside world. This is the subject on which Moore's double, a speaking elephant, meditates in "Black Earth." In one way, the elephant sounds comfortable in his ability to distinguish the inner from the outer, confident as he is, for example, that his soul, unlike his skin, "shall never // be cut into / by a wooden spear" (*BMM* 88). At the same time, however, he reflects that one must not wash away the river's sediment encrusting his joints, for "do away / with it and [he is himself] done away with" (*BMM* 87). The poem as a whole is structured around the difference between external manifestations of the self figured as "the / patina of circumstance" (*BMM* 87) and an intangible internal essence. Yet that difference cannot be satisfactorily established, for just as "the unity of / life and death has been expressed by the circumference // described by [the elephant's] / trunk" (*BMM* 88) so spiritual poise cannot be separated from the external poise by which it is expressed. The elephant's ears, for example, "are sensitized to more than the sound // of the wind," while the "beautiful element of unreason" (*BMM* 89) underneath his skin is what lends it its definitive thickness. One implication of this inseparability is that, if it is true, then in practical terms, in reference to poetry, there is no "self," no informing consciousness, isolated from its manifestation in a poem, and no poem that is not also a manifestation of a particular self. This insight, however, is deceptively neat, as there remains the question of how a "self" manifests itself and is in turn created by a poem—to ask only the most pressing questions: Is the self in a poem the same as the identity of the author? Must a "self" be represented by an "I" in a poem (a pronoun Moore gave up almost completely in her major poetry of the thirties, as Margaret Holley points out), and if it is not, how will we recognize it?[20] Perhaps most importantly, if the form of a poem, like the skin of the elephant, is "full of the history of power" (*BMM* 88) by virtue of its individuality as the mark of a discrete self, what sort of power is it, and how may the poet use it or be used by it?

A CAPACITY FOR FACT

Consider here two long poems, Stein's *Stanzas in Meditation* and Moore's "An Octopus." Each articulates the pleasures and hazards of staking a poetic claim on the power and individuality of the self that writes. Despite their manifestly different projects, each takes a similar stance in regard to the challenges it identifies for itself: principally, I am concerned with how each poem considers the nature of a unified writing self, and the relationship to an audience such a writing self might entail. Stein's *Stanzas in Meditation* was first published posthumously in the Yale edition of her collected writing, in which it runs to 151 pages. She wrote this long poem in 1932, at the same time that she was writing her *Autobiography of Alice B. Toklas*. The *Autobiography* was intended for public consumption; Stein wrote it to get money and fame, both of which it brought her. The *Stanzas* reflect on that process, both the writing and the being rewarded, in a language as hermetic as the *Autobiography's* is accessible. For example, in one well-known passage the *Stanzas* comment on the inside joke of the *Autobiography:* it was not written by Alice. Stein says in Part IV, Stanza XIV: "This is her autobiography one of two / But which it is no one which it is can know . . . she will be me when this you see."[21] These lines point to two fundamental principles of the writing self according to Stein. In the first place, they take on resonance when set next to her meditation on the "oneness" or "twoness" of the writer in *The Geographical History of America.* In this latter book Stein emphasizes that her doubleness in the *Autobiography* is the necessary, and debilitating, condition of any writer who undertakes to write premeditatedly, with a purpose in mind, instead of spontaneously and accurately recording internal experience. She comments on this phenomenon in relation to philosophy, writing:

> When I was at college I studied philosophy that was it they did not know what they saw because they said they saw what they knew, and if they saw it they no longer knew it because then they were two. . . .
> The minute you are two it is not philosophy that is through it is you.[22]

The ability fully to be "one," by which Stein means to remain completely within one's own experience as one writes, is a hallmark of genius, and the province of "the human mind and master-pieces."[23] Exercising "relentless accuracy" in regard to one's own exact perception is, according to Stein, a safeguard against the incursion of other people's responses to one's work: "I think that if you announce what you see nobody can say no. Everybody does say no but nobody can nobody can say so, that is no."[24]

In the second place, Stein's boast that she is one of two and "which it is no one can know" points to the power of extension she sees in a singular self. If her goal is to write without regard to the world of other people, and in so doing fully inhabit the "one" she is as she perceives, she is fascinated by the paradoxically incorporative power such oneness allows her. This power is suggested most graphically by the "autobiography" of Alice Toklas, the imposture of which raises many questions. Chief among them is, what is an identity if anyone can write an autobiography for anyone else? If a recitation of the facts of a life are insufficient to make clear whose autobiography is being written, and if knowing whose autobiography is being written is no guarantee that one will know who is doing the writing, might not any autobiography be everybody's autobiography? What if one could leave the facts of a life and take out the person? The *Stanzas* are in part an attempt to do so; in John Ashbery's words, "the story of *Stanzas in Meditation* is a general, all-purpose model which each reader can adapt to fit his own set of particulars."[25] Ashbery calls the *Stanzas* a "hymn to possibility;" I call them a poem that has, like Moore's octopus, a capacity for fact. In Stein's poem "facts" are the linguistic objects out of which we fashion the story of ourselves; in this sense it is the most commonplace words that are the basic facts of everyone's life. Stein called the stanzas her "real achievement of the commonplace," and one can see why in lines such as the following:

> Not what they do with not
> Not only will they wish what
> What they do with what they like
> But they will also very well state[26]

What do "they" do in these lines? They "do," they "will wish," and they "state." These open-ended verbs, free for the most part of definite objects, participate in a field of flexible grammar in which reference moves forwards and backwards. Should the first line read "Not. What they do with 'not.'" Or should we see "Not what they do with 'not,'" or should we be listening for puns and hidden maxims: "Naught [is] what they do with 'not.'" All of these are possibilities, and each possibility expands with each succeeding line. Stein says in *How to Write,* "The question is if you have a vocabulary have you any need of grammar except for explanation that is the question."[27] Stein loved grammar, claiming to have liked nothing better as a child than to diagram sentences. As an adult writer, however, she discovered to her delight that sentences "diagram themselves."[28] She describes the discovery she made in writing *How to Write* that "vocabulary in itself and by itself can be interesting and can make sense . . . it is extraordinary how it is impossible that a vocabulary does not make sense,"[29] a discovery she seems to have greeted with some pleasure; if the words would take care of making the sense, she was left the freer to play with the words themselves and in that play find out how the arrangement of words can make a world. Stein describes this work as "a violent kind of delightfulness,"[30] and as the word "violence" suggests, this play has a less playful side, in its hints at the power one might arrogate by "having a vocabulary." If grammar will of its own motion create all possible combinations of meaning, then the one who has the right vocabulary will encompass all varieties of experience. Stein frequently reflects on this possibility in the *Stanzas,* claiming that "They like whatever I like," "I have begun again to think everything," and "All this is to be for me."[31] As Susan Schultz trenchantly puts it, "to write everybody's autobiography is both to deny the difference between writer and reader and to assert control over the reader's reception of the text."[32] To the extent that Stein cannot perfectly maintain the sort of ideal abstraction this project requires, it is bound to falter, as she recognizes: "I am trying to say something but I have not said it. / Why. /

Because I add my I."[33] Part of "add[ing her] I" is giving in to a desire to be read and understood, which generates moments of despair out of which the poem must repeatedly lift itself, as when it says: "I have thought that I would not mind if they came / But I do."[34] Nevertheless, Stein's ambition persists that in writing the *Stanzas* she will create a poem capable of assimilating anyone's experience of daily life, while at the same time rendering that experience in a style that is at once impeccably abstract and, as she said of her *Tender Buttons,* "not unordered in not resembling."

Deliberate dislocation of the reader's expectations and field of reference is as much Moore's technique as Stein's, as my initial reading of the title of "An Octopus" was meant to show. The word "glacier" appears nowhere in that poem; instead it defines its subject by picking and choosing from the official literature written about national parks in the United States and Canada, as the octopus/glacier itself "pick[s] periwinkles from the cracks," and in so doing embodies the action of the octopus.[35] "Action," however, in any direct sense, is the wrong word to apply to the octopus, from whose slow, almost imperceptible effects the reader's attention is continually drawn away. It would be difficult to find another poem in which such a sense of energy and motion is created around a description of a state of activity so gradual as to resemble stasis: the poem describes the octopus in terms of what it has embedded within itself on top of "Big Snow Mountain," and the variety of life that can flourish on top of such seeming stillness. To the extent that the poem is thus in part about a medium that acts quietly but decisively, we should already hear an analogy to Moore's repeated description of her writing as "if not a cabinet of fossils, a kind of collection of flies in amber" (*CPr* 551). The analogy is important because, in my reading of it, "An Octopus" elucidates the particular implications of amber as a metaphor for a poem: amber is beautiful, crystalline, durable, slow-moving, and deadly to anything trapped in it. In all these ways amber is like ice, and, but for its deadliness, spiritually akin to the various "laborious" devices, "ab[le] to endure blows" (*BMM* 64), by which Moore represents her poetics in "Diligence is to Magic as Progress is to Flight." Of course, the difference that the ice's deadliness makes is enormous: whereas Moore's attitude in "Diligence" is one of unmitigated defiance, daring the critic to suppose her poems "ephemera," "An Octopus" simultaneously depicts her method and inquires into its moral ambiguities. My reading of "An Octopus" as a self-reflexive poem about Moore's own poetics is informed by Robin Gail Schulze's reading of it as Moore's dramatization of the limits of human knowledge in the face of nature. Schulze characterizes the mountain as "a beautiful but potentially unknowable thing whose dangerous power may teach only an 'awful doubt' of any benevolent design in nature."[36] My suggestion that "An Octopus" presents an allegory in which the reader stands in relation to a Moore poem as Moore stands in relation to the mountain takes Moore up on her own hint when she writes, "it is a curiosity of literature how often what one says of another seems descriptive of one's self" (*CPr* 514).

In its moral ambiguity the world of Big Snow Mountain might stand as a precursor to the Brooklyn of "The Steeple-Jack." In both poems the reader is encouraged to see both beauty and danger, the latter more difficult to recognize than the former. The attractive features of life on Big Snow Mountain are immediately apparent, as it is the habitat of "a diversity of creatures" that "maintain[s] many minds" (*BMM* 127). The mountain's diversity is represented by the idyllic life of the careful beavers and special antelopes who live there, and by the dazzling concatenation of "calcium gems and alabaster pillars, / topaz, tourmaline crystals, and amethyst quartz" (*BMM* 126) to be found in its bears' dens. This profusion might be taken as an emblem of positive multiplicity; like Moore the glacier is a collector with wide-ranging tastes and an ability to keep its own contributions hidden in the background. It is the gouging motion of the glacier that has created, for example:

> The Goat's Mirror—
> that lady-fingerlike depression in the shape of the left human foot,
> which prejudices you in favor of itself
> before you have had time to see the others;
> its indigo, pea-green, blue-green, and turquoise,
> from a hundred to two hundred feet deep,
> "merging in irregular patches in the middle lake
> where like gusts of a storm
> obliterating the shadows of the firtrees, the wind makes lanes of ripples."
> What spot could have merits of equal importance
> for bears, elk, deer, wolves, goats, and ducks?
>
> (*BMM* 126)

There is poetic harmony here too, a "complexity [that] is not a crime" (*BMM* 91) in the passage's exercise of Moore's characteristic strengths: enumeration and list-making, close observation of nuanced differences, and lengthy quotation.

However, even in the poem's first lines there is also menace in the description of the glacier, which "deceptively reserved and flat" "kill[s] prey with the concentric crushing rigor of the python," and lies in wait behind "tightly wattled spruce twigs / 'conformed to an edge like clipped cypress / as if no branch could penetrate the cold beyond its company'" (*BMM* 125–26). If the "spot" created by the glacier is supremely "important" in the sustenance it offers to the animals who live there, it is more ambivalently important for any of its human visitors. The octopus' beauty is both dazzling, "as in Persian designs of hard stones with enamel" (*BMM* 129), and a lure to people to make the climb to see it. Mere physical force is not enough to ensure their success, as the mountain is as "inimical to 'bristling, puny, swearing men / equipped with saws and axes'" as it is partial to "gentians, ladyslippers, harebells, [and] mountain dryads" (*BMM* 129). The mountain is a test, as a Moore poem is a test, of the mental agility and stamina of the person confronting it. To be liked by the casual climber would be for the mountain a calamity—it chooses to nourish wild plants and to be a place "where climbers have not gone or have gone timidly" (*BMM* 129). Thus if, as the poet claims, the octopus works by "unegoistic action," that does not mean that it is not rigorous in selecting its own society. More than this: it is inexorable in that selection, its tentacles impartially consuming whatever they encounter:

> "Creeping slowly as with meditated stealth,
> its arms seeming to approach from all directions,"
> it receives one under winds that "tear the snow to bits
> and hurl it like a sandblast,
> shearing off twigs and loose bark from the trees."
>
> (*BMM* 131)

In its exuberant heterogeneity as well as its implicit threat, the poem's multivalent description of the glacier serves as an analogy for Moore's own poetics in two senses. First, her poem is a force that is also "unegoistic," in which the "I" of lyric poetry is only loosely implicit in a poem visibly stitched from the words of others, with no central point of view, in which, as Carol H. Cantrell writes, "perspective [is] a problem rather than a given."[37] Second, also like the glacier, Moore's method claims a supremely absorptive power, capable of assimilating to its purposes any language that comes its way; making a poem out of quotations is another way of saying to the world of language at large "all this is to be for me."

One difference between Stein's *Stanzas* and Moore's "Octopus" is that where Stein's "capacity for fact" is a function of her poem's ability to meditate on all the smallest of all of our common words, Moore locates "fact" in the welter of already crafted writing that surrounds us. Her capacity, like that of the glacier, is for swallowing whole distinct, individually stamped pieces of writing, creating a poem with the power to turn all other writing into facets of itself. This poem and the poetics it exemplifies are, like the "treacherous glass mountain" (*BMM* 129), only to be attempted by those with a "love of doing hard things" (*BMM* 131), who will not be fooled by a deceptive neatness of finish. Moore provides a figure of such a reader in the original version of "An Octopus." In a section later omitted she describes:

> "Calypso, the goat flower—
> that greenish orchid fond of snow"—
> anomalously nourished upon shelving glacial ledges

where climbers have not gone or have gone timidly,
"the one resting his nerves while the other advanced,"
on this volcano with the bluejay, her principal companion.
"Hopping stiffly on sharp feet" like miniature icehacks—
"secretive, with a look of wisdom and distinction, but a villain,
fond of human society and the crumbs that go with it,"

(*BMM* 129–30)

This bluejay, an American bird who "knows no Greek," and who, unlike the Calypso orchid, is not the glacier's chosen favorite, emblematizes the necessarily practical, even unscrupulous nature of the reader confronted with the octopus whose smoothness is an illusion, always threatening to conceal chaos. As a reader, one must hack into such a surface as one can, remaining mindful of avalanches and tearing winds, as well as of its own arms that stealthily approach from all directions. The reader is in danger where the poet's method is guided only by "relentless accuracy" of individual perception and expression. Like Stein's *Stanzas in Meditation,* "An Octopus" works with a paradoxically impersonal insistence on absolutely personal technique: impersonal because the self as such is absent in many of its traditional lyric guises, and personal because all categories of the language and experience of others are made use of in poems whose accents persist unequivocally, no matter "by whom they are read." It is Moore's and Stein's awareness of this tension, even this irreconcilable contradiction, that defines and unites what I have called their stance as authors. Recognizing this commonality is part of resisting the literary-historical stereotyping that keeps these poets from being as widely useful as they might otherwise be: Stein is not, as is often asserted, categorically and consistently averse to the conventions of first-person representation; no more is Moore ignorant of the subsuming ambition, sometimes Steinian in scale, that underlies her own deployments of those same conventions. If my emphasis on the similarities between Moore and Stein has overlooked their manifest and multifold differences, that seems to me a permissible counteractive to the prevalent assumption that differences are all there are to see. In light of their uniquely well-articulated and shared sense of the poetic balance between self and other, between voice and abstraction, and between individuality and domination, we would do well to remark not on how different their projects were, but rather on the remarkable variety of forms and answers to which a mutual project may give rise when put into such extraordinary hands.

NOTES

1. The two citations are from *Observations* (New York: Dial Press, 1924), 83–90, and the *Dial* 77 (December 1924): 475–81 (I have examined them in reverse chronological or-

der). See *BMM* 125–32, 312–18. Further citations from *Observations* will be taken from *BMM*.

2. The exceptions to this division between Moore and Stein and the later poets with whom they are associated are few. Two of these exceptions suggest the affinity I will argue for here: first, John Ashbery, in the early, more avant-garde part of his own career, writes with equal enthusiasm and penetration about the difficulties of both poets. Of reading *Stanzas in Meditation* he writes, "if, on laying the book aside, we feel that it is still impossible to accomplish the impossible, we are also left with the conviction that it is the only thing worth trying to do" ("The Impossible," *Poetry* 90, no. 4 [July 1957]: 254). In his piece "Straight Lines Over Rough Terrain," (*New York Times Book Review,* November 26, 1967), he writes of Moore's poetry: "there are . . . cases in which I become aware before the end of a poem that Miss Moore and I have parted company somewhat further back. . . . We are brought up against a mastery which defies attempts to analyze it, an intelligence that plays just beyond our reach" (1). Second, the National Poetry Foundation in Orono, Maine, founded explicitly to study and promote experimental and avant-garde work ranging from the Objectivists, to the Black Mountain poets, to "Language" poetry, has dedicated to Moore a volume of its *Man/Woman and Poet* series, a series that includes volumes on Mina Loy, George Oppen, Carl Rakosi, Charles Reznikoff, and Louis Zukofsky among other poets more commonly cited as influencing contemporary non–voice centered poetry.

3. Moore reviewed *The Making of Americans,* which she says "comprehends . . . a psychology which is universal," and *The Geographical History of America,* which she called "a triumph." Both reviews are reprinted in *CPr* 128–31 and 339–41, respectively.

4. I take the phrase "fighting spirit" from a letter of Moore's to H.D., written in 1916 (*SL* 113). I have written elsewhere about the extent to which this spirit may be seen both as a feature of Moore's intellectual treatment of her subject matter and as a formal principle of her composition. See Heather Cass White, "Morals, Manners, and 'Marriage': Marianne Moore's Art of Conversation," *Twentieth-Century Literature* 45, no. 4 (1999): 488–510.

5. The refutation of this parody is the implicit or explicit basis for the feminist reappraisal of Moore, for example, as practiced by Rachel Blau DuPlessis and Carolyn Burke, among numerous others. Kristin Hotelling details the persistence of parts of this image in Moore criticism. See Kristin Hotelling, "'The I of each is to the I of each, a kind of fretful speech which sets a limit on itself': Marianne Moore's Strategic Selfhood," *Modernism / Modernity* 5, no. 1 (1998), 93, n. 1. In treating Moore's later work dismissively I am following the critical consensus, though I am aware that I am also making a value judgment that requires a more thorough defense than I will give it here.

6. See Marie Boroff, *Language and the Poet: Verbal Artistry in Frost, Stevens, and Moore* (Chicago: University of Chicago Press, 1979), 80–105.

7. Gertrude Stein, *Lectures in America* (Boston: Beacon Press, 1957), 220.

8. Gertrude Stein, "Composition As Explanation" (1926), reprinted in *Gertrude Stein-Writings 1903–1932,* ed. Catharine R. Stimpson and Harriet Chessman (New York: Library of America, 1998), 527. Citations are to the Stimpson and Chessman edition.

9. Gertrude Stein, *Four in America* (New Haven, CT: Yale University Press, 1947), 131.

10. Stein, *Lectures,* 221.

11. Gertrude Stein, *How to Write* (Paris: Plains Editions, 1931; Toronto, Canada: Dover, 1975), 19. Citations are to the Dover edition.

12. Stein, *Lectures,* 147.

13. Stein, *Four in America,* 119.

14. Gertrude Stein, *The Geographical History of America* (New York: Random House, 1936; Baltimore: Johns Hopkins University Press, 1995), 234. Citations are to the Johns Hopkins edition.

15. I am able to refer thus glancingly to an essential and complex question about Moore's quotations because of the richness of the work already done in this field. The analyses I have

found most useful in coming to my own sense of Moore's balance between homage and self-assertion are John Slatin's *The Savage's Romance: The Poetry of Marianne Moore* (University Park: Pennsylvania State University Press 1986), 1–19; Margaret Holley's *The Poetry of Marianne Moore: A Study in Voice and Value* (Cambridge: Cambridge University Press, 1987), 37–43; and Elizabeth Gregory's *Quotation and Modern American Poetry: "Imaginary Gardens with Real Toads"* (Houston, TX: Rice University Press, 1996), 129–85.

16. Marianne Moore, untitled May 1, 1940 lecture, Sarah Lawrence College, *RML,* quoted in Slatin, 211.

17. See Cristanne Miller, *Marianne Moore: Questions of Authority* (Cambridge, MA: Harvard University Press, 1995), especially Chapter 2; Sabine Sielke, *Fashioning the Female Subject: The Intertextual Networking of Dickinson, Moore, and Rich* (Ann Arbor: University of Michigan Press, 1997), 19–90; and Hotelling, "Strategic Selfhood," 76. Perhaps the most notable way Sielke's and Hotelling's analyses in particular differ from mine is in their arguments' grounding in poststructuralist feminist theory. Sielke reads Moore's poetry through the lens of Kristeva's theory of semiotic "body" language, for example, while Hotelling reads Moore through Judith Butler and Donna Haraway to show how Moore's poetry "deconstructs the lyric 'I,' and, even more radically, the sexed body through which this 'I' is made to seem essential" (Hotelling, "Strategic Selfhood," 76).

18. Stein, *Geographical History,* 51.

19. Hugh English, "'By Being Outside of America': Gertrude Stein's 'Geographical History' of Gender, Self, and Writing" in *Women, America, and Movement: Narratives of Relocation,* ed. Susan L. Roberson (Columbia: University of Missouri Press, 1998), 262.

20. See Holley, *A Study in Voice and Value,* 79–83.

21. Gertrude Stein, *Stanzas in Meditation,* in *The Yale Edition of the Unpublished Writings of Gertrude Stein,* ed. Carl Van Vechten (New Haven, CT: Yale University Press, 1956; Freeport, NY: Books for Libraries Press, 1969), 77. Citations are to the Books for Libraries edition.

22. Stein, *Geographical History,* 178.

23. Ibid., 179.

24. Ibid., 162.

25. Ashbery, "The Impossible," 251.

26. Stein, *Stanzas,* 61.

27. Stein, *How To Write,* 60.

28. Stein, *Lectures,* 211.

29. Ibid., 230.

30. Gertrude Stein, *Tender Buttons* (Los Angeles: Sun and Moon Press, 1990), 10.

31. Stein, *Stanzas,* 37, 96, 78.

32. Susan Schultz, "Gertrude Stein's Self-Advertisement," *Raritan* 12, no. 2 (Fall 1992): 73.

33. Stein, *Stanzas,* 183.

34. Ibid., 79.

35. I follow Moore in referring to the "octopus" as a singular being, though Moore was actually describing a large grouping of glaciers on Mt. Rainier. Patricia C. Willis's account of Moore's trips to the Northwest gives a detailed account of the poem's factual basis. See Patricia C. Willis, "The Road to Paradise: First Notes on Marianne Moore's 'An Octopus,'" *Twentieth-Century Literature* 30, nos. 2-3 (Autumn 1984): 242–66.

36. Robin G. Schulze, *The Web of Friendship: Marianne Moore and Wallace Stevens* (Ann Arbor: University of Michigan Press, 1995), 52–53.

37. Caroll H. Cantrell, "'The Roar of Ice': Motion, Language, and Silence in Marianne Moore," in *New Essays in Eco-Feminist Literary Criticism,* ed. Glynis Carr (Lewisburg, PA: Bucknell University Press, 2000), 159.

Mannerist Moore: Poetry, Painting, Photography

Stacy Carson Hubbard

AROUND 1920[1] MARIANNE MOORE, DRESSED IN WHAT WOULD BECOME her signature outfit of dark tailored suit and white, broad-collared blouse with bow tie, sat for a photograph at the Sarony studio, famous for theatrical portraits. The result is a beautiful and imposing portrait, one which fulfills perfectly Roland Barthes's description of photography as "an Art of the person" which is "founded on the pose" and concerned with "the body's formality."[2] Though Moore once complained in a letter to another of her photographers, George Platt Lynes, that she was "an elephant of stone to convey where intentional spontaneity is concerned,"[3] it is precisely "intentional spontaneity," or artificed reality, which is here conveyed. The paradoxical relation of reality to artifice is embodied in what I find to be the most alluring detail of this photograph: Moore's impossibly curving, beautifully elongated and conspicuously posed left hand. This hand is what Mary Ann Caws might call an "eye magnet."[4] Here is how one observer describes it: the hand is "distractingly ambiguous in appearance . . . a flattering visual paradox, . . . long, thin, tapered, delicate . . . posed in a way that seems anatomically difficult . . . its fingers arranged to make an aesthetically appealing pattern or design. . . . [It] turns away from natural appearance toward abstraction, [and can] be interpreted as [an] . . . indication of [the sitter's] physical and intellectual worth."[5] Though I have playfully appropriated this description to gloss the Sarony portrait, it is actually James Mirollo's description of Bronzino's 1560 painting of Laura Battiferri, a classic of Mannerist portraiture and one which exemplifies its fixation on the "bella mano," or beautiful hand, from which derives the term "Mannerism." To apply this commentary to a photograph of an actual historical figure is, perhaps, to produce what Bonnie Costello has called, with reference to Moore's poetry, "powerful incongruities and bi-directional signals."[6] A photograph—what Susan Sontag has called a "trace of the real"[7]—is here made to mimic a painting (or many paintings), an historical (and famous) body made to approximate the impossible contortions and idealizations of Mannerist art. And, not least, here an artist is made the subject of art, and not, it would seem, in a way that insists upon her authority as maker, but in a way that absorbs her into a recognizable body of made

Marianne Moore, 1920 (possibly 1924). (Photograph by Sarony, reproduced courtesy of the Rosenbach Museum and Library; XII:03:03a.)

objects. Add to this that a woman most decidedly not associated with amorous themes borrows from art history a locus classicus of erotic iconography: the hand and glove of Raphael, Bronzino, Parmigianino, Petrarch, Sidney, and Shakespeare. Such allusion raises complex questions about the meaning of imitation or quotation, the paradoxical relation of nature to artifice, and the ambiguities of feminine authority.

Of course, the strange allusiveness of the hand in the Sarony portrait is owed in part to a mere accident of anatomy, and like any photograph, this portrait both invites and repels interpretation as an aesthetic object, balancing between its documentary authority and its aesthetic impact, between the sense that it is real and the sense that it is mannered. Moreover, though Moore is the artist in the portrait, she is not precisely the artist of it, so that any gesture of hers must be understood to exist within another artist's composition. This is a situation ironically like that which Moore often imposed upon the authors of the variously arranged quotations out of which she accreted her poems. The many portraits of Moore by such well-known photographers as Lotte Jacobi, Henri Cartier-Bresson, Cecil Beaton, Carl Van Vechten, George Platt Lynes, Richard Avedon, and Diane Arbus testify equally to the distinctive styles of their various photographers, and to Moore's own self-styling (which included actively participating in decisions regarding the editing, cropping, and printing of the portraits, as well as—on at least one occasion—a trial run in a photo booth before a sitting).[8] However, despite these complexities, I want to suggest that the applicability of Mirollo's description to a photograph of Moore raises significant questions concerning the relations of Moore's poetry to visual art, her conception of herself as an artist, and the role that her many photographic portraits play in our understanding of her poetics. I want to ask whether this portrait and the many others for which Moore sat merely form part of the biographical context for her poems, or whether they might better be viewed as "poetry by other means," the product of the same aesthetic attitudes and procedures which have made the poems.[9]

Though I may be making too much of visual coincidences, it is precisely the "too muchness" of Moore's own analogical leaps, the uses she makes of incidental features and visual "rhymes," that invites such speculation.[10] As I have argued elsewhere, the gaze which Moore turns on the natural world is one mediated by history, legend, and art, and one which is attuned to odd resemblances and inventive mistakes.[11] It is this layering of contexts and images which accounts in part for the visual obscurities endemic to Moore's descriptive practice. The sort of eye that can see in the kiwi's beak an "awl" (*CPo* 134), in a sycamore tree an "albino giraffe" (*CPo* 167), or in the pangolin both an artichoke and a "wrought-iron vine" (*CPo* 117), is the sort that might see her own face and body as potentially rhyming features, elements of compositions calling up other faces, other poses, other portraits. Of course, we are not accustomed to thinking of Moore's body as a component of her poetry so much as that which her poetic persona and subject matter suppress.[12] However, other bodies thickly populate both Moore's poems and her prose: the bodies of animals, athletes, actresses, dancers, and subjects in paintings, as well as the various hides, skins, armors, and clothes which express, conceal, shield, and shape these bodies. The question of what a body is—how it looks, how it functions, what it can do, and how it is related to anything we might call an "interior"—is of paramount concern to Moore. The "legion" "nettings" of a katydid wing (*CPo* 134); an actress "influencing the skirt edge away from her foot" (*CPr* 598); a tree-creeping cat's "dangling foot that missed / its grasp" (*CPo* 106); the arctic ox that "browses goatlike on / hind legs" (*CPo* 193); the elephant's "held-up fore-leg for use // as a stair, to be climbed or descended with / the aid of his ear" (*CPo* 129); the guitarist's "dangling hand / . . . suddenly set humming fast fast fast and faster" (*CPo* 170), are just a few examples of the witty, particularistic, and functionalist gaze which Moore directs at bodies. The mechanical complexities of the body—animal or human—combine with its aesthetic potential to suggest its attractiveness as an object; however, its expressiveness as a vehicle of personality or of spiritual significance always tantalizingly underlies its objectification. It is not, therefore, surprising that Moore would choose to engage the paradoxes of passivity and agency, objectification and authority, appearance and identity by submitting her own face and body to the camera's gaze. In its "passion for actuality" (*CPr* 543), the photograph promises to bring us nearer to the "raw material" of reality so elusive to poetry (and to the naked eye); however, in the elusiveness of the sitter's identity and the imaginative interventions of the photographer's hand and eye, we encounter the question of art's selectivity, its formality, and its historicity. In the photographic portrait we may experience the distance between what Moore calls, in "Poetry," "the raw" and "the genuine"; we may experience the necessity of the camera's contrived garden to the effect of the sitter as "real toad" (*BMM* 72–73).

One might expect that hands would figure prominently in artist or author portraits, and indeed Moore's hands are given great emphasis in many of her photographs.[13] A portrait made by her favorite photographer, George Platt Lynes, in 1935, shows Moore leaning one elbow upon the curved back of a chair, her fingers artfully unfurled just below her left ear, where they echo the curves of her braided hair, soft tie, and full-cut jacket. Half in shadow, half in light (as is her face), Moore's delicate and mysterious hand centers the composition. The Rosenbach Museum and Library contains numerous images of Moore posing with gloves (held, never worn), taken from young womanhood through old age by a variety of photographers. In these photographs the gloves often serve to accentuate—or, strangely, to proliferate—the hands. For example, in another photograph taken by Lynes, this

Marianne Moore, 1935. (Photograph by George Platt Lynes, reproduced courtesy of the Rosenbach Museum and Library and George P. Lynes, II; XII:09:01.)

one from 1955, Moore stands with her left elbow resting upon the edge of an upturned drafting table, her right hand grasping her left wrist as well as a pair of stiff leather gloves whose fingers point upward in a mirror image of the dangling left hand. This tight cluster of three "hands" stands out against Moore's characteristically dark suit, the glove only faintly distinguishable from the real hands. The positioning of her hands so as to exploit the happy accident of their Mannerist styling and the habit of posing with gloves suggest that Moore is making of her own body a vehicle for aesthetic statement, allowing it to speak a language not its own.

In her portraits, Moore visually "quotes" a body of Renaissance art and literature which makes of the ungloved hand and the artful arrangement of double-jointed digits an intricate vocabulary of desire and power. The theme of the hand and the glove is a staple of Mannerist art as it is of poetry in the Petrarchan vein; it carries with it a complex network of meanings, generally bespeaking the virtue, beauty, and cruelty of women, and suggesting a tantalizing vacillation between the hiddenness and visibility of the beloved's body.[14] In a broader sense, the contrast between the gloved and ungloved hand—or the hand and glove themselves—emphasizes a tension between the "real and ideal, passion and restraint, creative fantasy and artful control."[15] However, as Peter Stallybrass and Ann Rosalind Jones have shown, the ubiquitousness of the theme of hand and glove in the Renaissance extends to representations of men, and serves to remind us of the period's nonessentialist notions of identity; the glove, as a transferable object imparting magical power or erotic fulfillment, or confirming the bonds of friendship, "materialized the power of people to be condensed and absorbed into things and of things to become persons."[16] Detached from its wearer's hand, or from the other member of the pair, the glove has the effect of multiplying and mystifying agency,[17] making its owner available for possession or circulation at the same time that it accentuates the elusiveness of such possession through its obvious emptiness. For a poet perennially fascinated by the relation of the visible to the invisible, the external to the internal, and whose ideal poem is less an assertion of visionary power than a recirculation of other people's linguistic property, such a symbol might have carried rich resonance.

Bonnie Costello has argued that "visual art offered [Moore] . . . a store of images and techniques from which she could draw in creating her own patterns of resemblance."[18] We might see such procedures at work in the creation of images of the poet as well. Studying the Sarony portrait, one notes the directness (though not openness) of Moore's gaze; the stiff uprightness of the body opposed to the sinuous curves of the hand; the fiercely tense quality of the right hand in contrast to the artful repose of the left; the austerely masculine attire, together with the crownlike braid of hair and the feminine sexual connotations of the glove, combining to make this portrait

Marianne Moore, 1955. (Photograph by George Platt Lynes, reproduced courtesy of the Rosenbach Museum and Library and George P. Lynes, II; XII:09:45.)

a study in finely poised oppositions. These are paradoxes of the kind that characterize the tensely ironic architecture of Moore's poems, and which infuse her own critical vocabulary: ardor and restraint; idiosyncrasy and technique; feeling and precision. Such tensions echo the "pulling both ways"[19] of Mannerist figures generally, in which the torquing of the hands

5559 · NAPOLI · La bella del Parmigianino · Museo Nazionale · *Anderson, Roma*

Parmigianino (Francesco Mazzola), *Antea*, 1535–37. Museo Nazionale di Capodimonte, Naples, Italy. (Reproduced by permission from Alinari / Art Resource, NY)

and body in the interests of design testify to the fragile control art exerts over nature, to the value of a "thing / made graceful by adversities," to lift a phrase from "The Pangolin" (*CPo* 118).

Though I cannot here elaborate all of the features of Moore's poetry which might lead one to label her a literary Mannerist, I want to sketch just a few ways in which the term resonates. Mannerism has been called "stylish style" for its hyperconsciousness regarding its relation to prior art and the complexities of reference itself (the emphasis on pointing fingers, what is sometimes called a "pointing at pointing,"[20] highlights this). It is a style that aims, above all, for a graceful resolution of extreme aesthetic complexities, resulting in compositions both elegantly beautiful and often unbalanced or strained in their attention to detail and their elaboration of intricate curves and lines. As John Shearman has said, Mannerism puts "a premium on variety, pull[ing] away from unity towards multiplicity."[21] The quintessential Mannerist object is the "figura serpentinata," the body or hand twisted in multiple directions, embodying an awkward gracefulness, what Moore herself might call "intentional spontaneity." A few examples from Moore's writings must suffice to suggest the relevance of this style to her own: to wit, Moore's delight in serpentine images (as well as actual serpents), including the winding mountain road of "An Octopus," the flowers like "pyramids / of mathematic / circularity" in "Smooth Gnarled Crape Myrtle" (*CPo* 103); the "shadows of the alps / imprisoning in their folds like flies in amber, the rhythms of the skating-rink" from "Snakes, Mongooses, Snake-Charmers, and the Like" (*BMM* 111); and the "wistaria-like . . . opposing opposed / mouse-gray twined proboscises' trunk[s]" of "Elephants" (*CPo* 128). These images—and the language Moore uses to capture them—point to a form of baroque intricacy which Moore repeatedly claims to deplore, but of which her poems are chock full. Her long sentences, winding lines (often too long for the width of the page), and her awkwardly graceful breakings of words across lines (a habit which Moore herself referred to as "mannered" [*CPr* 644]), suggest that the serpentine figure or line dictates not just much of the matter but the form of Moore's poems as well.[22] Though Moore advocates for what, in "A Face," she calls "uncircuitous simplicity" (*CPo* 141), few of her poems could be said to achieve this effect.[23] "When I am as complete as I like to be, I seem unable to get an effect plain enough," she famously complained (*CPr* 420). In the extremity of their observational precision, Moore's poems tend to approach a level of elaboration that can only be called baroque. The collector's sensibility in Moore tends toward multiplication of both the image and the perspectives through which it is viewed. Add to this the self-consciousness regarding looking and pointing which infuses Moore's poems (clearly apparent in titles such as *Observations*, "When I Buy Pictures," "Picking and Choosing," and "Critics and Connoisseurs"); the many poems which take as their subject other works of art; the tendency toward a proliferation of detail; and the tensions between unselfcon- sciousness and "fastidiousness" (*BMM* 77), and we have all the elements of a markedly Mannerist style. Leonardo, Raphael, Michelangelo, El Greco—these are artists Moore knew and admired and from whom she may have absorbed aspects of this style.

Characterized by the "strong-lined gesture calling attention to itself,"[24] inviting speculation about what it means to look and to represent, Man- nerist art (like its younger cousin, Surrealism) offers a rich vocabulary for self-representation, such as that exemplified in Il Parmigianino's famous *Self-Portrait in a Convex Mirror.* The magnification of the artist's hand laid inside the curve of the mirror's edge in the foreground of this painting, and overshadowing the artist's more distant face, may be seen as an exaggera- tion of the artistic function, a gesture which at once tantalizingly draws us in and excludes us from the painting's reflected world. Such self-conscious gestures, in verbal form, are often startlingly foregrounded at the "edges" of Moore's poems as well, such as in the opening of "Novices": "Novices // anatomize their work" (*BMM* 113); or "Poetry"'s "I too, dislike it" (*BMM* 72); or the initial pronouncement in "Picking and Choosing" that "Litera- ture is a phase of life" (*BMM* 97). In "When I Buy Pictures," the first per- son singular appears six times in the first four lines (including the title): "When I Buy Pictures / or what is closer to the truth, / when I look at that of which I may regard myself as the imaginary possessor, / I fix upon what would give me pleasure in my average moments" (*BMM* 101). "Buying," "looking," "regarding," "fixing" and (implicitly) "imagining" and receiv- ing "pleasure," the speaker foregrounds the processes of observation, arrangement, and imaginative appropriation (as well as self-revision—"or what is closer to the truth") which constitute the central tasks of the poet as Moore conceives of these. "[L]ook[ing] at that" with the penetrating gaze of the descriptive poet entails "regard[ing] [her]self" in the act, such that a poem about "pictures" (also boxes, parquetry, manuscripts, hiero- glyphics, and a depiction of what could certainly be a Mannerist gesture— "Michael taking Adam by the wrist") becomes, in the Mannerist mode, a contemplation of the "piercing glance" itself: "[o]f whatever sort it is, / it must be 'lit with piercing glances into the life of things.'" It is perhaps not merely coincidental that this glance, which in its original context belongs to the Hebrew poets,[25] enters the poem in the form of a quotation. Indeed, one might suggest that such self-consciousness about attention and selec- tion merely makes explicit the "metapoetic" dimension implicit through- out Moore's highly quotational poetry.[26]

That Moore often turns in her poems to descriptions of art objects by way of exploring poetic principles is clear. That she may also have thought of her own image within visual representations as a vehicle for addressing questions of self-referentiality, hyperconsciousness, and quotational practice is the possibility which I would now like to explore through closer examination of some of her photographic portraits. In order to elaborate the significance of what I have called a "pointing at pointing" in Moore's self-representations, I want to turn once more to the Sarony portrait and another look at the way its hands may be said to reference Moore's authorship by circuitous routes. An instance of what Moore calls in "People's Surroundings" a "personal-impersonal expression of appearance" (*BMM* 110), the Sarony portrait with its odd hands has intrigued eyes other than mine. In 1925, Marguerite Zorach painted a portrait of Moore which, though based on a series of sittings, seems to owe something in its depiction of pose, costume, and hands to the Sarony photograph. In 1956, Moore's good friend, Hildegarde Watson, also sketched Moore in a different pose but with this same hand rather awkwardly attached as if it has been transposed from the photograph. Looking backwards, the Sarony photograph seems to allude to a number of Renaissance paintings, most strikingly Bronzino's *Portrait of a Young Man* (1530s) housed at the Metropolitan Museum.[27] This portrait "rhymes" in a number of ways with the Sarony portrait, most powerfully in the pose, though also in the expression of the face, even to the arching of the eyebrows, and the crowning effect of the hat. Though I cannot say with certainty whether Moore ever saw this painting, one imagines that she would have appreciated, in addition to the subject's appealingly relaxed yet authoritative demeanor, the visual wit evident in Bronzino's placement of grotesque carved faces on chair arm and table leg, such that they undercut the elegant composure of the young man. Such playful animation of objects—and deflation of persons—is a staple of both Moore's descriptive and satiric poems. Yet, if Moore was indeed styling herself, consciously or unconsciously, after Bronzino's portrait, we might wonder why she chose to substitute a glove for the book (with finger imbedded) that signifies the cultured status of Bronzino's young aristocrat. The book would surely have provided a more appropriate emblem of authorship than the glove, with its connotations of refinement and/or eroticism.

Watson suggests that Moore was unaware of the beauty of her hands and posed with gloves in order to conceal them.[28] In an essay on Anna Pavlova, Moore gives extended attention to the positioning of the dancer's hands in photographs, noting that they convey both naturalness and artifice: "[I]n the photograph in which she is seated on the wide steps of a building in Italy— her hands on her sunshade which rests on her lap—the middle finger and little finger of each hand, higher than the finger between, adhere to classic formula but with the spontaneous curve of the iris petal" (*CPr* 389). Such an observation suggests that Moore gave considerable thought to the choices involved in the placement of one's hands. Indeed, the Pavlova essay gives, throughout, remarkable evidence of the connections Moore sees

Marguerite Zorach, *Marianne Moore and Her Mother,* **1925 [dated 1919]. (Reproduced courtesy of Jonathan Zorach and by permission from the National Portrait Gallery, Smithsonian Institution; NPG.87.217.)**

Hildegarde Watson, drawing of Marianne Moore, 1956. (Reproduced courtesy of the Rosenbach Museum and Library; XII:12:27.)

Bronzino (Agnolo di Cosimo di Mariano), *Portrait of a Young Man, possibly Guidobaldo II, Duke of Urbino,* 1530s. (Reproduced by permission from the Metropolitan Museum of Art, Bequest of Mrs. H. O. Havemeyer, 1929. The H. O. Havemeyer Collection. All rights reserved; 29.100.16.)

Unknown, formerly attributed to William Scrots, *Elizabeth I when Princess,* 1533–1603. (Reproduced by permission from The Royal Collection © 2004, Her Majesty Queen Elizabeth II; RCIN 404444.)

Elizabeth's hand—a detail from *Eliza-*
beth I when Princess. (Reproduced by
permission from The Royal Collection
© 2004, Her Majesty Queen Elizabeth
II; RCIN 404444.)

Marianne Moore's hand—a detail from
photograph by Sarony. (Reproduced courtesy of the Rosenbach Museum and Library; XII:03:03a).

between the form and movements of the body and character or personality.[29] Her description of Pavlova's hands makes explicit the psychological
significance of their styling: "'Her hands possess a life of their own,' it was
said. In the little finger apart from the fourth, one deduces independence; in
its double curve, poetic feeling; in the slightly squared fingertips, originality" (*CPr* 390). In her autobiography, Watson describes Moore's hands in
terms which, intriguingly, echo this description of Pavlova's: "[Her] fingers
are exceptionally long, with supple tips . . . her little finger separates widely
from the fourth—a sign, she told me, of self-sufficiency, adding sadly: 'And
I do not want to be self-sufficient.'" Watson sees in these hands a reminder
of a famous painting: "There is a portrait of Elizabeth I, when princess, in
which the long little finger curves away from the fourth. She, too, was a
redhead, and may not have wanted to be self-sufficient, either."[30] In the
painting to which Watson refers, by an unknown sixteenth-century artist,[31]
Elizabeth's body is turned slightly to the right, her left index finger is in-
serted into a book (as in Bronzino's *Young Man*), her headpiece crowns
her red hair (as Moore's braid does hers), and her right hand with its ex-
traordinarily tapering fingers and oddly arched thumb and little finger reads
like a mirror image of Moore's left hand as it appears in the Sarony portrait.
Queen Elizabeth was, of course, like Moore, a serial sitter (and it is worth
remembering that before photography, serial portraiture of this kind was
available only to royalty and a handful of the very wealthy or famous).
Queen Elizabeth was often portrayed with glove in hand; though where
women's gloves in Renaissance painting and Petrarchan poetry most often
signify the combined allure and inaccessibility of the beloved, or more generally acts of withholding or restraint, in representations of Elizabeth they
acquire the added charge of worldly power. The glove—a term which may
derive from "gift-love"[32]—given to Elizabeth's favorites was worn, upright, as a token on cap or sleeve, the insignia of queenly patronage. Though
the held glove is hardly a staple in portraits of authors (the pen or book be-

ing more typical emblems), Moore would not be the first woman poet to invoke Elizabeth, the queen-poet, as an empowering precedent for female authorship (one might think here of Anne Bradstreet's "In Honor of That High and Mighty Princess Queen Elizabeth," for example). An intriguing photograph by Evelyn Hofer of Moore's gloves in tissue paper might be read as a self-conscious manipulation of just such emblematic meanings: the gloves were a gift from another poet named Elizabeth, this one not a queen, but a Bishop. By 1983, when this photograph appeared in *Vanity Fair* alongside an essay by Bishop about Moore, the gloves alone could call up a whole range of Moorish connotations: manner, style, conduct, the luminous quality of gifted objects, the hiddenness of the poet's selective hand, the sense in which, as Moore says in "People's Surroundings," people's possessions both do and do not answer one's questions (*CPo* 55–57). As in the Renaissance custom of painting a sitter's clothing without the sitter present,[33] it seems that Hofer saw in Moore's accessories a more profound depiction of her self than even the face and body could convey (she photographed her famous cape and tricorn hat hanging on a coat tree at the same time that she photographed her gloves). Stallybrass and Jones have made the point that in Renaissance portraiture clothing and other possessions carry the burden of conveying particularistic identity, whereas faces were often filled in using templates.[34] Such a notion of identity conferred through possession and use resonates with Moore's authorial practice as well as her many self-representations. The muting of authorial identity in Moore's other-directed poetry bespeaks a notion of self contingent upon attention and observation, delineated by curiosity, predilection, or preference.

Mary Ann Caws has made the argument that Surrealism carries forward the central concerns of Mannerism in its emphasis on the self-consciousness of the aesthetic gesture, its interest in acts of pointing dissociated from their objects, and its embrace of paradoxically conflicting tendencies as definitive of beauty. It is not difficult to discern a continuity between what I have named Moore's Mannerist tendencies and her Surrealist sympathies. Like the Surrealists, Moore favored the found object and the object collage, disorienting titles, and portraits at one remove. Though her poetry has many allegiances with contemporaneous practices of "straight photography," such as those of Alfred Stieglitz, Paul Strand, and Edward Steichen, she was also drawn to intersections of photographic practice with Dadaist, Surrealist, and Cubist experiments in sculpture and painting.[35] Portraiture is generally understood to be the form of photography most constricted by referentiality; however, in the twenties and thirties, portraits of avant-garde artists and writers whose own practices challenged mimetic codes became staging grounds for photographers' extensions of their art into more abstract, compositional, and self-reflexive styles. Man Ray's 1933 photograph of Picasso in which the artist's hands recall those in his own paintings, or André Kertész's 1926 portrait of Mondrian showing nothing but his spectacles and pipe, might stand as exemplars of Surrealist portraiture.[36] As Linda Leavell has shown, the object arrangement is characteristic, as well, of Moore's own poetic portraits, as evidenced in "Those Various Scalpels," "To a Prize Bird," "To a Steamroller," and others.[37]

In a remarkable photograph housed in the Rosenbach collection (photographer unknown), Moore's ubiquitous and emblematic glove is translated into one of the aggressively animate objects characteristic of Surrealist collage. Moore is the object of multiple representations in this photograph, what she herself might have called a "well-nested effect" (*CPr* 399). Moore's body, on the left, is separated from her head, on the right, as sculpted by Gaston Lachaise in 1925; similarly, her hands are separated from her gloves which stand upright in an exaggerated gesture of pointing or alarm, reminding one perhaps of the "spiked hand" of "Marriage" (*BMM* 119) or the fingers like "a / bundle of lances" in "Those Various Scalpels" (*BMM* 103). The eyes of the bust seem to look at the poet, or perhaps at her gloves (though only the lighting of the photograph so as to form pupils out of shadows makes this little joke possible). This is the sort of punny composition and decomposition of the human form which delighted Marcel Duchamp and Man Ray (and which is characteristic of Mannerist painting and literature, as in the blazon). The parts and parallels and originals and imitations peopling Moore's poems can be seen to be in sympathy with such practices (one might think, in particular, of the parsing of the mind into eyes, ears, face, heart, feet, fingers, and feathers in "The Mind is an Enchanting Thing," a poem with some Surrealist qualities). In this staged encounter of carved head and aggressively bristling gloves, the actual woman stands aside like a statue (or the headless remains of one), while the objects conduct the photograph's little drama of recognition. The poet famous for observing, pointing, and selecting, gives over both looking and pointing to her surrogates—bust and gloves—which look and point at one another, while the poet, like the acacia lady of "People's Surroundings," "disappears" into the protective coloration of her habitat (*BMM* 109–10). As Moore's jerboa may resemble the claw of a Chippendale chair (*CPo* 15), and her monkey-puzzle tree a "glyptic work of jade" (*CPo* 80), so Moore herself can be represented by stylized objects, rendered expressive through a sly suppression of the supreme vehicle of self-expression, the face. Certainly this portrait, more than most, calls attention to the artistry of the photographer, his or her wit and style, and yet this style is so suggestive with regards to Moore's own, that it has the effect of visually enacting *her* typically analogical wit. The photograph becomes, in a sense, a multiply authored picture-poem, a collaboration among poet, photographer, and sculptor which quotes from both Renaissance portraiture (with its ever-present gloves and fondness for background statuary) and several decades of

Marianne Moore's torso with bust of Moore by Gaston Lachaise, 1948. (Photographer unknown, reproduced courtesy of Rosenbach Museum and Library; XII:04:05.)

experimentation in Surrealist art and photography. In a characteristically circuitous practice of allusion, Moore uses her own image (or allows it to be used) to refer to the camouflaged creatures and stylized objects which attract her interest in the poems. Further, the photograph portrays a complex model of artistic authority in the relation of the barely visible poet (and her oddly observant surrogate) to the invisible photographer who "finds" his material in Moore. Here Moore allows herself to become a piece of another artist's construction, trying out the role which she imposes on others in her poems.

We might want to read such a collage (and such a collaboration) together with a poem like "Silence," in which borrowed voices render virtually irretrievable the authorizing voice of the poem, but in which ironic juxtaposition of appropriated materials allows us, piecemeal, to discern the poet's destabilizing perspective.

> My father used to say,
> "Superior people never make long visits,
> have to be shown Longfellow's grave
> nor the glass flowers at Harvard.

> Self reliant like the cat—
> that takes its prey to privacy,
> the mouse's limp tail hanging like a shoelace from its mouth—
> they sometimes enjoy solitude,
> and can be robbed of speech
> by speech which has delighted them.
> The deepest feeling always shows itself in silence;
> not in silence, but restraint."
> 　Nor was he insincere in saying, "'Make my house your inn.'"
> Inns are not residences.

(BMM 124)

　The poet of "Silence" both participates in, and seems to endorse, her own silencing, and yet she rises above silence in the very composition of the poem's materials, and its undercutting of others' voices.[38] The speaker is not silent, but restrained; she speaks of and around her father's words, taking them as her prey. Just as the father is not "insincere" in quoting Edmund Burke—"'Make my house your inn'"—so the daughter is "not insincere" in her temporary occupation of her father's words, but the restraint of her own speech has the effect of both confirming and critiquing his—confirming its content, while implicitly criticizing its insistent overstatement. In this way, the daughter robs the father, in the process reinventing both silence and superiority. As an exercise in strategic self-silencing, however, the poem yields one more turn: Moore's notes to the poem indicate that this daughter is not Moore herself, but her friend, "Miss A.M. Homans," and that the poem's patriarch is in fact only on loan (Moore never knew her own father). Apparently Moore, at least, needn't be shown the grave of a dead poet in order to understand how silence may be made to speak.[39] Such strategies of mediated self-fashioning may illuminate the borrowing of gestures and the apparent undercutting of authority in Moore's portraits. The displacement into multiple voices made to play off against one another in a poem like "Silence" approximates the displacement of the face and hand in the "Surrealist" photograph, in which the strangely truncated and unidentifiable figure of Moore imposes itself, nonetheless, into the frame.

　Forced off the verbal path of expression, silently sitting for portraits, Moore finds ways to use the body's form to express the poet's function and the photographer's techniques to suggest the poet's values. No less subject to revision than the poems themselves, Moore's serial self-fashionings in photographs undermine the stability of the term "author," just as her frequently rearranged poems undermine the notion of an "authorized text." Complex, costumed, allusive, and historical, Moore seems to say of her image, as she might say of a favorite painting, or a dress, or a cherished clipping from a magazine, "'this is I'. . . . 'this is mine'" (Moore attributes these phrases to Gordon Craig in "Picking and Choosing," *BMM* 97). Such "self-possession," however, can only be imaginary in a world in which "accessibility to experience" (*BMM* 107) is preferred over "self-sufficiency." When Moore praises, in "Silence," those who are "self-reliant like the cat," it is Emerson's paradoxical notion of self-reliance to which she refers: let us not speak, says Emerson, of self-reliance, but "rather of that which relies," [40] thus emphasizing the gesture of self-collecting over anything that might properly be called a "self." In a related vein, Moore identifies "that of which I may regard myself as the imaginary possessor" (*BMM* 101) *as* the self, possessed imaginatively in the form of the image. The mousing cat of "Silence" is both silent and self-reliant because its mouth is full of another. So, too, the speaking silence of Moore's photographic selves bears testimony to all that the poet's eye has absorbed of others' looking; the limp glove clutched in her hand, like the dangling tail of the mouse in "Silence," tells of significance captured from other contexts, transplanted as a form of restrained (and mysterious) self-expression. Second skin, empty, yet overflowing with accumulated meaning, the glove—like a borrowed phrase— multiplies and circulates the self. So, too, the stylized hand of the poet herself, calling up the unreal hands of Mannerist painting, suggests that the very agent of writing is not entirely one's own, neither natural nor unique, but rather a conjoining of "abstract" identity to "idiosyncratic . . . personal presence."[41] Moore's portraits, so modern yet so historical, can be said to "trade simultaneously on the prestige of art, and the magic of the real."[42] For all the seeming immediacy with which they capture the poet's bodily presence, Moore's photographic portraits prove to be every bit as quotational as her poems.[43]

Notes

1. Some copies of this photograph in the Rosenbach archive are dated 1920, some 1924.

2. Roland Barthes, *Camera Lucida: Reflections on Photography*, trans. Richard Howard (New York: Hill and Wang, 1981), 79.

3. Marianne Moore to George Platt Lynes, November 2, 1950, folder V:38:09, *RML*.

4. Mary Ann Caws, *The Eye in the Text: Essays on Perception, Mannerist to Modern* (Princeton, NJ: Princeton University Press, 1981).

5. James V. Mirollo, *Mannerism and Renaissance Poetry: Concept, Mode, Inner Design* (New Haven, CT: Yale University Press, 1984), 140.

6. Bonnie Costello, *Marianne Moore: Imaginary Possessions* (Cambridge, MA: Harvard University Press, 1981), 212.

7. Susan Sontag, *On Photography* (New York: Farrar, Straus and Giroux, 1977), 54.

8. For overviews of Moore's life in photographs, see Evelyn Feldman and Michael Barsanti, "Paying Attention: The Rosenbach Museum's Marianne Moore Archive and the New York Moderns," *Journal of Modern Literature* 22, no. 2 (Fall 1998): 7–30; and Patricia C. Willis, "Images of Marianne," *Marianne Moore Newsletter* 3 (1979): 20–24.

9. Willis makes the point that, when sitting for photographs, Moore "composed a persona which became an equivalent of her poetry" in "Images of Marianne," 22.

10. See Hugh Kenner in *A Homemade World: The American Modernist Writers* (Baltimore: Johns Hopkins University Press, 1975), 92, for a discussion of Moore's "optical puns"; and Costello, *Imaginary Possessions,* 210, on "visual rhymes."

11. See Stacy Carson Hubbard, "The Many-Armed Embrace: Collection, Quotation and Mediation in Marianne Moore's Poetry," *Sagetrieb* 12, no. 2 (Fall 1993): 7–32.

12. Cristanne Miller discusses the perception of Moore as bodiless or sexless in "Sexology, Style and the Poet's Body," in *Cultures of Modernism: Marianne Moore, Mina Loy, Else Lasker-Schüler* (Ann Arbor: University of Michigan Press, 2005).

13. An interesting comparison might be made between some of these photographs and the series of photographs by Alfred Stieglitz which portray Georgia O'Keeffe's hands in stylized—one might even say Mannerist—poses. A tension between eroticized or idealized femininity and artistic agency inhabits both sets of images.

14. For a more extended discussion of the prominence of this theme in Renaissance art and poetry, see Mirollo, *Mannerism and Renaissance Poetry,* 125–59.

15. Ibid., 142.

16. Peter Stallybrass and Ann Rosalind Jones, "Fetishizing the Glove in Renaissance Europe," *Critical Inquiry* 28, no. 1 (Autumn 2001): 114–32.

17. The idea of multiplicitous agency, or many-handed authorship, might remind us of Moore's admiration for the woman called "Miss A," who could write simultaneously with both hands in multiple languages and two directions. Miss A's abilities are described in an issue of *Scientific American* from 1923, from which Moore transcribed notes into one of her poetry notebooks and which she used as a source for her description of Eve in "Marriage." See Marianne Moore, poetry notebook, 1922–1930, 1251/07, folder VII:04:04, *RML,* 10. For a fuller discussion of Miss A / Eve as a model for the woman writer, see my "The Many-Armed Embrace," 7–32.

18. Costello, *Imaginary Possessions,* 186.

19. Caws, *The Eye in the Text,* 76.

20. Ibid., 51.

21. John Shearman, *Mannerism* (Harmondsworth, UK: Penguin Books, 1964), 67.

22. See Caws, *The Eye in the Text,* 71–86, for a discussion of enjambment as a Mannerist practice.

23. See Costello, *Imaginary Possessions,* 196–97, for a discussion of Moore's criticism of baroque style as self-criticism.

24. Caws, *The Eye in the Text,* 50.

25. Moore's note to the poem identifies the source of this phrase as A. R. Gordon's *The Poets of the Old Testament* (*CPo* 268n).

26. Cristanne Miller, *Marianne Moore: Questions of Authority* (Cambridge, MA: Harvard University Press, 1995), 190.

27. I am grateful to Michael Barsanti of the Rosenbach Museum and Library for suggesting this parallel.

28. Hildegarde Watson, *The Edge of the Woods: A Memoir* (Rochester, NY, 1979), 131.

29. Moore's datebook for 1921 indicates that she saw Pavlova perform on November 2 of that year. See Marianne Moore, datebook, folder VIII:01:03, *RML.*

30. Watson, *The Edge of the Woods,* 131–32.

31. It is possible that Moore saw this painting on her visit to Windsor Castle in 1911, though her letters make no mention of it.

32. Stallybrass and Jones cite this as John Minsheu's derivation from "Guide to the Tongues" (1617) in "Fetishizing the Glove," 3.

33. Peter Stallybrass and Ann Rosalind Jones, *Renaissance Clothing and the Materials of Memory* (Cambridge: Cambridge University Press, 2000), 34.

34. Ibid., 38.

35. For in-depth discussion of Moore's interests in modern photography and painting, see Linda Leavell, *Marianne Moore and the Visual Arts: Prismatic Color* (Baton Rouge and London: Louisiana State University Press, 1995).

36. Pierre Vaisse, "Portrait of Society: The Anonymous and the Famous," in *The New History of Photography,* ed. Michael Frizot, trans. Helen Atkins, Susan Bennett, Liz Clegg, John Crook, and Caroline Higgitt (Koln, Germany: Konemann, 1998), 506.

37. Leavell, *Prismatic Color,* 96–134.

38. Others have offered more fully developed readings of this poem. In a rich and multi-layered interpretation, Elizabeth Gregory suggests that Moore is revising Emerson's practice of quotation in the multiply embedded voices of "Silence," and asserting the "realm of the secondary" as the ground of authority. She argues further that the poem's endorsement of silence may be a way for the woman poet to "[request] the silence of others in order that she may work." See her *Quotation and Modern American Poetry: "Imaginary Gardens with Real Toads"* (Houston, TX: Rice University Press, 1996), 141–54. In a related vein, Jeanne Heuving sees the poem as a critique of Emersonian self-reliance, arguing that "Moore simultaneously praises and criticizes a decorum of restraint, revealing the power relations that allow some to be restrained and condemn others to silence." See her *Omissions Are Not Accidents: Gender in the Art of Marianne Moore* (Detroit: Wayne State University Press, 1992), 115–20. In *The Savage's Romance: The Poetry of Marianne Moore* (University Park: Pennsylvania State University Press, 1986), John Slatin interprets "Silence" as Moore's attempt to both "circumvent" and "appropriate" the paternal authority of Emersonian and Eliotic traditions (150–55). Miller, in *Questions of Authority,* discusses "Silence" in the context of speech-act theory, arguing that it represents "a two-way process of communication." Though the father performs "an act of power" over the daughter in attempting to silence or restrain her, her repetition of his words constitutes a "new performative act" which insists on the possibility of response. "She manipulates the father's words so as to structure a 'polity of shared power' rather than a relationship of 'power over'" (180–84). Charles Altieri reads the poem as a "drama of affiliation and difference" in which the daughter "transform[s] the strengths of her internalized father figure into a precursor for her own sense of individual power." See *Painterly Abstraction in Modernist American Poetry* (Cambridge: Cambridge University Press, 1989), 270–71. Caroll Cantrell, in "'The Roar of Ice'" in *New Essays in Eco-Feminist Literary Criticism,* ed. Glynis Carr (Lewisburg, PA: Bucknell University Press, 2000), 157–74, sees "Silence" as a comment on Moore's life with her widowed mother, in which both were perennially visitors in others' households and thus subject to the "restraint incumbent upon nonresidents" (167).

39. The image of the cat may refer to yet another poet, both predatory and restrained. At around the same time that she was writing "Silence" Moore wrote a review of Wallace Stevens's work for the *Dial,* entitled "Well Moused, Lion," in which she criticized Stevens for his "deliberate bearishness" and "unserviceableness" (*CPr* 93), suggesting a connection to the silence-imposing and conditionally hospitable father, as well as to the mousing guest, in the poem. However, in the same essay, she praises Stevens for the "liberties" he, like Shakespeare (and perhaps like the quoting daughter in "Silence"), takes with words. In a later essay on Stevens, "Conjuries That Endure," Moore describes him in terms that again echo "Silence": his poems "prove to us that the testament to emotion is not volubility. Refusal to speak results in . . . eloquence" (*CPr* 349).

40. Ralph Waldo Emerson, *Selected Writings of Ralph Waldo Emerson,* ed. Donald McQuade (New York: Modern Library, 1981), 142.

41. Miller, *Questions of Authority*, 35.

42. Sontag, *On Photography*, 69.

43. An early version of this paper was delivered at "'A Right Good Salvo of Barks': The Marianne Moore Conference" at Pennsylvania State University in 2003 and I am grateful to the conference participants for their many helpful suggestions. Special thanks go to Barbara Bono, Elisabeth Joyce, Charles Carman, Linda Leavell, Cristanne Miller, Robin Schulze, and Chiaki Sekiguchi. Michael Barsanti and Karen Schoenewald provided valuable assistance with locating materials in the Moore archive; Marianne C. Moore, literary executor of the estate of Marianne Moore, and the Rosenbach Museum kindly granted permission to quote from Moore's letters, notebooks, and poems and to reproduce photographs.

"The magnitude of their root systems": "An Octopus" and National Character

Fiona Green

"THE TERM 'OCTOPUS' EMBRACES A LARGE NUMBER OF SPECIES," WROTE W. P. Pycraft in a World of Science article for the *Illustrated London News* in 1924. Careful to distinguish between the true octopus and its ten-armed relative the squid or cuttle-fish, Pycraft's "good news for the gourmet" included a warning that the "bewildering variety" of octopus-like creatures might tempt the unwary diner into choosing the wrong one.[1] In the same issue the *News* ran the tragic story of George Mallory and A. C. Irving's fatal attempt on the summit of Everest.[2] Pycraft's article offered Marianne Moore some of the verbal delicacies which she quoted in her 1924 poem "An Octopus," and whether or not the juxtaposition of the naturalist's column and the news from Everest prompted it, Moore's poetic hybrid of octopus and glaciated mountain is as various and bewildering as the species Pycraft had described.

"An Octopus" has a prominent place in readings of Moore's poetry, and has rightly been read within rich seams of literary history. It would be hard to think about a poem set in Paradise from which " 'disobedient persons [are] summarily removed' " without thinking of Milton, and there is good reason too for seeing this mountain poem as Moore's engagement with the romantic sublime.[3] But as well as summoning a literary past, Moore's poem is marked by the cultural and historical context in which it emerged. This essay situates "An Octopus" in relation to debates about national character and immigration that reached a crisis point in the early nineteen twenties. The poem's setting in the Mount Rainier National Park suggests Moore's engagement with the discourses of national vigor that the parks were designed in part to promote. However, the poem's emphasis on diversity counters conceptions of American racial purity, the eugenicist polemics that frequently accompanied calls to reinvigorate the American race. Like the other long poems of 1923–1924 ("Marriage" and "Sea Unicorns and Land Unicorns"), "An Octopus" is made up almost entirely of quotations. The root system of Moore's poem, the sources she quotes and their combination in the verbal texture of her verse, suggest a historical reading of "An Octopus" to set alongside those interpretations that consider the poem in terms of literary affiliation and aesthetic innovation.[4]

As many readers of Moore's poetry will know, the immediate biographical context for "An Octopus" was two trips Moore and her mother made in 1922 and 1923 to visit her brother Warner, a Navy chaplain then stationed near Seattle. On each of these trips the Moores visited the Mount Rainier National Park, taking the view of the Nisqually glacier from the subalpine meadow named Paradise Park.[5] The poem, though, does not derive from first-hand observation of Mount Rainier; its materials are other texts. Moore's self-styled "hybrid method of composition" in this case issues in a monstrously mixed creature.[6] The panoramic opening of the poem presents in large scale the progress of a massively powerful and yet delicately discriminating creature, an organism which is also a landscape, a natural body which is also a feat of technological brilliance:

An Octopus

of ice. Deceptively reserved and flat,
it lies "in grandeur and in mass"
beneath a sea of shifting snow dunes;
dots of cyclamen red and maroon on its clearly defined pseudopodia
made of glass that will bend—a much needed invention—
comprising twenty-eight icefields from fifty to five hundred feet thick,
of unimagined delicacy.
"Picking periwinkles from the cracks"
or killing prey with the concentric crushing rigour of the python,
it hovers forward "spider fashion
on its arms" misleadingly like lace;

(*BMM* 312)

Moore's Notes to the *Observations* version of the poem acknowledge W. P. Pycraft among the sources for this opening section (*BMM* 147): she adapts the phrase "spider fashion / on its arms" from the *Illustrated London News* article noted earlier. Moore selects from Pycraft's article the verbal morsel which her octopus-poem ingests, and she also learns from her source something about the slipperiness of naturalist observation. In Pycraft, as in the poem, attempts at precise octopod anatomy and measurement produce a species that is less than clearly defined:

The common octopus of our own seas may be taken as a type. This, when full-grown, has a flask-shaped body of the size of a large coconut, and eight long arms, bearing each a double row of powerful suckers. These arms, which are connected by a broad sheet of membrane extending some distance from the base, have an expanse of about eight feet. When "sauntering" along it walks on these arms in a spider-like fashion, very "creepy" to behold.[7]

An accident or infelicity in the source—eight arms misleadingly extending to eight feet—is exploited in Moore's poem. The anatomy of her octopus is hard to identify (does it have arms or legs? are its "feet" limbs or dimensions?) and as if to compound the difficulty Moore introduces yet further appendages—"pseudopodia"—that sound like, but aren't quite feet. We don't get the measure of "An Octopus" either if we scan its surface for metrical feet; this is one of those "hybrids of a flagrantly prose origin"[8] in which careful enumeration and measurement ("comprising twenty-eight ice-fields from fifty to five hundred feet thick") sound a note of distinctly prose-like pedantry, pushing the verse line to exceed even the generous breadth of the *Dial* page, and calling for runover lines in all subsequent printings. And yet there is formal pattern here nonetheless, a delicate system of muted sounds lacing across the surface of the verse: "of ice" finds a half rhyme in "it lies"; land and water dissolve in the sibilant "sea of shifting snow dunes"; "killing prey" picks up and manipulates the consonants of "'Picking periwinkles.'" If from an aerial perspective the glacier seems "deceptively reserved and flat" the poem works in three dimensions. Those samenesses and differences across its surface gradually form patterns for the ear, and at the same time, behind or beneath the sonic patterns lie the tangled roots of quoted materials, some still tethered to their origins by Moore's Notes. Tracing back through some of the textual sources of "An Octopus" reveals the concern with national character that underlies the poem.

   Among the quotations in the opening lines of "An Octopus," two in particular reveal roots that anchor Moore's poem in its contemporary moment and point to the poem's preoccupation with national vigor. Having surveyed the shifting glaciated ground of Mount Rainier from above, Moore comes in for a closer look:

> The firtrees in "the magnitude of their root systems,"
> rise aloof from these manoeuvres "creepy to behold"—
> austere specimens of our American royal families,
> "each like the shadow of the one beside it.
> The rock seems frail compared with their dark energy of life,"
>   (*BMM* 312)

Moore entangles Pycraft's "creepy to behold" with two other texts, each of which prompts her to look through the details of the landscape to the deep history, the origins and lineage of the nation. The first quotation, "'the magnitude of their root systems,'" comes from John Muir, the Scottish-born naturalist and most vocal wilderness preservationist of the late nineteenth century, whose national parks campaigns, including calls for the protection of Mount Rainier, continued until his death in 1914. In the source that includes his line about root systems Muir is not talking about fir trees, but about the sequoia, the giant redwood:

> the *root system corresponds in magnitude* with other dimensions of the tree, forming a flat far-reaching spongy network two hundred feet or more in width without any taproot, so suggestive of endless strength, it is long ere the eye is released to look above it.[9]

The redwood played an especially prominent role in the establishment of the national parks, contributing to the nationalist rhetoric which fueled the arguments of early preservationists. The discovery of the sierra redwoods in 1852 provided evidence that the scenic monuments of the American landscape could rival, in grandeur and in mass, the cultural monuments of Europe. In fact the very naming of the redwood was the occasion for transatlantic competition: British botanists classified the newly discovered tree as *Wellingtonia Gigantea;* Americans countered with *Washingtonia Gigantea. Sequoia Gigantea,* after the Cherokee Chief Sequoya, was the widely accepted compromise.[10] Since the mid-nineteenth century the redwood has been cited time and again to underwrite the nation's claims to antiquity, to prove America's natural wonders equal to the man-made heritage of Europe, and to make a compelling case for wilderness preservation.

Of course giant redwoods don't belong in alpine landscapes so Moore plants her glacier with fir trees. But her poem does preserve that sense of nobility and antiquity Muir ascribed to the Big Tree. He says that the sequoia "belongs to an ancient stock . . . and has a strange air of other days about it, a thoroughbred look inherited from long ago."[11] Against that background, Moore's initially puzzling designation of fir trees as "austere specimens of our American royal families" starts to make sense: what she has taken from John Muir, along with a snippet of direct quotation, is that nationalist argument whereby living monuments assume the position of aristocratic properties, lending the landscape the kind of ancestral depth that America otherwise lacks. And of still more significance to the immediate cultural context of Moore's poem is the question of belonging, which John Muir investigates as follows:

> the Big Tree always seems unfamiliar, standing alone, unrelated, with peculiar physiognomy, awfully solemn and earnest. Nevertheless there is nothing alien in its looks . . . the Sequoia, with all its strangeness, seems more at home than any of its neighbours, holding the best right to the ground as the oldest, strongest inhabitant.[12]

In the early decades of the twentieth century, and especially during the eighteen months in 1923–1924 that it took Moore to compose her poem, the question of who was properly "at home" in the United States, along with anxieties about "alien looks" and about the strength or weakness of the population, would have resonated strongly with concerns over immigration.

The second text on which Moore draws for the passage about fir trees also comes heavily freighted. Her source is John Ruskin:

> The firtrees . . .
>
> . . . .
>
> "each like the shadow of the one beside it.
> The rock seems frail compared with their dark energy of life,"
>
> (*BMM* 312)

In these lines Moore compresses and juxtaposes with John Muir some phrases from the fifth volume of Ruskin's *Modern Painters*. Ruskin's principal concern in this final volume was with organic unity, with what he called the "law of help," the highest law of the universe which, in the case of works of art, showed itself in the unity of pictorial composition. The greatest exponent of that unity was J. M. W. Turner. In the passage Moore quotes, Ruskin is looking at a particular drawing in the Turner bequest, *The Source of the Arveron* which shows a pine-clad glacier. Ruskin admires the drawing because "ordinary observers saw in [the glacier] only its rigidity; but Turner saw that the wonderful thing was its non-rigidity. Other ice is fixed, only this ice stirs."[13] This reading of Turner would have appealed immediately to Moore, who makes a comparable observation of her glacier's apparently rigid yet wonderfully flexible material in "glass that will bend—a much needed invention—". Ruskin's description of *The Source of the Arveron*, like Muir's of the sierra redwood, is sensitive to the relationship between trees and ground. Turner's genius was in capturing the movement of the ice on static canvas, but because he could not observe that movement directly ("the glacier cannot explain its own motion"), he focused instead on the oblique and distorted angles of the pine trees, and, reading these as indices of the glacier's progress, "fastened on this means of relating the glacier's history."[14] As in Muir's account, the land does not bespeak its own history. Instead, to get a sense of its phases of stasis and change, one must analyze the character of its inhabitants. And like Muir on the redwood, Ruskin emphasizes the pine tree's characteristic remoteness, its hardihood: "the pine rises in serene resistance, self-contained," he writes, and he goes on to imagine, in the passage from which Moore borrows,

> companies of pines . . . in quiet multitudes, *each like the shadow of the one beside it*—upright, fixed, spectral . . . with such iron will, *that the rock itself looks bent* and shattered beside them—fragile, weak, inconsistent, *compared to their dark energy of delicate life,* and monotony of enchanted pride:—unnumbered, unconquerable.[15]

Ruskin's pines and Muir's sequoias have a good deal in common: their legibility as signs of historical continuity or change, and their aristocratic remoteness, yet absolute right of residence. In the marriage of Muir's Big Tree and Ruskin's pine as the generic "firtrees" of Moore's "Octopus," the trees are likewise sturdier than the ground: "the rock seems frail compared with their dark energy of life." Whatever shifty or "creepy" maneuvers of the topsoil might threaten to dislodge them, these enduring, deep-rooted species hold their ground.

What Moore takes up from Muir and Ruskin, and what matters for a historical reading of her poem, is the way in which each source connects natural history and national life. The thoroughbred sequoia testifies to the antiquity and noble heritage of America. Ruskin makes a still more explicit connection between a nation's trees and the soundness of its constitution. He says that "the tremendous unity of the pine absorbs and moulds the life of a race" and goes on to explain that the Northern peoples of Europe gained their cultural superiority from having lived under the shadow of the pine forests:

> whatever elements of imagination, or of warrior strength, or of domestic justice, were brought down by the Norwegian and the Goth against the dissoluteness or degradation of the South of Europe, were taught them under the green roofs and wild penetralia of the pine.[16]

By the early 1920s, pseudo-scientific theories maintaining the superiority of the Northern races of Europe and the degradation of the South would have important consequences for America's immigration policy. The roots of these brief quotations from the beginning of "An Octopus," then, illustrate in small scale Moore's involvement in the immigration controversy of the first decades of the twentieth century that raised questions about how to promote the health and vitality of American citizens, and about what new racial strains should or should not be allowed to come within the nation's boundaries.

Written in response to Moore's sojourns in Mount Rainier National Park and taking "government pamphlets" as some of its founding documents, "An Octopus" is well placed to pick up on discourses of national vigor. Arguments for preserving areas of wilderness at Yosemite and Yellowstone in the mid-nineteenth century rested mainly on scenic nationalism. After the Civil War, however, a less buoyant cultural climate also lent weight to the preservationists' cause.[17] Turn-of-the-century degenerationists claimed that the yoke of big business had sapped American individualism and that an influx of "new" immigrants had weakened the American race. Degenerationists held that the pioneer spirit forged at the frontier had given Americans their distinctive character, and that in the absence of wild lands, with

mass migration to urban centers, that spirit had now dwindled and weakened. Areas of wilderness preserved in the national parks promised a source
of renewed virility and fitness for a supposedly enervated population. The
"out-of-door gospel" preached by John Muir, though it originated in a Romantic, quasi-transcendentalist belief in the divinity of the landscape, lent
itself readily to those "fundamental frontier virtues" promoted during the
Roosevelt administration, to the extent that in a much publicized encounter
in 1903 Muir and Roosevelt held "campfire talks" on an expedition to
Yosemite.[18] Moore casts glances in the direction of such wholesome, red-
blooded activities when she catches sight of "the mountain guide evolving
from the trapper" (*BMM* 314) and later in the poem when she catalogues
"eagle traps and snowshoes, / . . . alpenstocks and other toys contrived by
those / 'alive to the advantage of invigorating pleasures'" (*BMM* 316).

Degenerationist anxieties and prescriptions for renewed health were not
confined to reviving and exercising the spirit of the frontier. Equally ur-
gent, especially in the period when Moore was writing her poem, was the
problem of immigration, and the question of how to preserve the "purity"
of the American race. The confidence, during the Progressive Era, in America's capacity to absorb what was foreign to it and to assimilate whatever
alien strain might come in—indeed to draw strength from hybridization—
gave way in the early twenties to a more strictly racial conception of national identity. Eugenists warned that "throwbacks" and "reversions"
would result from the crossing of distantly related stocks, prompting calls
from nativist circles to limit the numbers of American immigrants whose
origins were non-Nordic.[19] 1924, the year Moore's poem was published,
was the year of the National Origins Act, the immigration bill that legis-
lated a quota system whereby the proportions of new immigrants would be
based not on patterns of recent migration, but on the distant national origins of the whole white population. The intended result was that by far the
largest proportion of new entrants would be from Northern and Western
Europe.[20] The close affiliation between these two patterns of thought—the
renewal of the frontier spirit and exclusionist immigration policies—finds
witness in the membership of Roosevelt's Boone and Crockett Club.[21]
Among the founding members of this big game hunting club in 1888 were
Madison Grant, later author of *The Passing of the Great Race* (1916), who
lamented the decline of Nordic influence in Europe and America and drew
on eugenicist arguments in his campaign for racial exclusion, and Henry
Cabot Lodge, who sponsored the adult literacy test in 1895 and went on to
become a member of Roosevelt's restrictionist Immigration Commission
in 1907.

From the perspective of such advocates of racial purity, Moore's fir trees,
those "austere specimens of our American royal families," aloof aristocratic specimens with the best right to inhabit and inherit the land, seem to

invoke disturbingly nativist connotations. As Moore's poem goes on, however, a counter-current to these connotations of homogeneity and purity begins to emerge. The poem catalogues in extraordinary detail—again largely from textual sources rather than direct observation—the flora and fauna of the mountain. One species is especially eye-catching:

> a stone from the moraine descending in leaps,
> another badger, or the spotted ponies with "glass eyes,"
> brought up on frosty grass and flowers
> and rapid draughts of ice water.
> Instructed none knows how, to climb the mountain,
> by "business men who as totemic scenery of Canada,
> require for recreation,
> three hundred and sixty-five holidays in the year,"
> these conspicuously spotted little horses are peculiar,
> hard to discern among the birch trees, ferns, and lily pads,
> avalanche lilies, Indian paintbrushes,
> bears' ears and kittentails,
> and miniature cavalcades of chlorophylless fungi
> magnified in profile on the mossbeds like moonstones in the water;
> the cavalcade of calico competing
> with the original American "menagerie of styles"
> among the white flowers of the rhododendron surmounting rigid leaves
> upon which moisture works its alchemy,
> transmuting verdure into onyx.

$$(BMM\ 315)$$

The glass-eyed ponies are indeed peculiar. Moore gleans her reference from W. D. Wilcox's *The Rockies of Canada* in which Wilcox describes the Indian pony, or cayuse. As she records in her Notes, the cayuse is a hybrid which "owes its origin to a cross between the native mustang and the horses introduced by the Spaniards." Wilcox celebrates the ponies' endurance and strength, but in passing also mentions that "some of these ponies have 'glass eyes': or a colorless condition of the retina supposed to be the result of too much in-breeding" (*BMM* 106).[22] Whereas those deep-rooted fir trees seem to signal the preservation of thoroughbred stock in Moore's poem, the ponies suggest anxiety about the consequences of in-breeding in a population which, originally hybrid, chooses to close the door to difference. The cayuse starts to disappear in this passage: first it is "conspicuously spotted" ("spotted" doubling as both variegated in color and easy to pick out) but in the very next line it becomes "hard to discern," the cayuse starts to blend into a background of which the most conspicuous aspect is that it, like the pony's eye, is colorless. Among the flora Moore notes chlorophylless fungi, white flowers of the rhododendron—verdure is indeed transmuted into onyx. And if this colorless environment, like the colorless condition of the retina, is the result of too much in-breeding, so too in this passage the resources of poetic language are impoverished. The striking thing about these lines, so unusual for Moore, is that they repeat themselves. Moore notes lilies twice ("lily pads," "avalanche lilies") and repeats the awkward phrase "cavalcade of" twice in three lines ("cavalcades of chlorophylless," "cavalcade of calico"). As the vocabulary reproduces itself, the sound patterns lose their delicacy so that the densely packed repetitions in these few lines tend to coagulate into a clogged alliterative mass.

The implication of this passage about the cayuse is that if in-breeding weakens the stock of poetic variety, then continued hybridization might renew its vigor: "the original American 'menagerie of styles'" has to compete for its ground, and again Moore's source points specifically to racial mixing. The phrase "menagerie of styles" comes from a light-hearted column in the London *Graphic* about evening wear. Skeptical of the notion that there might be such a thing as "faultless" evening dress, the columnist writes:

> In Parisian theatres, restaurants, and those gilded resorts where one sups and dances, anarchy reigns as far as evening dress is concerned—because Paris is Europe's playground, and the wearer of evening dress from Jugo-Slavia quaffs champagne alongside the wearer of evening dress from Stockholm or Lisbon. Nevertheless, even in the *Parisian menagerie of styles,* there remains this common feature—that evening dress is always unmistakably evening dress, in men's wear.[23]

The message Moore takes from this passage is that a singular style can be confected, and its identity retained, even when the components are anarchically mixed. Moore's source is especially pertinent to the debates about national character that underlie "An Octopus" in that it imagines a mix of arrivals from Northern, Southern, and Eastern Europe. When Moore changes the original text's *"Parisian menagerie of styles"* to "the original American 'menagerie of styles'" she Americanizes what her poem takes in, and yet, by giving an extract from the source in her Notes, she allows the text to retain something of its native identity.

A preference for diversity over homogeneity, for varied color over monochrome design, is also evident in a larger scale in Moore's poem. John Muir's primary concern for Mount Rainier was for its subalpine flower meadows. Listing the huge variety of plants in this "perfect floral elysium" he campaigned for their protection, whereas, he said, Mount Rainier's "icy dome needs none of man's care."[24] In the same spirit, Moore's poem preserves the lowland flora in catalogue form, detailing multifarious colors, textures, and species. The icy peak of the mountain, on the other hand,

characterized by crystalline whiteness or severe monochrome, defeats her
powers of description. "The perspective of the peaks" in "An Octopus" is
less a sublime aspiration than a treacherously unapproachable condition of
stasis.

Moore's preference for hybridity over "pure" bloodlines shows itself at
the verbal surface and in the conceptual roots of her approach to the mountain's peak, and her use of sources reveals a particular interest in the science
of eugenics.[25] We know from the published Notes to "An Octopus" that
Moore read the August 25, 1923 issue of the London *Graphic* because she
quotes directly from M. C. Carey's article "The Octopus in the Channel Islands," the source of her line "picking periwinkles from the cracks."[26] Two
pages after Carey's column in the *Graphic,* there is an article entitled "The
Laboratory of the S-Ray," a full-page feature about the Galton laboratory,
the eugenics research center at University College London, endowed by
Francis Galton in 1904 and chaired by mathematician Karl Pearson. The "S-
Ray" refers to Pearson's statistical method, as the *Graphic* explains: "the
Laboratory of the S-Ray; that is to say, the ray employed by way of fath-
oming statistics. As a searchlight it is turned on to masses of collected facts
and exposes the skeletal structure which is common to them all."[27] Pearson
traced patterns of heredity and attended especially to inherited abnormalities: "the walls [of the laboratory] are covered with charts showing how
night-blindness, or cataract goes down through families." The *Graphic*'s
mention of cataracts resonates with Moore's interest in those glass-eyed
ponies—and indeed with the waterfalls that mark the poem.

But perhaps the most striking aspect of the *Graphic* feature, and the one
that holds most significance for "An Octopus," is its illustrations. The page
is framed with silhouettes, profiles of Galton and Pearson and, most prominently, those the article calls "composite silhouettes." To produce these
"composites," the article explains, silhouettes of numerous subjects are
traced, so that each face can be described mathematically: "for every individual a series of numbers delineates exactly his or her profile." The components are then added together and divided by the number of sitters so that
"the result, when redrawn to scale, smoothes away irregularities of feature
and produces an almost Grecian profile," in other words, a faultless norm,
a eugenic blueprint. The *Graphic*'s phrasing here recalls the rather dense
passage toward the end of "An Octopus" in which Moore shifts from descriptive cataloguing to more discursive phrasing and in which she introduces the Greeks to her octopus-glacier. Though the patchwork of quotations makes the argument dense and elliptical, its general drift is to oppose
the lofty idealism of the Greeks to those practical, rough hewn skills and
virtues one might need to survive in a new country, and which one finds in
abundance in Moore's earthly paradise.[28] "The Greeks liked smoothness,
distrusting what was back / of what could not be clearly seen," Moore

writes, in one of those rare lines that is apparently not a quotation. Moore's phrase "the Greeks liked smoothness" recalls not only the Grecian love of beauty but Galton's conception of eugenic fitness. Francis Galton's research convinced him that the ancient Greeks had been the finest of all races.[29] According to the *Graphic* article, the "Grecian profile" smoothes away irregularities of feature, obliterates those surface abnormalities, those rough patches and invigorating pleasures that animate Moore's poetry and which she wanted to preserve, both in her verse and in the nation.

In 1852, James Fenimore Cooper observed that "the great distinction between American and European scenery, as a whole, is to be found in the greater want of finish in the former than in the latter."[30] Whereas Cooper thought of that rawness as a defect that time would remedy, it was precisely the American landscape's characteristic "want of finish," its wild ruggedness, that was preserved and celebrated in the national parks. Toward the end of her poem Moore exclaims,

> Neatness of finish! Neatness of finish!
> Relentless accuracy is the nature of this octopus
> with its capacity for fact.
>
> (*BMM* 317)

Read in the light of Moore's concerns about American nativism, "Neatness of finish!" sounds an exasperated or dismissive rather than celebratory note. Given her acknowledged borrowings from Ruskin elsewhere in the poem, a likely source here is his writing on Giotto:

> Giotto's genius is not to be considered as struggling with difficulty and repressed by ignorance, but as appointed, for the good of men, to come into the world exactly at the time when its rapidity of invention was not likely to be hampered by demands for imitative dexterity or *neatness of finish;* and when, owing to the very ignorance which has been unwisely regretted, the simplicity of his thoughts might be uttered with a childlike and innocent sweetness, never to be recovered in times of prouder knowledge.[31]

Moore's disdain for "neatness of finish," her suspicion of smooth surfaces and her implied nostalgia for the roughness of the primitive puts her in sympathy with the frontier rhetoric that galvanized the national parks movement. At the same time, though, she was wary of the normative science and restrictionist immigration policies that were also intended to reinvigorate the American character. Doubtless Moore was fascinated by research into heredity, her training as a biologist attracting her to Mendelian breeding experiments and her capacity for fact and number, her own "relentless accuracy," drawing her attention to Galton's and Pearson's data-sifting statistical methods. But the colorless environment that threatens to engulf the "menagerie of styles" in "An Octopus" and the catastrophic curtain of whiteness at its end suggest that attempts to weed out the strange and the alien lead only to poetic and national sterility.

Marianne Moore sited her magnificent poem at the intersection of several trains of thought about national character, eugenics, and immigration; but she did not simply encrypt a message about race in the guise of a poem about a mountain. What "An Octopus" clearly shows is the interrelation of poetics and politics in Moore's art. Moore's experiments with poetic language— her experience of the unexpected felicities that occur when you make unlikely matches between different species of writing or, on the other hand, of what happens when poetic language is deprived of variation and allowed to reproduce only itself—those experiments emerge from and speak to a nation that risks closing itself to the enlivening effects of new blood and cultural change. For Moore, preserving America's character meant preserving its heterogeneity, its inventive flexibility and its capacity to remain, like "Big Snow Mountain," "the home of a diversity of creatures."

NOTES

1. W. P. Pycraft, "The World of Science: Good News for the Gourmet," *Illustrated London News,* June 28, 1924, 1218.

2. "Everest the Merciless and Still Unconquered: A Climbing Tragedy," *Illustrated London News,* June 28, 1924, 1231. The article is illustrated with photographs of the Everest expedition crossing the glacier beneath the "merciless" summit.

3. Quotations from the main text of "An Octopus" are from its first published appearance, *Dial* 77 (December 1924): 475–81. References to Moore's published notes are to the version printed in *O,* 105–7. Both texts are reprinted in *BMM,* 125–32; 147–49; 312–18. John Slatin suggests affiliations between Moore's poem and Emerson, Poe, Ruskin, Henry James, and William Carlos Williams as well as Milton. See *The Savage's Romance: The Poetry of Marianne Moore* (University Park: Pennsylvania State University Press, 1986), 156–75. Robin Schulze has argued that in "An Octopus" "Moore joins Stevens and Shelley in composing a great poem of romantic winter vision." See *The Web of Friendship: Marianne Moore and Wallace Stevens* (Ann Arbor: University of Michigan Press, 1995), 60.

4. Among recent accounts that have emphasized Moore's relation to the visual arts, Elisabeth Joyce considers that "'An Octopus' takes the international approach of collage form and applies it directly to America" (*Cultural Critique and Abstraction: Marianne Moore and the Avant-garde* [Lewisburg, PA: Bucknell University Press, 1998], 80–85); and Caroll Cantrell traces the affinities she finds between Moore's poem and Northwest Indian art in "'The Roar of Ice': Motion, Language, and Silence in Marianne Moore," in *New Essays in Eco-Feminist Literary Criticism,* ed. Glynis Carr (Lewisburg, PA: Bucknell University Press, 2000), 157–74.

5. For details of the biographical circumstances of the poem, see Patricia Willis, "The Road to Paradise," *Twentieth-Century Literature* 30, nos. 2–3 (Autumn 1984), 242–66.

6. Marianne Moore, "A Note on the Notes," *CPo* 262.

7. Pycraft, "Good News for the Gourmet," 1218.

8. Pearl Andelson, an early reader of Moore's *Poems* (1921), complained in these terms about her style. Cited in Harriet Monroe, "A Symposium on Marianne Moore," *Poetry* 19, no. 4 (January 1922): 211.

9. John Muir, *Our National Parks* (Boston: Houghton Mifflin, 1901), 272; emphasis mine.

10. Alfred Runte, *National Parks: The American Experience,* 2nd ed. (Lincoln: University of Nebraska Press, 1987), 26–27.

11. Muir, *Our National Parks,* 268. Among the closing lines of Moore's poem is another phrase that originates in Muir's description of the redwood, though in the poem it is applied to Mount Rainier: "the white volcano with no weather side" is adapted from "[the redwood] shoots forth its limbs with equal boldness in every direction, showing no weather side" (270).

12. Muir, *Our National Parks,* 272.

13. John Ruskin, *Modern Painters: 5* (1860), vol. 7 of *The Works of John Ruskin,* ed. E. T. Cook and Alexander Wedderburn (London: George Allen, 1905), 105.

14. Ibid.

15. Ibid., 7:105–6 (emphases mine).

16. Ibid., 7:110.

17. See Roderick Nash, *Wilderness and the American Mind,* 3rd ed. (New Haven, CT: Yale University Press, 1982), particularly Chapter 9, "The Wilderness Cult," 141–60.

18. Ibid., 138.

19. Mark H. Haller, *Eugenics: Hereditarian Attitudes in American Thought* (New Brunswick, NJ: Rutgers University Press, 1963), 148.

20. Ibid., 157.

21. Nash, *Wilderness,* 152.

22. For the source of Moore's quotation, see W. D. Wilcox, *The Rockies of Canada* (New York: Putnam's, 1901), 130.

23. "The Mystery of an Adjective, and of Evening Clothes," *Graphic,* June 21, 1924, 1006, my emphasis. The adjective in question is "faultless."

24. John Muir, "The Wild Parks and Forest Reservations of the West," *Atlantic Monthly* 81, January 1898, 26.

25. David Kadlec has detailed Moore's reading about heredity and eugenics in "Marianne Moore, Immigration, and Eugenics," *Modernism/Modernity* 1, no. 2 (1994): 21–49. Especially pertinent to my argument is Kadlec's discovery that Moore was taking notes from an interview with plant hybridizer Luther Burbank during her 1922 trip west, and reading *Journal of Heredity* during the National Origins period (40–41). Kadlec does not discuss "An Octopus."

26. See M. C. Carey, "The Octopus in the Channel Islands," *Graphic,* August 25, 1923: "It can pick a periwinkle out of a crack, and yet crush a larger prey with the grip of a small python" (282).

27. "The Laboratory of the S-Ray: Where Statistics Are Made Fascinating," *Graphic,* August 25, 1923, 284.

28. Patricia Willis identifies several of the source texts for this section of the poem in Richard Baxter, W. D. Hyde, and J. H. Newman. See "The Road to Paradise," 247–59.

29. Haller, *Eugenics,* 11.

30. James Fenimore Cooper, "American and European Scenery Compared," in Washington Irving et al., *The Home-Book of the Picturesque: or American scenery, art and literature* (1852; facsimile reproduction with an introduction by Motley F. Deakin [Gainesville, FL: Scholars' Facsimiles & Reprints, 1967]), 52.

31. John Ruskin, "Review of Lord Lindsay's 'History of Christian Art'" (1847), *Works,* 12:222, my emphasis.

The "Not-Native" Moore:
Hybridity and Heroism in the Thirties

Charles Berger

THROUGHOUT THE NINETEEN THIRTIES, MARIANNE MOORE PARTICIPATED, at a distance, but with fierce engagement, in all the crucial debates revolving around the role of the poet in a time of economic, social, and political crisis. Her poems, essays, and letters from this decade constitute a crucial contribution to aesthetic thought in a period when verbal artists felt it a duty to defend certain kinds of poetry against Marxist critique, even while they often absorbed valid aspects of leftist polemic into their own work. Reading *The Selected Letters of Marianne Moore* and concentrating on the early thirties, in particular, will give any reader an indelible sense of how closely, shrewdly, and idiosyncratically Moore tracked the awful news emanating from home and abroad. Writing to expatriate American friends in the early years of the Depression becomes something of a moral duty for Moore, as she takes it upon herself to comprehend the devastation around her and render it through description to Americans abroad. The range of reference in her letters, and her pragmatic comprehensiveness, marked by innumerable displays of shrewd judgment, present a fascinating stylistic contrast to her many literary reviews from the same period. The reviews embrace an ethos of epigrammatic constriction, saying much through crystallization and intimation. In the aggregate, the reviews and brief essays comprise an invaluable assessment of modern American writing, with particularly sharp evaluations of James, Pound, Williams, and Stevens. Moore used these occasional assignments to brood on the same problem that faced Stevens: how to move from the experimental ethos of 1914–1924 to the demands of the thirties, where poets felt compelled to provide an ideological defense of poetry's necessity.

Moore's poetic output during the 1930s did not approach the torrent of verse she wrote in the teens and early twenties, but it is substantial, to put it mildly, and it shows clear signs of a poet consciously altering her style: the poems become more discursive, edging toward more openly public themes, even as they retain her commitment to that wrought idiosyncrasy of figurative encapsulation without which poetry, as Moore thought, loses

150

its distinction and purpose. But it remains true that scholar/critics of modern American poetry, unless they have a special interest in Moore, tend not to think of her as someone who wrote "thirties" poetry. By contrast, Stevens is known, by admirers and detractors alike, to have had a thirties phase. One can debate the influence of his poetry on other poets of the decade, or the importance of that phase within his oeuvre as a whole, but his peculiar visibility during the thirties is not open to dispute. It is a different story with Marianne Moore. Due to the oddities of Moore's publishing history, she has no single volume of poetry that can be readily associated with the thirties, no *Ideas of Order* or *The Man with the Blue Guitar*, or *Owl's Clover.* Her *Selected Poems* came out in 1935, but it included many poems written considerably earlier; no effort was made to indicate which of the poems were produced in recent years. In 1936 she published *The Pangolin and Other Verse*, a small, limited-edition book. *What Are Years* appeared in 1941. Stevens resisted topicality by mastering a form of topical obliquity. Moore, for whatever reason, did not manage her career with the aim of bringing about, by book publication, a conspicuous coincidence between her figurative meditations on scarcity, oppression, nationalism, race, identity, and the "low, dishonest decade" of the thirties, as Auden put it.

Grace Schulman's new edition of Moore's poetry—*The Poems of Marianne Moore* (2003)—is organized chronologically, after the fashion of Holly Stevens's *The Palm at the End of the Mind*, and this will help, along with the work of criticism, to remind readers that Moore's characteristic response to events of the thirties is not replaceable by any other poet's. This essay examines a range of poems, from "The Steeple-Jack" to "Virginia Britannia," every one of which engages central issues of contention from the decade. I concentrate on Moore's efforts to counter pernicious ideologies of nationalism and hero-worship, not by surrendering the concept of the hero or the nation, but by subjecting such affirmations to the rigor of poetic skepticism (in this, she and Stevens are one), a credo that asserts the necessity of cautious belief, for without some form of assent, poetry is neither read nor written. Moore demands that such belief must not become exclusive, must not ground itself on obsolete metaphors, must not spawn hatred, and must be able to withstand critique through defensive sallies of wit, not contempt. Poets excel at metaphor and wit, hence become most necessary at times when the enemies of poetry—who gather on the left, the right, and in the middle, as well—regard such work as utterly irrelevant.

Auden, of course, was a far more influential voice for poetic skepticism in the thirties, especially since he had a brief Marxist phase. His frontal assaults on nationalist allegiance culminate in the witheringly satirical "Letter to Lord Byron" (1936) and "Sonnets from China" (1938), where the technology and the bureaucracy of war (in anticipation of Pynchon) make of patriotic sacrifice an absurdity. Neither Moore nor Stevens wrote on this scale during the decade, though Stevens came close with his minimalist epic-sequence, "The Man with the Blue Guitar" (1937). Instead, both poets wrote a number (greater, for Stevens) of resistance-pieces, taking stands against mutually canceling ideologies—Marxism and Fascism—which negated, with equal viciousness, assertions of value through particularity and individuality. Stevens thematized the threats to his poetry and his quest for countervailing figures, tropes, and personae, more publicly than did Moore, and throughout his poetry of the thirties he looks for ways of installing persuasive speakers, who will not turn the poet's stomach, before a public that they might also captivate. Moore, though preternaturally sensitive to the degradations visited upon the language by avatars of democracy and fascism alike, nowhere in her poetry fabricates a fictive speaker who might persuade otherwise. After all, she chose to end her 1935 *Selected Poems* with "Silence," a poem whose gender plot from an earlier time becomes transformed, by virtue of placement in the volume, into a closing benediction aimed at ending the shrieking from all sides. Based on the treatment of Daniel Webster at the close of "Marriage," we have some idea of Moore's disregard for public speakers. She was particularly immune to Franklin Roosevelt's radio voice (*SL* 283). On the other hand, she found Yeats and Frost to be captivating speakers on the subject of poetry— unacknowledged legislators, always the best kind of public person for Moore, and not for Moore alone (*SL* 286, 300).

The *Selected Poems* of 1935 begins with "The Steeple-Jack" and "The Hero," poems that foreground the difficult effort to locate a version of heroism that can withstand skepticism, as well as discourage dangerous exaggeration. This pairing is then followed by "The Jerboa," a profound indictment of imperial arrogance and excess, which brings forward its own unlikely emblem of heroic resistance, "the sand-brown jumping rat." All three poems were published in 1932. "The Steeple-Jack" and "The Hero" appeared, along with "The Student," as a triptych in *Poetry,* under the less than splashy title, "Part of a Novel, Part of a Poem, Part of a Play." "The Jerboa" appeared in *Hound and Horn.* Moore replaced "The Student" with "The Jerboa," an arrangement followed in subsequent collections, as if the latter—which she called "maybe the one and only thing I have ever written" (*SL* 265)—staked out a greater urgency of theme.

"The Steeple-Jack" opens with the line: "Dürer would have seen a reason for living" (*CPo* 5). It's worth pausing at that first word, the first name, and taking a look backward at how Moore opened *Observations* in 1924: "You make me think of many men / Once met, to be forgot again / Or merely resurrected / In a parenthesis of wit" (*BMM* 51). ("To an Intra-Mural Rat," the opening poem of the earlier volume, did not survive into the *Selected* or *Collected Poems.*) The foregrounding of Dürer here at the beginning is clearly more than a parenthetical gesture. But whatever affinities one ad-duces between Dürer and Moore, and I would vote for the quality Moore points to when she speaks, a few lines later, of "water etched / with waves," clearly the artist stands out because he is not one of "many men," but is a *confrère* upon whom one can rely in a time of desperation, when one needs to find "a reason for living." Thoreau, the American isolate, explains in *Walden,* "Where I Lived, and What I Lived For," but Moore wants a spiritual vademecum from further afield, and in 1932 it seems especially important that such a figure be German and male. For Moore was deeply worried about Hitler in 1932. On April 4, 1932, writing to Bryher, she phrases her concern: "Hitler's defeat indeed seems necessary. Otherwise we might all 'leave forever.' You would be surprised to know how anxiously the Hindenburg election was awaited and hoped for in America" (*SL* 263). As indicated by the quoted words in my title, "not-native," I center on Moore's quest throughout the thirties to locate an aesthetic not bound to nationalistic identifications, and the opening turn to Dürer establishes this motive as a priority. In a more word-wizardly way, we might also seize on the possibilities offered by the French pun on the artist's name, *dur,* which serves as a curious sort of apotropaic address to the reader, warning him or her that the book in hand will be "hard," a danger-sign at the beginning of the poem to match that placed by C. J. Poole at the end.

Affinities offered by Dürer himself may never add up to more than a screen for other, more pressing concerns, if only for the reason that he is long dead, but Moore's choice of a fellow artist to serve as entrée to the *Selected Poems* indicates her career-long practice of reading her contemporaries and near-contemporaries as a way of gauging her own feasible choices. Moore wrote a series of short reviews and appreciations in the early thirties that enabled her to define her own course of attack, by contrast and by consanguinity. Two pieces stand out for their intensity of engagement: her first review of *A Draft of XXX Cantos* (*CPr* 268–77), published in 1931, and her essay, "Henry James as a Characteristic American" (*CPr* 316–22), published in 1934. Pound and James, along with Stevens, whose publication of *Ideas of Order* in 1936 occasioned an equally trenchant review from Moore, served as touchstones for her, though her relation to Pound's work was always fundamentally oppositional. Stevens and she were the purest intellectual allies throughout the decade, as Robin Schulze reminds us in *The Web of Friendship: Marianne Moore and Wallace Stevens,* and they wrote brilliantly about each other, for what they wrote, in brief appreciations, served as a form of poetic/spiritual autobiography. But even though James was a crucial figure for her since her Bryn Mawr days he was distant enough to elicit sustained, elegant analysis. The *Cantos* can only be said to have burst upon her as a negative epiphany, a masterful charting of poetry's baleful sublimity when grounded on grievous error and abetted by astonishing technical originality.

Moore notes what many poets have gathered from Pound: his ruthless hunt for examples of beauty, the precision of his phrasing (if not his thinking), and his musical range. But on a deeper level, where Pound exists as a force-field, she turns to words such as "mastery," "master-appreciation," or "master-quality." She associates him with "certitude" and "decision." She quotes from the Malatesta cantos to reinforce these linkages, and the block Latin lettering drives home the ideology of monumentalism: "SIGIS-MUNDUS HIC EGO SUM / MALATESTA, FILIUS PANDULPHI, REX PRODITORUM" (*CPr* 275). The attitude necessary to hoist these assertive blocks into place may serve as a convenient motto for everything that Moore opposed, though it also compelled fascination. And then there was the question of his representation of women: "apropos of 'feminolatry,' is not the view of woman expressed by the Cantos older-fashioned than that of Siam and Abyssinia? knowledge of the femaleness of *chaos,* of the *octopus?*" (*CPr* 272). As she moved toward the fashioning of her own version of heroism, Pound might be kept in mind as a useful, if large, example of how not to proceed. James, on the other hand, offers innumerable lessons in how to be American and cosmopolitan, a citizen of the world and a local. Unlike Pound, James felt no need to vilify what he left behind, for the simple reason that he did not exaggerate the virtues of old culture. James celebrated neither monuments nor touchstones. Moore adopts something of a Jamesian style as she layers and unlayers the complex folds of James's relation to America, remembering always his statement in *Notes of a Son and Brother:* "one's supreme relation, as one had always put it, was one's relation to one's country" (*CPr* 318).

Moore is noticeably interested in the boyhood of Henry James, as if the example of James's late, professed allegiance, in *Notes of a Son and Brother,* to the earliest manifestations of his encyclopedic sensibility, might serve as a paradigmatic corrective to patterns of American masculinity. For what is at stake in Moore's essay on James is not only a certain way of being American without being provincial (and dangerous), but also a way of being a man in America without surrendering boyish qualities that have less to do with Huck Finn than with the boy who loved the theater and who risked bluff mockery when he made "the least attempt at personal adornment" (*CPr* 320). In other words, the example of Henry James leads to the issue of how to define masculinity in a way that will not result in an American who "glow[s] belligerently with one's country" (*CPr* 321). That, in turn, leads to the figure of Ambrose in "The Steeple-Jack."

Ambrose comes into "The Steeple-Jack"—when he is, indeed, in the poem, for Moore removed him in the 1951 *Collected Poems*—rather abruptly, signaled in advance only by alliterative consanguinity with the "ambition" that this town is said to dispel:

> The diffident
>
> little newt
>
> with white pin-dots on black horizontal spaced-
> out bands lives here; yet there is nothing that
> ambition can buy or take away. The college student
> named Ambrose sits on the hillside
> with his not-native books and hat
> and sees boats
>
> at sea progress white and rigid as if in
> a groove. Liking an elegance of which
> the source is not bravado, he knows by heart the antique
> sugar-bowl shaped summer-house
>
> (*CPo* 6)

The not-natively named Ambrose, who seems to have been christened in accordance with the same spirit that gave Stephen Dedalus his odd name, may attend an unnamed college in this town, or perhaps is on vacation from the college which provided him escape from this complacent village, beset by dangers it thinks to tame by naming. The quoted passage reminds us that "elegance" and "college" come from the same Latin root: "legere," to choose. The conjunction of "elegance," "college," and "source" provides verbal evidence for the reader to construct a tale of chosen, rather than inherited, nativity. Moore pushes the issue even further by endowing Ambrose with a high-falutin' name, testifying to cultural pretensions held by at least one of his parents. It could indeed be dangerous for someone named Ambrose to be living in a town like this, since a name so defiantly oppositional to male bravado, like the foppy, not-native hat he wears, can get a boy into trouble, especially a college boy. In a town of "jacks," he dares to be the jill on the hill. Whether this town would prove a "fit haven" for an apparent misfit like Ambrose, is left for the reader to decide.

As the principle of the "not-native," Ambrose is, nonetheless, said to feel "at home" in a town like this. Nor is he the only not-native transplant or entity to be catalogued. As John Slatin has remarked, many of the flowers mentioned in the poem are not native to North America, but have become domesticated in coastal areas.[1] They take root, as the living memory of Dürer takes root in the poet's mind while she surveys the stranded whales. At the beginning of her thirties volume, Moore establishes the importance of what Wallace Stevens, in reviewing *Selected Poems,* noted in the following terms: "She hybridizes . . . by association. They are an intermingling."[2] Hybridity and intermingling, as ideological commitments, provide a strong antidote to nationalistic bravado.[3] Another word for these concepts is "confusion," and that is what Moore singles out for praise: "it is a privilege to see so / much confusion" (*CPo* 5). Not for her the kinds of order, grounded on dangerous notions of authentic identity, celebrated by fascists and fascist sympathizers.

At the time she was writing "The Steeple-Jack" and its companion poem, "The Hero," Moore was also absorbed by Yeats. Her task of reviewing *The Winding Stair* and *Words for Music Perhaps and Other Poems* allowed her to indulge a desire that she expressed this way: "I have been wanting all my life to write about Yeats" (*SL* 294). Yeats and Pound offered innumerable examples of male poets identifying with, or measuring themselves against, violent men of action. Think of Yeats's portraits of violent, prepossessing rich men who know what they want. Yeats, as poetic recorder, drunk with daemonic images, measures himself against such, and finds both himself and the other wanting, to a degree. But a residuum of respect for the rooted man of power remains, as much for the strength of his will as for his commitment to place. This cannot be Moore's way. But she, like Stevens, acknowledges the necessity of writing a poem of heroism as the thirties gathered force, since it was clear that large societies were darkly drawn to such figures, with or without the poet's permission. "The Hero" was written five years before Stevens' own examination of the poet in a time of Depression, "The Man with the Blue Guitar," and there are interesting stylistic similarities between the two poems, with short, choppy lines, jingling and jangling against each other:

> going where one does not wish
> to go; suffering and not
> saying so . . .
>
> Jacob when a-dying, asked
> Joseph: Who are these? and blessed
> both sons, the younger most . . .
>
> It is not what I eat that is
> my natural meat,
> the hero says. He's not out
> seeing a sight but the rock
> crystal thing to see

(*CPo* 8–9)

The revisionary difference in Moore's approach to all things heroic is clear throughout the poem. Emblems and anecdotes of the "not-native" abound, as the hero is cut off from natural affinity with nation and people. "The Hero" has a listlike look to it, but the genealogical stories it tells are all broken, vexed, marked by error and refusal: "Moses would not be grand-son to Pharaoh." When Moore chooses to define the hero in terms that might be understood by others, she employs elemental language, as if she were clearing the ground of ideological debris and getting to the heart of abstract action: her hero is caught "standing and listening where something is hiding." There is almost a folkloric quality to this tableau, but Moore is not interested in fashioning a *volk* out of such narratives.

"The Hero" begins with a statement of where we, the nonheroic ones, like to go, so that we may be reminded that "liking" is not part of the abstract hero's makeup. Moore's wide reading in Yeats would doubtless have led her to his various expressions of what he termed "antithetical selfhood," defined most openly in *Per Amica Silentia Lunae:* "Of all things not impossible, the most difficult." That credo is one Moore could indeed abide, since it avoided linking the heroic with national or indeed, natural affiliations: "It is not what I eat that is / my natural meat, / the hero says." The final two stanzas of "The Hero" turn and turn the screw of parable-like complexity, short lines making it hard for readers to escape the knotty task of interpretation. Many readers, I would imagine, are made uneasy as another folkloric tableau enters the picture, in this case, almost a speaking statue. I refer to the "decorous frock-coated Negro / by the grotto," employed by the caretakers of a sanitized Mt. Vernon national shrine and slave site:

> The decorous frock-coated Negro
> by the grotto
>
> answers the fearless sightseeing hobo
> who asks the man she's with, what's this,
> what's that, where's Martha
> buried, "Gen-ral Washington
> there; his lady, here"; speaking
> as if in a play—not seeing her; with a
> sense of human dignity
> and reverence for mystery, standing like the shadow
> of the willow.
>
> Moses would not be grandson to Pharaoh.
> It is not what I eat that is
> my natural meat,
> the hero says. He's not out
> seeing a sight but the rock
> crystal thing to see—the startling El Greco
> brimming with inner light—that
> covets nothing that it has let go. This then you may know
> as the hero.

                                                                    (*CPo* 9)

The twentieth-century man who serves as stationed and stationary tour guide to the white (we can assume) sightseers, answers, without being directly asked, the woman's battery of questions to her mute male companion. Costumed but nonetheless authentic, he is described as "not seeing her," because he is intent on "the rock crystal thing to see." Which is exactly what? That is not an easy question to answer, because the Negro is also said to have, as hero, a "reverence for mystery." Moore's political conservatism sometimes threatens to become a kind of passive resignation, except when she imbues it, as here, with a foreboding sense of anger being held back, unreadability being put forth. The speaking shadow adheres to politesse and dignity, but doesn't completely veil the possibility that next time it will be the fire that speaks. Forced assent breeds a quality we might better label stoic, not heroic; suffering and not saying so will not stay so forever. I believe that the fearless sightseeing hobo, the woman, takes the point of the message. And I certainly concur with Cristanne Miller, who identifies the "hobo" with Moore herself.[4]

Remarkably, for a poem called "The Hero," this text is flush with negatives (the not-native, for example), as if for Moore, the via negativa were the proper road for heroic journey. The last stanza of "The Hero" stresses the valor of beholding "the rock crystal thing to see," reminding of Emerson's declaration that "Imagination is a very high form of seeing." The last stanza is more coherent and self-flattering to the artist and to the artistic principle, but such praise comes at the cost of not seeing the political, which may indeed be one of the things that the hero must "let go." It is one thing for a Cincinnatus, or a Washington, to leave the capital and return to the plow; quite another for a dressed-up descendent of slaves to accept his role in an updated minstrel show. But since Moore never grants violence a therapeutic role, accept he must, at least in the precincts of her poem. Epiphanic force is achieved when "the startling El Greco / brimming with inner light" bursts into the poem, reminding of Pound's Provencal retrievals, but without the attendant narrative of military campaigns. El Greco can be read as both product and producer—shorthand for the work, or the name of the artist (actually the nickname of the artist). To become the name for the thing you produce is to abolish the alienation between work and commodity that marks modern manufacture. At bottom, rage against such alienation drove Pound to fashion fictions of cultural coherence, and he did not shrink from the force required to do so. Moore celebrated the vigor of an El Greco, and the triumph of the artist who can turn himself into a work of art, by not coveting all that such compressed intensity must let go. But, as her previous stanza reminds us, some figures are accorded names in the roll call of history, others are not: Gen-ral Washington, El Greco; Moses, Pharaoh; but, his lady, here, and the decorous frock-coated Negro, there, in a "doubled vision," as Miller puts it, of minoritized racial and gender positions.[5]

Moore's hero, and heroine, are said not to covet a named presence on the historical stage, sacrificing the fame that most heroic narratives, even into the twentieth century, regard as the hero's reward. No name, no fame. Instead, there is the abiding iteration of the anonymous example—"this then"—which holds a place that anyone meeting Moore's new criteria for admission may enter into. Stevens follows Moore's lead when he refuses to name his heroic figures; as he says of his tramp-hero (another fearless hobo) in "Notes Toward a Supreme Fiction": "Give him / No names."[6]

The quest to expound a counter-heroics continues in "The Jerboa," where the emblem of freedom and inviolability, "the sand-brown jumping-rat," emerges from the camouflage of empire-obliterating sands (*CPo* 13). "The Jerboa" exemplifies the quintessence of Moore's aesthetic and political (though never personal) quarrel with Pound, for it is the poem of hers that most closely resembles the *Cantos* in verse-structure. Writing a lengthy poem of imagistic retrieval and foregrounding, Moore uses the poetic occasion to mount a strong attack on Pound's technique of plundering the past in search of imagistic aura, verbal and pictorial, which might be used to indict the modern bourgeois state. Moore's findings are put on display in a curatorial tour de force culled from the greater glories of New York's museums. She anticipates James Clifford in recognizing the museum as a contact zone. As Moore visually handles her objects, she succumbs to the spell of the outlandishly small and the outlandishly large, until the scandal of scale leads her to the ethical scandal underlying grandiose projections of political colossi, whether found in Rome, Egypt, Milan, or Berlin, whether designed by Pharaoh or Führer or Duce: "a fantasy / and a verisimilitude that were / right to those with, everywhere, // power over the poor" (*CPo* 12).

The keenest edge of the dart aimed at colonizing empires and the patriarchal values they always uphold, as well as the part of the poem most acutely directed at Pound, comes at the beginning of the second section of the poem, entitled *Abundance:* "Africanus meant / the conqueror sent / from Rome. It should mean the / untouched" (*CPo* 13). Under the guise of chastising the spirit which furnishes Scipio with the cognomen of conquest, Moore steers her revisionary condemnation toward the would-be modern Scipio, Benito Mussolini, who had his own designs upon North Africa in 1932, when the poem was written, designs which culminated in the invasion of Ethiopia in 1935, when *Selected Poems* was published. But Moore's real target was Pound, apologist for Mussolini. Reluctant to engage Pound's politics directly in her correspondence with him, Moore resorts to terse demurral in a postscript from November, 1931: "P.S. The Italian stamps—Roman wolf and Caesar—make a hit with me that the Fascisti do not" (*SL* 261). And the poem's association of "sand-brown jumping-rat" with "the blacks, that choice race," as exemplars of the true heroism of resistance, continues an old dispute between Moore and Pound, once again centering, interestingly enough, on Ethiopian qualities. Back in 1919, when Moore sent Pound a copy of "Black Earth," he baited her by asking if she was a "jet black Ethiopian." On that occasion, Moore responded by denying that she was black, but mixing categories nonetheless in a deliberately confusing manner: "I am altogether a blond and have red hair" (*SL* 122). Over a dozen years later, Moore goes further, identifying herself as, if not black, then at least "sand-brown," "altogether" an opponent of European colonial exploitation.

The jerboa is a native, granted, but Moore favors the creature because it is vulnerable and its indigenous qualities serve as a defense against extinction, not as a claim against the rights of others. When the native moves in the direction of nativism, and proprietary claims that exclude and oppress others, some of whom may even hold the edge in priority, then Moore's sympathies and strategies work to reveal the presence of hybridity at the source. Moore's most ambitious ode to the "not-native" as constitutive of the ground of identity, of ground-as-identity, comes in "Virginia Britannia," first published in the English magazine *Life and Letters Today* in December 1935, then included as part of the sequence "Old Dominion" in *The Pangolin and Other Verse* in the following year, appearing five years later in 1941 as part of *What Are Years*. I mention this publishing history because Moore worked hard to get her statement right in the final stanza of the poem, offering a significantly different version at the end of the process. John Slatin has ruled that "the nostalgia which overpowers the late poems also wrecks 'Virginia Britannia' in revision," even though 1941, when the revision is made, can hardly be called "late" in Moore's career.[7] More importantly, Slatin bases his judgment on a preference for the visual element in Moore, assigning nostalgic, moralistic qualities to abstraction. Bonnie Costello's reading also favors a naturalistic framework for interpretation: "the end of the poem describes the advance of evening."[8] But "abstraction" is always present in poetry, so the question must be phrased in the following way: what did Moore gain in the 1941 version and why was she so intent on defining the welter of issues surrounding "identity" in the late thirties?

Before adjudicating the battle over revisions—and "Virginia Britannia" teaches nothing if not wariness with regard to priority—a sense of the poem's scope is in order. Returning to one of the secular-sacred grounds of European-American origin, Jamestown Colony, Moore employs a measure and a style unlikely to inspire *frissons* of identification. In addition, she deliberately avoids what many other poets (Yeats, the Eliot of "East Coker," Lowell) might have succumbed to: the opportunity to strike a stance, to assume an authoritative pose or position on the grounds of origin. Moore, by contrast, writes the poetic "speaker" out of the poem. "Pale sand edges England's Old / Dominion," is an apt emblem for faded empires as well as the bleaching-out of identity (*CPo* 107). The poem's diction promotes hybridity by spinning out an astonishing number of hyphenated words describing flora and fauna. (Moore seems eerily prophetic of the later tendency to assert hyphenated forms of American identity.) As soon as the Europeans arrived—indeed, sooner—there was always already a hyphenated division at the source. "Priorities were cradled in this region," indicates that the founding site was already plural. The proliferation of hyphens throughout the poem points horizontally, deferring the quest for vertical hierarchies, just as the poet declares that Black idiom confounds the hunt for sources by speaking of "advancin' back- / wards in a circle" (*CPo* 109–10). Moore's shrewdest move to disrupt mystifications surrounding the issue of native origins comes with her treatment of Pocahontas. Even a poetic radical such as Hart Crane, in the section of *The Bridge* entitled "Powhatan's Daughter," wrote of Pocahontas in terms of the red earth, seeing her body as the underlying substance of the American continent, her breasts as mountains, and so forth. Moore will have nothing to do with such constructions. Her Pocahontas is described, three times, as "odd":

> Odd Pamunkey
> princess, birdclaw-ear-ringed; with a pet raccoon
> from the Mattaponi (what a bear!). Feminine
> odd Indian young lady! Odd thin-
> gauze-and-taffeta-dressed English one!
>
> (*CPo* 109)

Moore encourages her reader to look up the etymology for "odd," which turns out to come from an Old Norse word for "third," as in the construction, *odda-mathr*, third man, odd man out. Pocahontas, then, is neither one nor the other, neither Indian nor English, but an essential third principle, the principle of hybridity. The line break, "Feminine / odd," takes the oddness of femininity, from the male perspective, and gives it an added dimension. From this passage, it would appear that, for Moore, true hybridity results not from the perfect blending of two cultures, but from the production of a new and different thing, an odd man, or woman, out. When hybridity does not take, you get "strangler figs choking / a banyan" (*CPo* 110).

Turning to the significant revisions enacted upon the last stanza, it is important to note that Moore invested this closing section with what is for her an unusual degree of summary importance. She reworked the stanza from 1935 to 1941 in a search to define, as precisely as possible, the nature of hybrid identity upon a site where the prototypical modern nation was constructed through the "colonizing" of native Americans and the forceful "establishing" of "the Negro" on the banks of the Chickahominy. I will concentrate on the first half of the last stanza, for that is where Moore concentrated the conceptual force of her revision.

Here are the relevant lines from *The Pangolin and Other Verse* (1936):

> The live oak's rounded
> mass of undulating boughs, the white
>   pine, the agèd hackberry—handsomest vis-
> itor of all—the
>   cedar's etched solidity
>   the cypress, lose identity
>   and are one tree[9]

By 1941, in *What Are Years,* the closing stanza had undergone a dramatic change of emphasis and phrasing:

> The live oak's darkening fila-
> gree of undulating boughs, the etched
>   solidity of a cypress indivis-
> ible from the now
>   agèd English hackberry,
>   become with lost identity,
> part of the ground,[10]

The 1951 *Collected Poems* restores "filagree" and "indivisible" to wholeness by eliminating the hyphens—a shame, in my opinion—and the 1967 *Complete Poems* restores normative orthography to "filigree," correcting the mock-feminized variant of "filagree" (more noticeable in the hyphenated version)—also a shame, I would argue. The major changes to the stanza, clearly, come with the remarkable finding of "darkening filagree" as a replacement for "rounded / mass," and the decision to make the hybridized loss of identity not issue in the unity of "one tree," but return to the undifferentiated ground. Moore constructs the sentence so that it becomes difficult to see—precisely the point—what blends into the ground, since the ornamental filigree dissolves into the tree. Rather than standing up from the ground, as if vaunting its own strength, the hybridized entity strengthens the ground from which it emerges, as one possibility among others. So-called "lost identity" is now seen by Moore not in terms of cenotaphic, monumental splendor, but as the humbled ground, proving that "'Don't tread on / me'—tactless symbol of a new republic"—misconstrued the true locus of the republic's vigor. "Filagree" or, indeed, "filigree," is similarly mottled with complexity designed to undo facile nationalist genealogies (*CPo* 110). For filagree is a word designed to trigger association with other words it will then seek to dissolve. In particular, Moore guessed that within the context of a poem about the site of national origins, filagree would encourage contamination by "filiation" and "pedigree," as if Moore were creating a nonce-word. Instead, by emphasizing the ornamental aspect of filagree work, and relying on her most curious readers to hunt for an etymology that reveals teasing affiliations to genealogy—"thread" and "grain"—Moore creates a resistance to heroic accounts of nation-founding. The thread of genealogical relation is ornamental, a work of fictive weaving. This, then, you may know as the ground of the hybrid hero.

My attention, thus far, has been focused on the first half of the poem's final stanza, but the concluding lines add significantly to the critique of nationalistic arrogance, not so much through overt, moralistic condemnation, as by the far-fetching of an overt allusion to the Wordsworthian child:

> sunset flames increasingly
> against the leaf-chiseled
> blackening ridge of green; while clouds, expanding above
> the town's assertiveness, dwarf it, dwarf arrogance
> that can misunderstand
> importance; and
> are to the child an intimation of what glory is.

(CPo 111)

Costello is correct to point out how this allusion differs from anything other than allusion in Moore, for it is more overt and more overtly "literary," but she fails to interpret the allusion in its full complexity; worse, she accuses Moore of treating the allusion as an "unqualified 'poetic' solution . . . presented as 'truth,' not as language."[11] Slatin does a much more thorough job of tracing the allusion through the intricacies of the "Intimations Ode" itself, but his commitment to naturalizing interpretation means that he will miss, inevitably, Moore's deepest motives for bringing Wordsworth into the scene of instruction: namely, the fact that "Priorities were cradled in this region."[12] The whole of "Virginia Britannia" scrutinizes nationalistic claims growing out of this first act of settlement, showing again and again, through insertions of hyphenated hybridity, that the only purity possible on such a site would be the purity of "assertiveness" and "aggressiveness." Why, then, turn to Wordsworth at the end, and to the "Intimations Ode" in particular? What guides Moore to this allusion is her judgment, shared by Gertrude Stein as well, that heroic accounts of nationalistic origins and nativist identities are not only childish, but are meant, precisely, for the child in us who looks for simple identifications. Allusive recovery leads to a moment of epiphany, as Moore, trailing the clouds above the town with Wordsworth's "clouds of glory," trumps the tour guide's pitch to the natural children of America with Wordsworth's strong universalizing argument meant to remind all children, everywhere, that we "cometh from afar," that our priorities were always cradled elsewhere, certainly not at any site deemed a national birthplace.

Moore's place in the poetry of the thirties will become increasingly clear, just as her central role in creating what we regard as first-wave modernist

poetry is now indisputable. The literary history of the thirties looks different when Stevens and Moore are regarded as central players, not periph-
eral annotators. Even though both poets avoided contributing to the general afflatus emanating from the left and the right, casting themselves as
revisers of outsized claims, whether made on behalf of the nation-state or
the proletariat, the very resistance they displayed toward assumptions of
identity has made them into major figures of post-modernist skepticism.
Moore's difficult but not exclusive poetry of critique, which employs wit,
rhetorical disjunction, upheaval of categories, as well as categorical up-
heavals, and refuses to embody a centered consciousness in the form of
speaking personae—how different this is from Yeats, Eliot, and Pound—
appears now to fit almost seamlessly into more advanced interrogations of
identity formation. One is struck, over and over again, observing the radical carefulness governing her output in the thirties, by the thought of how
many poems she must have denied herself during these years, scrupulous
as she was to avoid the commission of error at a time when the last thing
the world needed was dangerously false ideology.

NOTES

1. John Slatin, *The Savage's Romance: The Poetry of Marianne Moore* (University Park:
Pennsylvania State University Press, 1986), 187.

2. Wallace Stevens, "A Poet That Matters," review of *Selected Poems* by Marianne
Moore, in *Opus Posthumous,* rev. ed., ed. Milton J. Bates (New York: Knopf, 1989), 220.
Stevens's review first appeared in the December 1935 issue of *Life and Letters Today.*

3. Susan Stanford Friedman's *Mappings: Feminism and the Cultural Geographies of
Encounter* (Princeton, NJ: Princeton University Press, 1998) and Robert J. C. Young's *Colonial Desire: Hybridity in Theory, Culture and Race* (New York: Routledge, 1995) are two
of the best recent theorizations of cultural hybridity.

4. Cristanne Miller, *Marianne Moore: Questions of Authority* (Cambridge, MA: Harvard
University Press, 1995), 154: "And yet it is difficult not to see Moore in this figure, with her
distinctly masculine way of life (as hobo), her untiring interest in the mundane and popular,
her factual questions and her desire to see sights slightly off the beaten track that give unac-
cented attention to women—asking, for example, 'Where's Martha / buried' rather than for
George's grave."

5. Miller, *Questions of Authority,* 153.

6. Wallace Stevens, *The Collected Poems of Wallace Stevens* (New York: Knopf, 1954),
388.

7. Slatin, *The Savage's Romance,* 210.

8. Bonnie Costello, *Marianne Moore: Imaginary Possessions* (Cambridge, MA: Harvard University Press, 1981), 104.

9. Marianne Moore, "Virginia Britannia," in *The Pangolin and Other Verse* (London:
Brendin Publishing Co., 1936), 9–10.

10. Marianne Moore, "Virginia Britannia," in *What Are Years?* (New York: Macmillan,
1941), 31.

11. Costello, *Imaginary Possessions,* 105.

12. Slatin, *The Savage's Romance,* 210–20.

Flamboyant Reticence: An Irish Incognita

Laura O'Connor

Binn a mbriathra, gasta a nglór,
    aicme rerab mór mo bháidh;
a gcáineadh is mairg nár loc:
    mairg adeir olc rís na mnáibh.

Sweet their voices, true their tact,
    Their kind wins my allegiance;
Scorn on them I will not brook:
    Woe to those who malign women
        —Gearóid Iarla ("Earl Gerald") 1338–1398

[E]very man is a quotation from all his ancestors.
        —Ralph Waldo Emerson, "Quotation and Originality"

RICHARD AVEDON'S PORTRAIT OF MARIANNE MOORE, RESPLENDENT IN A mantle and tricorn and bearing a bouquet of flowering quince, conveys the mixed messages of her authorial persona as a "spinsterish anti-poetess": the woman who in the late forties "walked into a milliner's shop and asked to be fitted as Washington crossing the Delaware" cuts a dash as the national founding father and fairy godmother of American letters.[1] Moore sports her signature mantle in a spirit of camp: she postures boldly (*se camper*) and stands out (*campeggiare*) in the fashionably démodé garb that also serves as protective armor and camouflage (*kamp*, what is curved, flexible, articulated) for rhetorical subterfuge.[2] This essay explores how Moore deploys an Irish-Scythian mantle as a narrative technique for restoring underground oppositional narratives to mottled visibility and for commenting upon the sexual politics of the English Pale in Ireland and Scotch-Irish isolationism.

Moore's "Sojourn in the Whale" and "Spenser's Ireland" mix the defamatory commonplaces the poet-speaker has "heard men say" about Ireland into oblique declarations of Irish affiliation that simultaneously represent the dynamics of racial and gender discrimination and camouflage personal disclosure. The poetics of indirection Moore employs in these designedly

mantled representations of her ethnic homeland provide a metapoetic commentary upon the need for clandestine ingenuity and reticence under repressive conditions and contributed to her reception as an Irish "incognita."
I would like to render Moore less of an incognita by showing her extensive
engagement with Irish colonial history, which, in part because it is mantled, has received scant critical attention.[3]

"Spenser's Ireland" sweeps from an arresting treatment of Ireland as a
distant ethnographic object—"Spenser's Ireland / has not altered; — / a
place as kind as it is green, / the greenest place I've never seen" (*CPo*
112)—to a resounding, if ambivalent, declaration of Irishness: "I am troubled, I'm dissatisfied, I'm Irish" (*CPo* 114). Moore mediates her avowal of
Irishness through a dialogical arrangement of ethnographic discourse about
Ireland in a virtuosic performance of the idiosyncrasy she sees as the
essence of her poetic identity. Moore admires idiosyncrasy in the precise
etymological sense of *idio* (one's own, distinctive) *synkrasia* (mix), that is,
one's take on one's material lends it distinction. Moore's own combinato-
rial verve, lambent irony, and brio of delivery imbues her material with
gusto, which in turn can impart to readers the idiosyncratic "spin" that she
has wrought on her subject matter. Gusto is ambiguously a property of the
verse and a quality discerned in it by the reader who is expected to catch
and savor the implicit messages flowing through Moore's writerly inscrip-
tion of a dazzling conversational style. The loose-knit conversational hum
reassures one that it isn't necessary to catch *every* nuance, while the brac-
ing "fragrance of iodine" spurs one to intuit "implicit" ironies ("If tributes
cannot / be implicit, // give me diatribes and the fragrance of iodine" *CPo*
151). Deeply attuned to how reception determines what and how things get
said, Moore is fully committed to trusting personal predilections, even at
the risk of obscurity. She confesses in a 1960 interview with Donald Hall
that "the most difficult thing for me is to be satisfactorily lucid, yet have
enough implication in it to suit myself."[4] The carapace of quotation that
can make her verse appear opaque "seems under compulsion to set down
an unbearable accuracy," and this tension between public engagement and
private meaningfulness, clarity and allusiveness, propels the "hybrid
method of composition" of her poetics.[5] The "flamboyant reticence" of my
title attempts to name a quality that results from this productive tension in
Moore's poetics of idiosyncrasy, her gift for beguiling us with ramifying
detail and the "shimmer of the unsaid" while yet prepossessing us with the
exuberant punch of the poem as a whole (*CPr* 435).

Trusting personal predilections for Moore often means being "prepos-
sessed" by the "impassioned explicitness" and "infectious" compressed
ambiguity of those peers who obey her moral injunction to go "right on doing what idiosyncrasy tells [them] to do . . . to see the vision and not deny
it; to care and admit that we do" (*CPr* 422–23, 426). She offers as an ex-

ample how in "Mr. Colum's telling of the story of Earl Gerald, gusto as objectified made the unbelievable doings of an enchanter excitingly circum-
stantial," adding that she felt compelled to cite Colum's parenthetical aside
about Irish storytelling verbatim in a poem she was about to write in order
to preserve its pith and gusto (*CPr* 426). Colum's aside, which Moore
covertly places in "Spenser's Ireland" to link oral history about Spenser's
antagonist, Earl Gerald, with Craig-Moore family lore, itself has the form
of an idiosyncrasy of Irish speech, the Irish bull. Here Moore takes her cue
from Anglo-Irish novelist Maria Edgeworth, who coauthored *An Essay on
Irish Bulls* (1802) with her father and whose citation of the Irish-Scythian
mantle in *Castle Rackrent* (1800) Moore reads as an extended bull.[6] Similarly, Moore's multidimensional citational practice in "Spenser's Ireland"
creates a poem that has the gusto and pithy éclat of an Irish bull and yet
packs in enough "implication" to gratify the troubled and dissatisfied poet-
speaker and to provide an encrypted genealogy of subaltern Irish historiography. The Irish-Scythian mantle that shows and hides Moore's affiliation to Ireland has the double-voiced structure of the Irish bull. Moreover,
the "gusto as objectified" by Moore's use of this idiosyncrasy of Irish
speech may illuminate the flamboyant reticence of Moore's citational
strategies in other contexts.[7]

When Ezra Pound wrote asking the poet he had hailed the previous year
as an exemplar of logopoeia if she were "a jet black Ethiopian Othello-
hued," Moore replied by portraying herself as hailing from the relatively
dull background of a devout and close-knit Presbyterian family: "I am *Irish
by descent, *possibly* Scotch also, but *purely Celtic* . . . and contrary to your
impression, I am altogether blond and have red hair" (*SL* 122). Significantly,
however, her self-description suppresses the colonialist and sectarian over-
tones of Scotch-Irishness to identify with the colonized Irish and to lay
claim to the considerable cachet of a Celtic background in Anglo-American literary circles at the time. Marianne Craig Moore's matrilineal roots
can be traced back to the Warner great-grandparents who left Ireland in the
1815–21 diaspora, and to the Craig family who participated in the 1610
Stuart plantation of Ulster and resettled in the colony of the Penns in 1719
(they were denied entry at Boston) with the four other "Dissenter" families
whose collective history is documented by Mrs. Moore's cousin, Mary
Craig Shoemaker, in *Five Typical Scotch-Irish Families of the Cumberland
Valley.*[8] Shoemaker documents an unwaveringly high level of intermarriage among the five families over six generations, and when Moore wrote
Pound her family was recovering from the impact of her brother Warner's
marriage in 1918, a trauma presaged in 1915 when Mrs. Moore objected to
his courtship of a woman who was "not of [their] 'race.'"[9] The Moores cat-
egorized their clannishness, perseverance against adversity, impatience,
and adversarial identity as "Irish" traits, and apparently saw their some-

what beleaguered ("Dissenter") minority culture as an extension of their precarious yet resilient homestead. "Irish" ("Ire-ish")[10] is a loaded word, part of the family argot that Warner admiringly detects in Moore's writing "in our own special 'language' but so marvellously handled that the 'aliens' could & can understand them & enjoy it."[11] The family argot operates as a kind of communal "thick skin" to insulate the preternaturally close three-some from the outside world. This argot suggests that the Irish poems may be rife with hidden family narratives but also shows how "special 'languages'" can create vernacular subcommunities.

Moore published odes to Shaw, Yeats, and George Moore, and a regular "Irish Letter" when she edited the *Dial,* and was exceptionally well-informed about Irish history, literature, and politics. "Sojourn in the Whale" (1917) ironizes the attribution of "'feminine temperament'" to Ireland in a parable of resurgence that covertly links Moore's emergence in the New York avant-garde with the 1916 Irish insurrection and identifies her as a player in the Irish literary renaissance. In "Spenser's Ireland" (1941), she affiliates herself to two improbable precursors for an American modernist poet, fourteenth-century Gaelic poet Gearóid Iarla, and Maria Edgeworth, a writer Moore admired so much she adapted Edgeworth's novel *The Absentee* (1812) into her only play, *The Absentee* (1962). Through recondite allusions to Edgeworth's citational practice, Moore establishes an Irish-Scythian-Amazonian sorority with Edgeworth that links their mutual endeavors to represent the suppressed histories of the colonized Irish who have "dis / -appeared" beyond the Pale of the colonialist historical record to Herodotus's task of reconstructive historiography.

The phrase "beyond the Pale" is rife with conscious and unconscious memories of the linguicism that went hand-in-glove with the Englishing (later Anglicization) of Ireland. English was harnessed as an instrument of linguicide (eradicating Gaelic) and of linguicism (the social differentiation that legitimates the proper English of the Anglo elite and stigmatizes Celtic languages and accented and vernacular Englishes as "dialects"). The Statutes of Kilkenny (1366) prohibited English settlers from using Irish language and customs among themselves, but this ineffectual "English-only" legislation was enforced under the aegis of a King's Justiciar who was none other than the Gaelic poet, Gearóid Iarla. Poynings law (1494) required settlers to build a double ditch around the Dublin enclave, the Pale (O.F. *pal,* stake), as a means of preventing them from assimilating into Gaelic culture and of excluding the hostile transplanted Gaels from the inner sanctum of colonial society. Edmund Spenser seeks to generalize the Pale's dual function of restraining the colonizer and excluding the colonized in *A View of the Present State of Ireland* (1596) by laying out a master plan for gaining absolute control over cultural memory by "translatinge" the Irish natives into subordinate Anglicized serfs before they translated the settler caste into Gaelicized degenerates.[12] By the eighteenth century, the English Pale designated the social pecking order that exalted the Anglo elite over their *audibly* different inferiors. One notes an imaginary Pale in that the circulation of Irish bulls demarcates the ethnicized class hierarchy that elevates the Anglo-Saxons over Celts.

Irish bulls are solecisms that are circulated as laughable failures at verbal passing by the semi-Anglicized Irish. They are cited for the purpose of bolstering the intrinsic superiority of proper-English speakers and putting down those whose brogues and idiomatic speech are mocked as inadvertent disclosures of their low and provincial Irish origins. Although the intended meaning of these utterances is clear and straightforward, they are so infelicitously expressed as to be manifestly absurd and self-contradictory.[13] They are translational catachreses, formed when the desire to express an Irish idiom in English generates a solecism that is apparent to the English-speaking auditor but not to the speaker of Irish-English whose thinking is shaped by Gaelic syntax.[14] Many are anacolutha that arise out of the incompatibility between an English grammar based on subordination and an inflected Gaelic language whose syntax can be freely reordered for emphasis (e. g., "I haven't taken a drop tonight but one drink") and euphonious redundancy ("this house will stand as long as the world does, and longer"). Such anacoluthic license is a feature of the implicit conversational style of vernacular usage, which eschews the sequential and explicit logic of a print-standardized communicative style to dart ahead, shift emphasis, make positive assertions through antiphrasis, exaggerate, abruptly change tack, and leave gapped or dangling phrases to be completed by interlocutors who can grasp what the speaker means to impart. "Those who are quick and enthusiastic . . . are apt to make elisions in speaking, which they trust the capacities of their audience will supply," the Edgeworths note, offering as an example "the best way of boiling potatoes is in cold water."[15] Bulls are cited, not spoken, if I may use a bull to define the speech genre. It is only when the discerning collector wields the utterance as an eminently *quotable* blunder, and supplies an occasion for insiders of the blunder Pale to form a bond of pleasurable superiority at the disparity between their verbal mastery and the blunderer's ineptitude, that the utterance becomes a bull. The tendentious citation of these boomeranging punch-lines highlights how the figurative felicity of the original utterance is received as artless bungling when spoken by a provincial, and is applauded as artful wit only when it is cited by a raconteur or ethnographer from inside the ranks of the Pale.

In their *Essay on Irish Bulls,* the Edgeworths cite not to ridicule, but to reform the reflex discrimination against the audibly Irish—"whenever we hear the brogue, we expect the blunder," as Jonathan Swift describes it—by displaying the figurative wit and bilingual double-consciousness of these idiosyncrasies of Irish speech.[16] In a revealing parable entitled "An Irish Incognito" they recount how a highly Anglicized Irishman loses a wager that he can pass as English because he keeps betraying himself with bulls.[17] The title of "the Irish Incognito" is meant as a contradiction-in-terms—that is, as a bull—by the Edgeworths, who evidently hope that the Irish will continue to betray themselves with the irrepressible exuberance of their non-standard speech. Their indignation that the Irish should be denied the social clout to persuade others to attend carefully to what they mean to say is mixed with proleptic nostalgia about the likely future demise of these distinctively Irish ways of skewing English. This ambivalence about how the social mobility of Anglicization is achieved at the cost of cultural homogeneity is of great interest in relation to Moore's reworking of the Irish bull in the context of a multiethnic U.S. bent upon an English-only *"e pluribus unum"* makeover.

Moore uses two bulls in "Spenser's Ireland," which occupy crucial strategic positions in the poem's overall economy of citation. The poet-speaker's opening admission that Ireland is "the greenest place I've never seen" (*CPo* 112) undermines her credibility as an ethnographer, and makes her seem less authoritative than her precursor ethnographers who lived in Ireland. At the same time, since one cannot logically assert that an unseen place is the greenest, the admission paradoxically authenticates her as an Irish autobiographer by uttering an Irish bull. The ingénue-speaker is an outsider, but Irish culture is inside her, secreted within her idiosyncratic English. Avowing ethnicity with an Irish bull, a genre that ridicules the Irish in written form and is coded as an inadvertent betrayal of Irishness in speech-act form, opens up the ambivalent fissure between spontaneous and cited speech-acts in which cultural identity is fashioned. The friction produced by the never / ever substitution and the antithetical yoking together of solution and need ("greenest place" / "never seen") produces a catchy slogan in "plain American which cats and dogs can read" to illustrate how bulls' straightforward implicit meanings, enhanced by at-oddness with their explicit sense, have the "terseness and that simultaneous double meaning of the pun" that lends diction irresistible "contagion" according to Moore.[18]

The hyperbolic "greenest" is charged with the pejoration of Irish bulls as green in the compounded sense of credulous and uncultured and Irish, and the utterance rebounds to brand the speaker as herself the "greenest," the most Irish and the greatest dupe. She is the greenest because, to cite the second bull, which Moore quotes verbatim from Padraic Colum, "Hindered characters / seldom have mothers / in Irish stories, but they all have grandmothers" (*CPo* 112). The syntax of exemptive afterthought in the "but they all have grandmothers" aside, (a frequent source of contradiction in Irish bulls and a feature of Moore's syntax), mimics its atavistic message by eliding the intermediate link with an ulterior antecedent.[19] Instead of deriving Irishness from residency ("the same people in the same place," as Leopold Bloom puts it) the diasporate speaker redefines it as the same hindrance in different places. Moreover, the borrowed bull restates the immigration "principle of third-generation interest, 'what the son wishes to forget the grandson wishes to remember,'" in terms of atavistic matrilineal hindrance.[20] All Irish bulls are pregnant, and the motherless-but-grandmothered bull tropes on the mutations of reproduction that scramble stable hierarchies of antecedence. Many bulls treat the self-reflexive topics of identity and literacy. A greeting like, "when first I saw you I thought it was you, but now I see it is your brother" abashes personal egotism, and "I should have written a better letter, only I had not time to take a copy of it before I wrote it," another generic staple, highlights how bulls are used to mock the Irish as semiliterate.[21] Irish hindrance is transmitted through genes (grandmothers), quotations (stories), and the social web of interlocution that determines who is green.

Moore obliquely cues the reader into how the very quirkiness that provokes cultural condescension may also camouflage ulterior agendas. In the opening lines of "Spenser's Ireland," she makes an annotated obtrusive reference to Edgeworth's citation of Spenser on Irish mantles in *Castle Rackrent:* "They're natural,— / the coat, like Venus' / mantle lined with stars, / buttoned close at the neck,—the sleeves new from disuse" (*CPo* 112). *Castle Rackrent* features the scene of the ethnographic encounter in which an editor-amanuensis transcribes, prefaces, footnotes, and concludes the apparently guileless oral narrative of "an illiterate old steward," Thady Quirk.[22] Quirk's claim that the shabby "great coat" he wears as a sleeveless mantle belies that he is the father of a gentleman (a son he professes to disown for usurping the Rackrent family he loyally serves) is contravened by the editor's parallel ulterior script which cites Spenser on the seditious Irish mantle in a footnote.[23] Spenser wants mantles outlawed because they frustrate surveillance and facilitate covert subversive activity: "'the commodity [versatility] doth not countervail the discommodity [camouflage] . . . for [the mantle] is a fit house for an outlaw, a meet bed for a rebel, and an apt cloak for a thief'"[24] (Edgeworth citing Spenser). The editorial footnote surrounds Thady's "stream of anecdote told in an idiom incapable of translation into plain English" with quotation marks, lending his quirky English the double-voiced parasitism of the Irish bull to suggest that "honest Thady" may—but equally may not—mean the opposite of what he ostensibly n/ever says.

Moore's "Venus' / mantle lined with stars" quotes Edgeworth citing Spenser citing the Greeks in an ostentatiously "fair" use of classical erudition in the dialogue-format of Spenser's *A View of the Present State of Ireland.* In *A View,* Spenser's Eudoxus cites the Greek precedent of Venus' mantle to qualify Irenius' assertion that the sumptuary custom, along with the customs of nomadic pasturage, keening, and war cries, proves Irish descent from the Scythian barbarians.[25] "The Greekes also vsed yt [the mantle] ancyentlie," Eudoxus remarks, citing Herodotus and other classical authorities, "as appeareth by venus mantle lyned with starrs, though afterwards they changed the forme thereof into theire Cloakes called Pallia as some of the Irishe also vse."[26] Moore's triple-deckered citation of Edgeworth/Spenser/Herodotus suggests that Spenser's showy bipartisanship not only masks the exclusionary use of "classical quotation [as] the literary *parole* of literary men all over the world,"[27] but also represses a dread of the baleful "feminine" and "native" influences that are held at bay by the Venus allusion. In the context of *A View*'s preoccupation with forcibly Anglicizing natives before they Gaelicize settlers, "Venus" overlays the specter of mantle-clad "monashuts" (from *mná siubhail,* vagrant women) and foster mothers who expose the settler community to the "three most dangerous Irish infeccions" of intermarriage, foster-nursing, and "the evill custome of the language" because "the speache beinge Irish, the harte must needes bee Irishe."[28] A second labyrinthine link to Edgeworth on the Scythians in "Spenser's Ireland" supports the thesis that Moore reads the erotic subtext of the Venus-mantle debate as the colonizer's disavowed fear of the assimilative powers of Irishwomen's "sucke." In Moore's reading of *The Absentee*'s pivotal scene where the hero forswears absenteeism (act 2, scene 1 of Moore's play; chapter 8 of Edgeworth's novel), Moore allegorizes the host's parting gift of angling-flies as a cryptic Scythian rejoinder that assimilates the hero and excludes his English-militia companions in the same gesture.[29] Moore puts the most radically anticolonial spin on Edgeworth's Scythian allusions, and then mantles their joint radicalism by representing the cryptic bait as beautifully wrought angling-flies to be appreciated *qua* angling-flies in the poem (*CPo* 113, lines 38–45). By so doing, she salvages the Irish-Scythian mantle "as a strategy which imposes a way of life," a way of nomadic warfare, camouflage, and *aporia* that is so devised, according to Herodotus, "that none who attacks them can escape and none can catch them if they desire not to be found."[30] By doubly inscribing an Irish-Scythian-Amazonian sorority with Edgeworth, and adapting Edgeworth's quirky narrator to her own covert citation of Earl Gerald, Moore reads "'venus mantle lined with starrs'" as "hid[ing] fear of an inversion of the colonial enterprise in which the domestic triumphs over the state, female over male, and Irish over English."[31] The Pale is constituted in relation to what is repelled "beyond" it as barbarous and Other, but it is also the case, Moore shows in her Irish poems, that the excluded Other confronts the Pale with a display of reticence, "omissions [that] are not accidents," and opaque cultural practices that mark "the beyond" as a *withheld* limit, a mantled domain of unknowable reserves.[32] In Moore's poem,

"Venus' / mantle" archly glosses the "altogether blond" and red-headed poet's signature dress, and comments on her poetics of idiosyncrasy, the exclusionary politics of the English Pale in Ireland, and the disaffection she feels toward her ancestral homeland.

"Spenser's Ireland" juxtaposes two empirical reconnaissance texts, Spenser's blueprint for subjugating Ireland and Irish expatriate novelist Donn Byrne's glossy photo-essay, "The Rock Whence I Was Hewn," in the *National Geographic Magazine,* with Edgeworth's novels and Colum's "fictions," stories whose quirky styles of narration provide a vernacular for reading against the grain of the panoramic ethnographies.[33] The title of "Spenser's Ireland" calls attention to the colonizer's attempt to control the dissemination of Ireland's cultural identity at the same time as it oddly distances Moore from ownership of her poem. The omission of the "extra" title-line from the 11–line isosyllabic stanza for the following five stanzas retroactively gives "Spenser's Ireland" a kind of phantom status in the quantitative prosodic economy. This has the curious effect of marginalizing the overweening "Spenser" to the paratext, so that "Spenser" appears in the explanatory framework of the title and the footnotes but isn't fully integrated into the body of the poem. By contrast, "Earl Gerald" is secreted in the heart of an onionlike series of symmetrical parentheses, enveloped behind the paired citations of the Irish-Scythian mantle in lines 9–12 and 61–63.[34] "Spenser" is the highly visible author of the influential *View* and the canonical *The Faerie Queene,* texts that circulate in the dominant English print-culture. "Earl Gerald" is the opaque signature of the fugitive shape-shifter whose story Moore heard from Padraic Colum and who survives in folk memory as a millennial avatar and as a wizard in a children's trickster tale. For many Irish readers, "Earl Gerald" summonses "Gearóid Iarla," one of Spenser's Anglo-Norman precursors who "grewe insolente and bent . . . as degenerate . . . as the wilde Irish, yea and some of them have quite shaken off theire English names, and putt on Irishe, that they might be altogether Irishe."[35] In *A View,* Gearóid Iarla represents the specter of "Old English" degeneracy; in Irish folk memory he is heroized as a colonist who became "more Irish than the Irish" and joined forces with natives against the colonizer. Moore's weak lead to Earl Gerald in her note to line 58 of her poem, "From a lecture by Padraic Colum" (*CPo* 280), hides this historical-political subtext from her general readers, thereby marking the Irish-American poet as one of an Irish circle who know that to cite Earl Gerald is to cite over five centuries of colonial oppression. Moore has manifold motives for the mantled citation of Earl Gerald. She provides barely enough citations for Anglo-American readers to piece together the correspondences of allusion that would unearth the political history, and does so in a way that would provide such readers with an object lesson in the art of subaltern historiography. The poem allows for genealogical readings, ei-

ther by Irish cognoscenti who are predisposed to detect an anticolonial narrative between the folds of the quirky mantle or by literary sleuths who can
discover how to read the poem by studying how the poet-speaker reads
her cited precursor texts. Part of Moore's ambition in hiding the historic
"Earl Gerald" seems to entail creating a poem that can convey its meaning
independently of politico-historical glossing. By so doing, she reproduces
the contrastive transmission histories of the dominant written and underground oral texts and decenters the former's magisterial overview with the
latter's legendary ethos.[36] Though profoundly implicated in one another,
Spenser's *View* and Geraldine lore were both composed and circulated outside one another's earshot, and in Moore's poem the mutually entangled
"Spenser" and "Earl Gerald" are likewise intimately contiguous yet not
quite "present" to one another.

"Earl Gerald" is a composite folk-historical figure based on a prominent
family of assimilated Anglo-Norman settlers, the Fitzgeralds of Munster
and Kildare, who were deposed by the Elizabethans.[37] Tradition depicts
Gearóid Iarla as the son of the local sovereignty goddess, Áine, (in a coded
representation of rape, the first Earl, Maurice, is reputed to have mated with
her only because he first managed to seize her mantle) who placed her son's
family under taboo (*geis*) against showing surprise at anything he might
do.[38] By the time the fourteenth Earl, also named Gerald, was released
from prison in London in 1573, the lore had mythologized him into a messianic hero, a role he acknowledged upon his arrival home by the ritual divestment of English dress and donning of the Irish mantle. The fourteenth
Earl Gerald was the symbolic quarry of the 1580–82 campaign of terror
that Spenser helped Lord Grey execute in Munster, and his defeat cleared
the way for the plantations of Munster (in which Spenser was granted an
estate at Kilcolman) and, indirectly, to the 1610 plantation of Ulster (in
which Moore's Craig forebears were allotted estates). According to the lore,
Earl Gerald disappeared under the fairy mounds (in the Kildare version),
and into Lough Gur, under the slopes of Knockainey, Aine's hill or breast
(in the Munster version), whence he occasionally resurfaces to ask if it is
the time yet (to overthrow the usurper). The disappearance into the feminized landscape not only encodes the typological fantasy of a future return
to locality-based sovereignty, but it also graphically parodies Spenser's
neurosis about Irishwomen's sucke imploding the colonial enterprise. The
story that Colum published as "The Wizard Earl" is a trickster tale for children, albeit one that alludes to the political messianic trope by mentioning
that the Earl resurfaced "just before Earl Gerald's descendent, Lord Edward Fitzgerald, was making the people ready for an uprising [in 1798]."[39]
In Colum's tale, the Wizard Earl's wife begs "to know [him] in all [his]
shapes" and assures him that she won't "be made afraid of the change," but
when he metamorphoses into a stag, a cat-of-the-mountain, and a minia-

ture version of himself that is then seized upon by a monkey she breaks the taboo by screaming and he disappears underground.[40] By restricting her representation of Earl Gerald to the far-fetched whimsy of the tall tale, Moore recreates in the poem the discombobulating effect of the proverbial Irish bull, "of course I don't believe in fairies, but they're there."

In "Spenser's Ireland," Earl Gerald appears in the guise of hearsay, clandestine coded allusion, and folktale in which the lore survived and was received by Moore. Like all folklore, these feminized oral genres are "handed on from one person to another either by memory or practice rather than written record."[41] Moore quotes Colum's axiom about atavistic matrilineal hindrance verbatim, but without acknowledgment, and by so doing covertly links Geraldine typology with Craig-Moore lore. (Moore writes "secret sly hint" beside the bull in draft.) Much as legendary grandmothers elide mothers, remote clan lore can mask more immediate family narratives, and generalized cultural explanations like "it was Irish" afford safe distance from inadmissible knowledge:

> Hindered characters
> seldom have mothers
> in Irish stories, but they all have grandmothers.
>
> It was Irish;
>   a match not a marriage was made
>   when my great great grandmother'd said
> with native genius for
> disunion, "Although your suitor be
>   perfection, one objection
> is enough; he is not
> Irish." Outwitting
>   the fairies, befriending the furies,
>
>   (*CPo* 112–13)

Spenser's beleaguered garrison outlook was transmitted by great-great-grandmothers to the U.S. where it survives in U.S. nativist ideology and as a clannish "Irish" attitude among those who favor the reproduction of sameness ("a match") over "a marriage." Though Moore's citation of the Edgeworthian mantle celebrates the cryptic genius of the Amazons' repulsion of invaders, "Outwitting / the fairies, befriending the furies" presents a critical stance toward women's role as ethnic border guards. The phrase refers to another sumptuary camouflage, which, like Venus's mantle, conflates a clandestine Irish dress custom with a classical Greek allusion. "Outwitting the fairies" refers to a picture in Donn Byrne's *National Geographic* photo essay that documents how Irish mothers protect their sons from fairy abductors by dressing them in red petticoats: "Along the Connemara coast," reads the accompanying text, "boys were dressed in red flannel skirts up to the age of twelve . . . in order to deceive the fairies who are supposed . . . to run away with male children if they have the opportunity, but who will not touch little girls."[42] The masquerade of worthless femininity by the prepubescent boys intimates the cost exacted upon daughters by such vigilant maternal protectiveness and "hindrance."[43] The permissive taboo placed on Earl Gerald by Áine, which Colum delightfully renders as "if anyone who loved [him] was made afraid of the change, [he'd] have to disappear," stands in salutary and poignant contrast to such custodial conservatism.[44]

The mantled citation of Earl Gerald shows how occluded history returns under an occult guise that Moore associates with hindrance and with gusto. Concentration, which Moore characterizes as the infectious, impassioned explicitness of compressed ambiguity, heightens gusto (*CPr* 422–23). The exciting circumstantiality she admires in Colum's storytelling style is achieved by the compressed ambiguity with which she mantles the lore, which has "impassioned explicitness" when explicated in relation to the texts it hybridizes and whose withheld disclosure emulates the optimal deferral of the "but they all have grandmothers" punchline. It is possible to reconstruct the history behind Moore's "'Venus' / mantle,'" but the mantling of Gearóid Iarla effectively overlays the filiative modes of classical quotation and historical genealogies with the subterranean circuits of the oral tradition and folk customs. Most readers approach Earl Gerald analogously to the surrounding montage of meticulously crafted artifacts like angling flies and the array of unusual sumptuary items culled from *National Geographic* photographs, including a damask weaver, a grandmother knitting in front of a "purple-coral" fuchsia tree, and an assortment of megalithic twisted gold torcs and lunulae.[45] Those who can discern the "great amount of poetry in unconscious / fastidiousness" (*CPo* 38) exhibited by these folk ways, and appreciate "a private zany experience of the thing" in "the fly for mid-July" are likely to intuit how the exquisite "pride" and "care" invested in these artifacts is "like the enchanter's" and to catch on to what Ireland is "like" for the poet-speaker.[46] For the cognoscenti of "purely Celtic" American camp, the angling flies are neither fish bait nor a cryptic allusion to something else, though they may also be these things, but a flamboyant act of citation that signifies an affiliation to a marginal or subcultural group that shares their ironic relation to the mainstream. Like "An Irish Incognito," who prefers *not* "to practice the art of 'not to admire,' so as to give a justly high opinion of his taste,"[47] the poet-speaker imparts her enthusiasm for repossessing what one would keep by citing it and putting one's own distinctive spin on it. The discrete appeals to camp cognoscenti (who respond to the signifying éclat of idiosyncrasies of speech and shape-shifting camouflage) and to Irish cognoscenti (for whom the bull and Gearóid Iarla are charged with memories of linguicism) are arranged in a way that potentially facilitates a crossover of reading styles between the contrary modes of interpreting Earl Gerald. If Moore can reproduce the "gusto as objectified" she admires in Colum's "telling of the story of Earl Gerald" and in Edgeworth's quirky narrator, readers can be "hindered to succeed" (*CPo* 121) by hobbling their tendencies to read "Spenser's Ireland" either as "purely Celtic" textual pastiche or as Manichean anticolonial allegory.

Bulls and idiosyncrasies have intrinsic value for Moore as "fossil poetry" and as an exemplary style of interpreting the world from an odd vantage. At the same time, and paradoxically, bulls only come into existence when they are cited as such, and thus are void of intrinsic worth. When the Irish Incognito commends a Romney portrait as "absolutely more like than the original" he makes a metapoetic observation about bulls, which also applies to camp taste: both are predicated on the assumption that the reproduced utterance or image "is absolutely more like than the original." The playful imposition of "one's own spin" on an utterance or a thing is at the opposite end of the spectrum to the concept of idiosyncrasy as a resistant cache of indefeasible otherness, and yet both aspects have a role in creating "nomadic" coteries among those excluded from the gentlemen's club. Blatant bulls are cited as laughable failures at verbal passing, but milder bulls (like the two in "Spenser's Ireland") can operate as a passing code, "a freemason sign by which we Hibernians know each other."[48] Just as camp taste inverts the dominant art of "not to prefer" to form a cult that excludes, for once, those who are otherwise dominant, vernacular quirks can be made into a clandestine code to strengthen a marginalized group. By treating the bull as a didactic tool, Moore effectively resignifies it as a kind of "bloother," a verbal blunder circulated among the Irish themselves for self-instruction and entertainment. Whereas the (implicitly monolingual) auditor of the bull detects an inadmissible mode of thought disrupting the proper one, the (implicitly bilingual) auditor of a bloother detects a collision between two incompatible linguistic consciousnesses that is simultaneously funny and enlightening, since it allows one momentarily to occupy a third space for perceiving the play between the two. True to her precept that "A poet does not speak language but mediates it" (*CPr* 379), Moore cites the Irish bull and Earl Gerald in a manner that acknowledges the linguicism that was perpetuated by the English Pale in Ireland while yet preserving the contagious iterability of the speech genre and of Earl Gerald's ability to make a comeback.

Earl Gerald's "magic" inheres in the "gusto-as-objectified" by his extraordinary persistence in popular memory and in his remarkable capacity to resurface across generations and cultures as a quotation. His transversals back and forth "beyond the Pale" or beneath the mantle recapitulate how the Justiciar-*cum*-Gaelic poet was figured in the lore as the offspring

of military rapine and native magic, how his adoptive literate Gaelic culture was forced into underground oral channels and then underwent a
change of vernacular and a diaspora, and how he can now be cited as a
"purely Celtic" totem by anyone who would like to flaunt her ancestral ties
to the Emerald Isle by "wearing the green." By weaving an Irish-Scythian
warp into the ultra-American woof of her Washingtonian mantle, Moore
shows how the Irish bull, which is customarily cited for the injurious purpose of putting down the Irish and fixing the exclusionary mechanisms of
the English Pale, has a capacity for saying many things simultaneously and
implying what cannot be stated explicitly, which can be exploited to cele-
brate the capacity of the incognita to rebound, surprise, disarm, and to register dissatisfaction. The ingénue who bears her wish to be Irish on her
sleeve, or rather on the greenest, most "purely Celtic," sleeveless mantle
since "venus mantle lyned with stars," is deeply skeptical about the extravagant reciprocity of Irish hospitality: "The Irish say your trouble is their
/ trouble and your / joy their joy? I wish / I could believe it; / I am troubled,
I'm dissatisfied, I'm Irish" (*CPo* 114).

NOTES

I would like to dedicate this essay to the late Edward Said, who directed the dissertation on
which it is based and whose tragic and untimely death occurred as I was completing the essay. In our discussions of the "postcolonial" Moore, Said—who came to know Moore's poetry through R. P. Blackmur—was deeply engaged by her poetics of subaltern historiography and her critiques of ecological imperialism. This essay is drawn from a book-project,
Haunted English: The Celtic Fringe, the British Empire, and De-Anglicization, which explores how several Anglo-Celtic modernists "de-Anglicize" their literary vernaculars in an
attempt to work through and remake their conscious and unconscious memories of the linguicism that accompanied the Anglicization of the British Isles.

   1. On Avedon's portrait, see Richard Avedon, *Evidence, 1944–1994,* ed. Mary Shana-
han (New York: Random House, 1994), 62–64. On the "spinsterish anti-poetess," see San-
dra Gilbert, "Marianne Moore as Female Female Impersonator," in *Marianne Moore: The
Art of a Modernist,* ed. Josph Parisi (Ann Arbor: UMI Research Press, 1990), 35. On the
Washington tricorn episode, see Bonnie Costello, *Marianne Moore: Imaginary Possessions*
(Cambridge, MA: Harvard University Press, 1981), 248.

   2. See editor Fabio Cleto's reflections on the etymology of "camp," especially his discussion of the Indo-European root, *kamp,* and its connection with the Greek *mètis* in *Camp:
Queer Aesthetics and the Performing Subject: A Reader* (Ann Arbor: University of Michigan Press, 1999), 30 passim.

   3. See Patricia Willis, "The Notes to 'Spenser's Ireland,' " *Marianne Moore Newsletter*
4, no. 2 (1980): 2–9. Willis traces forty of the poem's sixty-seven lines to Moore's cited
works. See also Cristanne Miller, *Marianne Moore: Questions of Authority* (Cambridge,
MA: Harvard University Press, 1995), 156–59.

   4. See Donald Hall, "Interview with Marianne Moore by Donald Hall," in *Poets at Work,*
ed. George Plimpton (New York: Penguin, 1989), 87.

   5. See *CollP* 262, for Moore's famous prefatory "A Note on the Notes": "But since . . .

in anything I have written, there have been lines in which the chief interest is borrowed, and I have not yet been able to outgrow this hybrid method of composition, acknowledgements seem only honest." A contemporary, Randall Jarrell, captures the effect: "But the most extreme precision leads inevitably to quotation; and quotation is armor and ambiguity and irony all at once—turtles are great quoters. Miss Moore leaves the stones she picks up carefully uncut, but places them in an unimaginably complicated and difficult setting, to sparkle under the Northern Lights of her continual irony." See Randall Jarrell, "Her Shield" in *Marianne Moore: A Collection of Critical Essays,* ed. Charles Tomlinson (Englewood Cliffs, NJ: Prentice-Hall, 1969), 120.

6. See Maria Edgeworth, *Castle Rackrent,* ed. George Watson (New York: Oxford University Press, 1964) and Maria and Richard Lovell Edgeworth, *Essay on Irish Bulls* (Philadelphia: William Duane, 1803).

7. Almost all of Moore's critics have explored some aspect of her citational strategies. In *Quotation and Modern American Poetry,* Gregory writes that while Moore's quotational poetics, like those of T. S. Eliot and William Carlos Williams, revalues the secondariness associated with their status as American modernists, it does so most markedly in terms of gender and analogously to hierarchies of all kinds (130). Miller's analysis of Moore's gendered interpretation of "authority" in *Questions of Authority* resonates with my sense of Moore's idiosyncrasy and Edgeworth's poetics of "anecdote." Miller anatomizes how Moore combines intricate formalism, erudite allusion, and sententiousness with "culturally 'feminine' aspects of language use" more commonly associated with inconsequential orality in "a feminist metapoetics of appreciative and non-hierarchical exchange." Miller identifies Moore's "culturally 'feminine' aspects of language use" as "substitution of multivocality for an authoritative voice; inclusion of trivial, apparently irrelevant, information; excessive detail and excessive restraint; overemphasis on the mundane through marked quotations from the private sphere; and a didactic tone without accompanying transparent clarity" (192). Costello's study of Moore's "rhetoric of reticence" and "gusto" in *Imaginary Possessions* also informs my interpretation. In "'For inferior who is free?': Liberating the Woman Writer in Marianne Moore's 'Marriage,'" in *Influence and Intertextuality in Literary History,* ed. Jay Clayton and Eric Rothstein (Madison: University of Wisconsin Press, 1991), 219–44, Lynn Keller argues that Moore plays off the nonhierarchical nature of intertextuality against a patrilineal model of influence in her masterpiece "Marriage." Keller's reading resonates with Robert Young's observation in *Colonial Desire: Hybridity,* in *Theory, Culture and Race* (New York: Routledge, 1995) that hybridity, including Anglo-Celtic hybridity, always carries an implicit politics of heterosexuality (25). In "Marianne Moore, Immigration, and Eugenics" (*Modernism/Modernity* 1, no. 2 [April 1994]: 21–49), David Kadlec argues that Moore's post-Darwinian pragmatist understanding of "the instability of generational transmission" has ethical and metapoetic repercussions, and informs both her opposition to essentialist eugenics and restrictive immigration policies and the contingency of her isosyllabic stanzaic forms.

8. See Mary Craig Shoemaker, *Five Typical Scotch-Irish Families of the Cumberland Valley* (1922), *RML.* According to Evelyn Feldman of the Rosenbach Museum and Library (*RML*), the book was begun in the 1890s and published in 1922 (publisher not cited). I am grateful to Feldman for her help with the Moore family history. See my *Haunted English* for more on Moore's "purely Celtic" ethnicity and on how Scotch-Irish ethnogenesis elucidates the "junior partner" role of the Celt in British imperialism.

9. For the Moore family correspondence covering the year 1915, see folder V:21:13, *RML.* In that year, Warner Moore announced his engagement to a woman named Mary White. Mary Warner Moore did not approve of the match and disparaged it in racial terms. In a letter dated December 22, 1915, Mary Warner Moore wrote to her son of Mary White: "Should she ever marry into my 'race,' God would help me to love her and count her as al-

together mine; but such things God alone can accomplish. . . . May God indeed make you 'worthy' of Mary; [but oh! God! I pray thee let her never have him—let her never come near to having him.] (That prayer must needs write itself down)." She added a postscript to say that Marianne felt the letter would cause him displeasure. Warner (whose family nickname was "Badger"), responded in a letter dated December 23, 1915 by assuring his mother that he knew both his mother and he to be of "the same 'race'" (a word that he, like his mother, placed in quotation marks). In a letter to his mother dated July 9, 1916, Warner announced that he had ended the relationship with Mary White and that he, Marianne, and Mary Warner would move "as 3 in 1" to "Badger Hollow" (his future manse), adding "we are not of a race to flinch" at the sacrifice involved (folder VI:22:08, *RML*). The crisis over Mary White (whose "race" I have been unable to ascertain) coincided with the breakthrough visit to Manhattan that Marianne labeled her "sojourn in the whale" in ecstatic letters to Warner.

10. In drafts of "Spenser's Ireland," Moore doodles with a hyphenated "I'm Ire-ish," a play on the Elizabethan pun "land of Ire" and Shakespeare's "What ish my nation?" to accent the *I wish / Ire-ish* rhyme. See folder I:04:21, *RML*.

11. Warner Moore to Marianne Moore, 1 May 1920, folder V:23:19, *RML*.

12. Edmund Spenser, *A View of the Present State of Ireland,* ed. W. L. Renwick (London: Eric Partridge, 1934), 197.

13. On the reception of bulls from *Teagueland Jests* (1680) to recently, see Brian Earls, "Bulls, Blunders, and Bloothers. An Examination of the Irish Bull," *Béaloideas* 56 (1988): 1–92.

14. A good example of translational catachresis arises from the Gaelic *marbhadh* (to kill but also to hurt or wound), which is responsible for many bulls about Irish who are kilt and murdherred but who survive to tell the tale. From an Anglocentric point of view, such bulls are crazy hyperbole; from a Gaelocentric point of view, they contain information about degree of injury, because as *Castle Rackrent*'s editor, George Watson, notes, to be "kilt all over with rheumatism" is to be in a far worse state than to be merely "kilt with the cold." See his footnote to the comic scene when "lady Rackrent was all kilt and smashed": " 'She'll never ride no more on her jaunting car, (said Judy) for it has been the death of her sure enough.'—'And is she dead then?' says his honor.—'As good as dead, I hear'" (Edgeworth, *Rackrent,* 85).

15. Edgeworth and Edgeworth, *Bulls,* 164.

16. The Edgeworths cite Swift, "On Barbarous Denominations in Ireland" (1740). See Edgeworth and Edgeworth, *Bulls,* 14.

17. See Edgeworth and Edgeworth, *Bulls,* 185–224.

18. See "England," *CPo* 46, and *CPr* 435. Moore adds, "Robert Bridges insisted that words be in keeping—or, we might say, deliberately out of keeping" (435). The quality is close to Gilles Deleuze's concept of disjunctive synthesis, which he connects with nomadism, in *The Logic of Sense* (New York: Columbia University Press, 1990), 46.

19. In Moore's writing, exceptions tend to retroactively qualify the rule, e.g., "Voltaire objected to those who said in enigmas what others had said naturally, and we agree; yet we must have the courage of our peculiarities" (*CPr* 398). The contorted syntax of "we cannot say we are not enchanted with disenchantment in *The Plough and the Stars*" (*CPr* 197), as though Moore labors under extraordinary censorship when she is invoking the *Dial*'s royal "we" to make a positive assertion, attests to a deeply ingrained adversarial style. The tendency to make positive assertions through negation is a significant cause of Irish bulls. The tendency derives in part from the patterns of paraphrastic affirmations and denials in Irish bulls, which can be traced to the residual influence of the wide semantic range of the Gaelic for "but" *(ach)* and the absence in Gaelic of words for "yes" and "no." It seems a stretch to relate Moore's grammar of "hindrance" to such remote Gaelic contact, but the profusion of

negative compounds in "Spenser's Ireland"—"dissatisfied," "discommodity," "invisible," "disappeared," "disuse," "unlearning obduracy," "'I'll never give in,'" "native genius for disunion"—makes it clear that Moore associates her ethnic homeland with a rhetoric of Dissent. Elizabeth Bishop speculates that "the use of double or triple negatives, the lighter and wittier ironies" stemmed from her mother's "conversational style." See her "Efforts of Affection: A Memoir of Marianne Moore," in *The Collected Prose of Elizaebeth Bishop*, ed. Rober Giroux (New York: Farrar, Straus and Giroux, 1984), 129.

20. On what later became known as "Hansen's law," see Werner Sollors, *Beyond Ethnicity: Consent and Descent in American Culture* (New York: Oxford University Press, 1986), 215.

21. Edgeworth and Edgeworth, *Bulls*, 166, 164.

22. Edgeworth, *Castle Rackrent*, 3.

23. Ibid., 7.

24. Ibid., 8.

25. Spenser, *A View*, 66, 77.

26. Ibid., 66.

27. James Boswell citing Samuel Johnson. See James Boswell, *The Life of Samuel Johnson*, 3rd ed. (London: C. Dilly, 1799), 4:105.

28. Spenser, *A View*, 88–89.

29. To summarize Edgeworth's scene, Colambre and some newly quartered English militia visit patriotic antiquarian, Count O'Halloran, and Colambre distinguishes himself to his host by catching an allusion to Herodotus's account of the Scythians' cryptic gift of a mouse, a frog, a bird, and five arrows as a warning to the invading Persians. O'Halloran gives the English militia the angling-flies they admire (with the Swiftian barb that they are of Irish manufacture), and Colambre, by then dissociated from the militia, receives the funerary urn that eventually proves his beloved's honorable birth. See W. J. MacCormack and Kim Walker's introduction to Maria Edgeworth's *The Absentee*, ed. W. J. MacCormack and Kim Walker (New York: Oxford University Press, 1988), especially xix–xxi on the Scythian allusions.

30. See Herodotus, *The History*, ed. David Grene (Chicago: University of Chicago Press, 1987), 4:46; and Francois Hartog, *The Mirror of Herodotus: The Representation of the Other in the Writing of History*, trans. Janet Lloyd (Berkeley: University of California Press, 1988), 202.

31. See Peter Stallybrass and Ann Rosalind Jones, "Dismantling Irena: The Sexualizing of Ireland in Early Modern England," in *Nationalisms and Sexualities*, ed. Andrew Parker et al. (New York: Routledge, 1992), 161–64.

32. The epigraph to Moore's inaptly titled *Complete Poems*, "omissions are not accidents," is fitting for her work. Moore's mantled poetics engages Gayatri Spivak's question, "Can the subaltern speak?" (1988). Spivak's argument in *A Critique of Postcolonial Reason: Toward a Vanishing Present* (Cambridge, MA: Harvard University Press, 1999) that "[Coetzee's Friday] is the arbitrary name of the withheld limit" (193) applies to Moore's deployment of the triple-deckered citation of "Venus mantle."

33. See Donn Byrne, "The Rock Whence I Was Hewn," *National Geographic Magazine*, March 1927, 257–316.

34. The opening and closing sentences ("Spenser's Ireland," lines 1–4; 65–67), the only ones without annotated sources, provide an autobiographical frame that makes any ultimate separation of speaker and poet difficult. Ireland *is* "the greenest place I've never seen" for Moore, who first visited Ireland in 1964, when she was in her late seventies, and draft marginalia indicate that she *is* troubled, dissatisfied, and Irish. These lines envelope Donn Byrne's discussion of Gaelic-derived vernacularisms and interactive styles in the *National Geographic* photo-essay ("Spenser's Ireland," lines 5–8; 63–65); the citation of Edge-

worth's mantle-footnote ("Spenser's Ireland," lines 9–12; 61–63); and Geraldine lore ("Spenser's Ireland," lines 13–20; 57–61).

35. Spenser, *A View*, 83–84.

36. The coupling of the two texts in a manner that respects their contrastive modes of transmission creates the kind of hybridity Homi Bhabha defines in *The Location of Culture* (London: Routledge, 1994) as one "that reverses the effects of colonialist disavowal, so that other 'denied' knowledges enter upon the dominant discourse and estrange the basis of its authority" (114).

37. On the lore, see Dáithí Ó'hÓgáin, *"An é an t-am fós é?,"* *Béaloideas* 42–44 (1974–76): 213–308. Gerald's grandson, Thomas, the eighth earl, ruled Munster like a Gaelic king, and Spenser blames the Norman-Irish alliance on the "huge wronge" of his execution in 1468 (Spenser, *A View*, 85). Ó'hÓgáin dates the dissemination of Geraldine lore to the traumatic aftermath of the eighth earl's death, when the oral tradition merged the folk-motif of an enchanted hero who awaits an opportune moment to deliver his people from bondage with shape-shifting lore about the third earl, Gearóid Iarla, who was famed as a magician. In the fifteenth and sixteenth centuries, the typological lore had the political prestige of "history" and foundational myth, as demonstrated by the first earl's planting of the legend of Gerald's birth and the fourteenth earl's citation of the myth by donning the outlawed mantle. After the 1585 Act of Oblivion, which provided for the surcease of suits concerning anything occurring before 1583, the myth receded into the fugitive genres of clandestine coded allusions, rumor, and messianic typology. The constant elements in the lore are revealing: the naming of a native or assimilated Irish chief, the embedding of that name in a known locale, and the emphasis on the untimeliness of the reigning political order evinced by the question posed to or by the earl on his rare sightings: *"An é an t-am fós é?"* ("Is it the time yet?").

38. Conversation with Máire Mhac an tSaoi. The first earl evidently encouraged this tradition because a poem by the family bard, Gofraidh Fionn O'Dálaigh, names him "the son of Áine's knight" (*"a mheic marcaigh fionnÁine"*) when Gerald was a child.

39. As Patricia Willis suggests (see "The Notes to 'Spenser's Ireland,'" 8), the undocumented lecture is probably based on a Kildare variant of the lore that Colum published in *The Big Tree of Bunlahy: Stories of My Countryside* (New York: Macmillan, 1933), 101–15. Gearóid Iarla's fame as a poet and magician was such that Moore was probably made aware of the Munster connection. She may not have known Gearóid Iarla's poetry, since it wasn't widely disseminated, and she also may not have known the lore about his birth, though Colum's story features the maternal taboo. For the 1798 allusion see Colum, *The Big Tree*, 112; Colum adds that Earl Gerald was asked, "Has the time come?" and he replied, "Not yet, not yet!"

40. Colum, *The Big Tree*, 108–9.

41. *Funk and Wagnalls Standard Dictionary of Folklore, Mythology and Legend* (1949), s.v. "Folklore" (by Stith Thompson).

42. Byrne, "The Rock Whence," 314.

43. An unpublished draft version of "Spenser's Ireland" riffs, "so kind to everyone else / to itself so inhumanely blind." On the exogamy theme, Moore likens Ireland in the marginalia to a "[distrustful] hedgehog," adding darkly: "I used to hear them say / Blood is thicker than water / It is but not in just the way in which they meant." See folder 1:04:21, *RML*. In "The Paper Nautilus," restraining and constrained mothering is associated with productive hindrance: "her glass ram'shorn-cradled freight / . . . / was hindered to succeed, / the intensively / watched eggs coming from / the shell free it when they are freed" (*CPo* 121). On Moore's unusually close relationship with her mother, whom Linda Leavell justly characterizes as her "censor and muse," see Leavell, *Marianne Moore and the Visual Arts: Prismatic Color* (Baton Rouge: Louisiana State University Press, 1995), 40.

44. Colum, *The Big Tree,* 109.

45. See "Spenser's Ireland," lines 45–50, 52, 51–52, 31–32 and Byrne, "The Rock Whence," 264, 279, 372, 314.

46. See Moore, "Critics and Connoisseurs" (*CPo* 38); Susan Sontag's "Notes on Camp" (1964), reprinted in Cleto, *Camp,* 57–58; and lines 40, 43–45 of "Spenser's Ireland."

47. Edgeworth and Edgeworth, *Bulls,* 203.

48. Ibid., 217–18.

Poems by Jeredith Merrin

Bat Ode

Downtown Columbus, Ohio, rush hour

Dead, of course, but with soft,
egg-sized black body and
scalloped, coal-satin wings—
so pretty, it was hard

not to be happy to
have the rare city sight
of it. Hyper-real
(the way death always is),

and mildly exotic;
a sidewalk frisson, break-
ing middle-aged boredom.
(Everyone, everyone

becomes predictable—
especially the young
rebels, so timidly
indistinguishable,

and the "mature" beige ones:
alike in their terror
of appearing foolish
at all costs, at great cost,

inestimable cost.)
The bat was new, intact.
Heart flutter suddenly
stopped, dropped to the pavement.

O Delicately Veined,
Neat Eared, Night Wandering.
Neither epiphanic
lark, nightingale, nor rook.

—Published in *Bat Ode,* University of Chicago Press, 2001 (appeared in *Slate* online magazine).

Parasailing in Cancún

—December 2000

Why go up? Why not?
When the breeze on the beach
agrees with the heat of your skin,

you can welcome a shock.
Other senses mild, muted,
dozy and dim, what's vivid

in this place is sight:
cobalt sea, bleached sand,
quartzy green surf,

and damned if it's not
a Harte Crane-azure sky!
Might as well take a look

—an hour or so after lunch?—
from a steep, staged angle.
The speedboat picks up,

the particolored chute blooms
above circling brown pelicans
taking turns crashing

into surf, wings akimbo:
raffish fishers, disproving
the modernist notion

that the most elegant
form follows function.
Now the dried-frond *palapas*

are specks underneath which
—just two days from home
and serious weather—

turistas no longer
remember whether
it's Thursday or Wednesday

as they drink flat *cerveza.*
And now the chunky hotels,
in tight single file

for miles to the south,
reveal themselves as
exotic play pieces

—mango, pineapple, lime—
in a limited-edition
set of Monopoly.

Then—in hard, solid
sunlight—all of a sudden
the Yucatán's gone.

It's anywhere, nowhere;
you're weightless and still,
at dreamy alert,

tethered and free . . .
ten minutes in warm wind,
above a groomed world

where at dawn the surf-wrack
is raked up into bags
and no bug-life is seen.

Now the boat slows,
the Mexican beach boy
waves at the winch

and cranks the rope in:
back to the *Zona Hotelera*
and real, unreal Cancún!

If places have rhymes,
as they sometimes do,
this one rhymes "well" and "ill":

here where, unthinking,
you drink the water as ice
in one *margarita* too many,

hand over too many
half-guilty *propinas;*
where coconut palms,

cartoon resort props,
grow with chemical streaks
and chrome-yellow fruit;

where, on the mainland,
children playing in dirt yards
are skinny and sickly;

where your chairs are good wicker,
your wide window frames
a "Mayan," cement pyramid

against unpainted waves
as hidden speakers waft in
the same songs each day,

and, from a ceiling vent,
none-too-clean water,
in steady drops, slants

across the limestone-tiled
and *centavo*-bright
wall of your room.

—Published in *Poetry International,* as part of an essay entitled *And Damned If It's Not A Harte Crane-Azure Sky!,* Issue 6 (2002), 168–70.

Poems by Joanie Mackowski

View from the Bluff

This view's too big to see. Far below,
the scrap of beach looks like a pillow,

the breakers an uneven white fringe
on a blue bedspread, topped with an orange

bell buoy, and also see a schooner
there, gliding from the outer seas to inner,

its sail set on the ripples like a tooth.
And all rimmed by the Cascades, made smooth

by distance: watching the ducks fly Vs,
the shifting hackles of the waves,

and feeling one's idiosyncracies dissolve,
those inconvenient edges growing soft

as that band of cirrus stretching over
the San Juans. And a great blue heron

unfolds from beneath a briar, awkwardness
part of its gracefulness; it flaps away

and dwindles to a dot against the mountains,
becomes the period to close the sentence

of its own complex-compound loveliness.
Wouldn't it be nice to fly off into the distance,

to shed the body's tinsel and disappear
while a speedboat pulls open a long wake like a zipper

on the water, and then the waves zip it up
again? To blend, each ear an eddy,

each thought some floating clumps
of kelp, and the eyes a million glances

of sunlight refracting irregular argyle
patterns across the waves, while a gull

catches a fish: to be immense and miniscule. The breakers
roll themselves up between my fingers

like cigarettes, knock swirls of agitation
from swirls of calm, while the mountains jut

from the horizon like torn newspaper, their jagged
peaks crumpled against the sound as if someone could

set it aflame, kindle its deep blue cool
and white-tipped lizard skin, checkered

with light and seaweed. Peace is oceanic,
vulnerable, oddly giddy, and not

easily distinguished from chaos, but seven islands crouch in a terrible
green secret, arranged over the water

like rocks on a picnic table to anchor the tablecloth,
to keep it from blowing away and toppling

the paper platefuls and cans of beer
(as the earth and its irregular perfections

are pressed in the swirling palms of our hands,
the means absentmindedly fondled by the ends);

all kinds of truth are anchored by these islands.

Wild

The egret stands still as a glass of milk
by the lagoon, beneath a saw palmetto.
The lagoon shimmers with a school of mackerel,
and then a hand lifts up to close the blinds,
a chorus line of slender bands of metal.
The things we see rarely conform to plans.

Now a paw of sunlight edges through a crack
in the blinds and expands across the wall.
It prowls among the corners, grazes the crackers
on the table, uncurls toward the sofa,
where we sit. And once this lucid animal
devours us, it glides off, satisfied.

Zeros, veers,

one iridescent glimpse,
unsteady on my stalk and one hand clumsily

untying a snarl of twine—the vanishing point comes
to get me, swerves from a clump of camellias

and tiger lilies: green-crowned, ruby-throated
hummingbird. How odd to be threatened

by such imperious diminutiveness, its wings translucent,
orders of sky and foliage unloosening

from either side of it, the guttural
buzz of its flight throbbing my ear. I'm on a ladder,

its feeder in one hand, the other feeling for the eye
among papery handfuls of wasp nest barely

within reach, syrup (one part sugar to four
parts water), running down my arm. *Fear*

not, for thou art blessed among—must
have been something like this, almost

knocked to the ground by grace itself, the edge
of grace, its beak within an inch

of grazing my hand outstretched, groping—
what ungainly dread creeps in

under such wings, under the eaves
and swooped at by love's

razor glinting in the sunlight?

—Published in *The Zoo,* University of Pittsburgh Press, 2002.

El Greco's Daughter:
Necessary Deflection in Marianne Moore's "For February 14th" and "Saint Valentine"

Elizabeth Wilson

> To write is to make oneself the echo of what cannot cease speaking—
> and since it cannot, in order to become its echo I have, in a way, to
> silence it. I bring to this incessant speech the decisiveness, the
> authority of my own silence.
> —Maurice Blanchot, "The Essential Solitude"

R.P. BLACKMUR FAMOUSLY COMMENTS THAT MARIANNE MOORE WAS BORN CHASTE:

> there is no sex anywhere in [Moore's] poetry. No poet has been so chaste; but it
> is not the chastity that rises from an awareness—healthy or morbid—of the
> flesh, it is a special chastity aside from the flesh—a purity by birth and from the
> void.[1]

Blackmur construes Moore as inhabiting an original chastity whose stasis precludes the exigencies of knowledge of self or the world, implying that Moore's decision to remain detached from sexual or marital commitments was the concomitant of an innate state of being, a given disengaged from the problematics of the flesh. Moore did assert chastity as a condition of existence, but to assume such a choice is the automatic consequence of an innate condition of being is to reduce and demean the intellectual processes of a strong and successful writer, intent on establishing herself as a literary force alongside her male counterparts, most notably Pound and Eliot, Stevens and Williams. Moore's career path entailed pragmatic decisions to remain detached, not from knowledge of the world or of pleasure or desire, which her writing always demonstrates, but from the constraints of commitments beyond those of friends and family.

Moore's decision, not uncommon for her time, to remain as companion to her mother, finds resonance in Williams's assertion that Moore was "a rafter" of support, and "our saint."[2] Moore, however, conversely protested,

192

"I never was a rafter holding up anyone."[3] That same resistant tone is heard in "Efforts of Affection": "You know I'm not a saint!" (*CPo* 147). Appearances to the contrary, Moore insists that neither support of others nor saintliness were conditions she chose to ascribe to herself. Resistance to conventional perceptions of Moore as "asexual spinster" is indeed always best found in Moore's own work.

Two poems, "For February 14th" and "Saint Valentine," suggest that throughout her career Moore, contrary to Blackmur's contention that hers was "not the chastity that arises from awareness," continued to question and debate the issue of relationships, and the choices she herself had made. These poems, published in 1959 and 1960 respectively, postdate the death of Moore's mother in 1947 and fall decidedly in the period considered "late" and often thought by critics to lack the stringency of her earlier work.[4] In 1960 Moore was seventy-three. Nevertheless, "For February 14th" and "Saint Valentine," tied as they are to Valentine's Day, highlight issues of sexual and "marital" involvement that remained relevant to Moore's status as a professional woman committed to being companion to her mother and to a career in writing, the success of which sexual or marital relations may well have compromised. Both poems present a tonally complex layering of thought, each layer having the capacity to dominate and at times mask other positions within the poem.

Mary Warner Moore referred to her daughter's first volume, *Poems,* as a "veiled Mohammedan woman," implying that Moore's texts withheld as much as they disclosed (*SL* 172). By 1972, however, Moore's papers had been sold to the Rosenbach Museum and Library, Philadelphia where they were lodged after Moore's death in 1972.[5] Access to archival material complicates the public/private binary of an author's writing, and in Moore's case makes claims for an unbreachable private coding less persuasive. Moore's archive, which includes her "Conversation Notebooks," establishes what Roland Barthes deems the "circular memory" of the intertext, which regards Janus-like both the discursive habits of the Moore household and the verse itself.[6]

Moore's "Conversation Notebooks" particularly pinpoint the dynamics of conversation in Moore's life. They show Moore systematically transcribing conversations between herself, her mother, and others. Moore often puts her own voice in parentheses as she records comments attributable to "Mole," Mary Warner Moore, so that the "Conversation Notebooks" establish shifting voices set in counterpoint. Mary Warner's comments are wry, witty, and epigrammatic, and, if tone is to be trusted, acerbic, cutting: "Nobody else's child should ever be named for you."[7] Recording the comments of others is itself a form of response, and Moore's "Conversation Notebooks" suggest a place of silent yet decisive engagement with her mother's opinions, echoing and so controlling the voice of the conversational other. The "Notebooks" enact narratives of family and self, in a conversational pattern of assertion and counterassertion where writing functions as consolatory riposte to what might otherwise be unanswerable: "I would disapprove of you more [thoroughly] than of any person in [the] world if you were not my child."[8]

Moore used her "Conversation Notebooks" extensively as a source of material. Her poems reshape the sharp comments of which Mary Warner Moore was more than capable. The brusque moniker that Mary Warner gives to Marianne, "come on snipe legs," for example, echoes the "snipe-legged hieroglyph" of "When I Buy Pictures" (*CPo* 48).[9] The tag, reclaimed, is turned to different ends. Instead of the "fond" jibe, conflation with "hieroglyph" constructs an image of aesthetic pleasure linked, through Mary Warner's nickname for her daughter, to a sense of self reconfigured as complex, hieroglyphic.[10]

Two other well-known instances of Moore's use of the "Conversation Notebooks" show assertions by Mary Warner Moore contradicted in the poem into which Moore collages the comments. In "A Grave" (*CPo* 49) Moore uses Mary Warner's statement about a "man in the aisle" that "it is human nature to stand in the middle of a thing."[11] The image of the sea that follows sustains the poem's overt line of thought, yet also operates as riposte: "but you cannot stand in the middle of this." Mary Warner's remarks denigrating poetry, "there are things important beyond all this fiddle" and "a perfect contempt for it," migrate to "Poetry" (*CPo* 266–67).[12] The poem's opening response to the conversational other, whose comments by inference initiate the poem's speaking, is ostensibly one of agreement: "I, too, dislike it." The speaker, however, soon turns seeming agreement into the first feint in a process of rebuttal. "Poetry" interrogates the genre's value. It also asserts Moore's commitment to her particular kind of writing in the face of her mother's often voiced disapproval. Robin Schulze notes Mary Warner's "harsh words" in relation to Moore's poetic output: "Moore . . . copied them into her conversation diary next to other comments that reflected the extent of Mary Warner's consistent critique of Moore's early verse" (*BMM* 21n). While "Poetry" remains a statement of poetics it is also biographically specific, tied to Mary Warner's struggle to comprehend the kind of poet her daughter repeatedly demonstrated herself to be. In "Poetry" polite agreement, couched conversationally, marks a moment of dissembling which initiates rebuttal of the conversational other. This is conversation's disputatious underbelly, which the parings-down of "Poetry" (*CPo* 36) demonstrate, each version of the poem moving closer to the crux of the matter: response at its most crystalline refutes and silences.

Moore's poems, then, read in alignment with the "Conversation Notebooks," retain their links through collage with family scenarios which the

"Notebooks" map. Whatever else they articulate, Moore's poems, marked as sites of contestation and resistance, offer Moore a means of responding to a strong, opinionated companion whose authoritative voice, though valued, is also at times contentious. Moore's conversational poems are often spoken with all the lightness of tone and shifts of tack long acquaintance might summon. They also, "silently" and without destabilizing the dynamics of family relationships, "answer back."[13]

Access to Moore's archive, then, makes visible otherwise indiscernible patterns within her poetic practice and establishes her poems, as does Moore's annotative practice generally, as palimpsests which always contest a text's disengagement from context and the biographical. Furthermore, though family might be construed, or construe themselves, as first (ideal) readers, initiates closely conversant with the text's secrets, "one must also consider the possibility of an active reader who decides to read a text univocally."[14] Despite Mary Warner's assertion of her daughter's "veiled" intent, it is not impossible to imagine that Mary Warner herself might have been less than fully conversant with Moore's layered poems. Indeed, Moore's writing always addresses itself, in publication and by means of her omnibus archive, to a readership beyond the family circle under whose "harsh" eye a veiling of the "already veiled," an unperceived hieroglyphic complexity, might be *sine qua non.*[15]

The "Conversation Notebooks," then, firstly enact an interplay of voices operating conversationally. Secondly, they establish a reclamatory dynamic between poems and "Notebooks." Thirdly, they provide a model for poems that demonstrate a rhetorical pattern of assertion and response, or of assertion and counterassertion, whose tonal complexities echo conversational shifts of voice. Both "For February 14th" and "Saint Valentine" demonstrate this form, where shifting "voices" argue in counterpoint through debate and contestation. Even after her mother's death, Moore continued to use as rhetorical strategy a pattern of argument between tonally distinct voices where one position within a poem is seen finally to refute and silence another.

"For February 14th" is both conversation piece and occasional poem, the title invoking Valentine's Day as "the poem's cause," as did its publication in the *New York Herald Tribune* on 13 February 1959.[16] That Moore frames her text as Valentine's Day verse might also be thought to support the contention that her late work became increasingly populist. However, while the occasion is demotic, the poem written for Valentine's Day is firstly a gift that might be given. The status of the gift, seen by Cristanne Miller as emblematic of a culture of exchange, engaged Moore's attention throughout her career, and questions about gifts for Valentine's Day dominate "For February 14th."[17]

For February 14th

Saint Valentine,
although late, would "some interested law
impelled to plod in the poem's cause"
        be permitted a line?

Might you have liked a stone
from a De Beers Consolidated Mine?
or badger-neat saber-thronged thistle
        of Palestine—the leaves alone

        down'd underneath,
worth a touch? Or that mimosa-leafed vine
called an "alexander's armillary
        sphere" fanning out in a wreath?

Or did the ark
preserve paradise-birds with jet-black plumes,
whose descendants might serve as presents?
        But questioning is the mark

of a pest! Why think
only of animals in connection
with the ark or the wine Noah drank?
        but that the ark did not sink.

                                                (*CPo* 198)

The speaker asks herself if, for Valentine's Day, she might have liked a De Beers stone, a diamond. Such a gift suggests the conventional gesture of commitment to marriage. Diamonds, however, were not Moore's favored gems. Introducing a reading of the poem "Voracities and Verities Sometimes Are Interacting" (*CPo* 148) Moore spoke of the line, "I don't like diamonds; / the emerald's 'grass-lamp glow' is better," in a self-deprecating way: "sour grapes I'm afraid when I say I don't like diamonds."[18] Yet the question's syntax, the (counterfactual) conditional of "might you have liked" asserts the poem's presentness as it opens up an irrevocable past to ongoing debate.

"For February 14th" proposes three if not four gifts in quick succession, though none as present possibility: the De Beers diamond, a thistle of Palestine, a mimosa-leafed vine, and perhaps a vignetted armillary sphere. Each gift is a worthy conversation piece, yet inference complicates the items, their viability, and any possible response to the governing, "Might you have liked . . ." One might, given the day, desire the diamond for what it signifies, or desire it for its monetary value. One might decline it, if consideration were given to the circumstances of its production. Minimum wages and cavity searches mark the conditions of labor for De Beers diamond miners. Saying no becomes morally and politically appropriate, yet the desire to say yes remains always lodged as potential in the question itself.

Such associations "in connection / with" these hypothesized gifts differentiate them and implicate the reader in this game of gifts and the conundrum of choosing. Moore's thistle of Palestine might be *Carduus Benedictus,* the blessed thistle, considered an antidote to the bite of venomous creatures, though *Rhamnus Palaestina* is also a contender. From the genus Rhamnac came the crown of thorns, that same species found in the "neglected vineyard of the sluggard."[19] Etymological teasing offers tempting explications of vine and armillary sphere, though "Even gifted scholars lose their way / through faulty etymology" (*CPo* 151). The "down'd" undersides of leaves "worth a touch" suggest, with self-aware wit, sensate delight set in a play between touch and withdrawal against *Mimosa Pudica,* which, in a "mimicry of conscious life shown by the Sensitive Plant" shrinks from touch, its pudicity a by-word for delicacy, chastity.[20]

The jet-black plumes of the paradise bird similarly tempt. What hat might not willingly flaunt such finery? Yet given her familiarity with seventeenth-century writers such as George Herbert and Francis Bacon, Moore's use of the paradise bird as figure calls adornment ironically to task. The seventeenth century conventionally saw *Paradiseidae* as signifying the desire for heavenly rather than earthly glory. Loaded onto the ark to be brought from cataclysm to decoration, *Paradiseidae* carry their own etymological baggage, making of hats and heaven a troubling conjunction.[21] The debated gifts delineate Moore's engagement with typological nuances and with the problematics of possession and collection: her aesthetic delight in fashion and adornment as with the things that the earth offers, its plants and precious stones, the pelts and feathers of its creatures, which function in Moore's writing to reinscribe the glory of the creation, its pleroma.

The poem's momentum, however, is curtailed. The act of questioning is itself called to account in a tonal shift that suggests the protocols of polite conversation may have been breached: "But questioning is the mark // of a pest!" This summary assertion of impropriety shifts the text's trajectory and the intellectual activity whose logic in debating the gifts has brought the speaker to the conundrum of the paradise-birds. If there is thought to be had, it should be of this order: "that the ark did not sink."

Silencing the questioning tone, the poem ends with an acknowledgment of the precision and care of "right making" as its first and final rule, over and above all other considerations, including the gift of a diamond on Valentine's Day.

Right making, constructing the ark in obedience to God's mandate so that it does not founder, returns us to our inheritance, the ground of our being, the plenitudinous world of things offered as a sign of God's grace. Here the artificer's sense of the value of a thing's construction, poetry included, argues an overarching commitment to craft and vocation. Right making, the ark built intentionally to precise specifications,[22] and right thinking, asserted by the interjection, intersect. The ark or the poem itself safely afloat remain always nothing short of miraculous.

As trope the ark carries consolatory force, and again Moore's commitment to seventeenth-century writers aligns her use of the ark figure with typology familiar to them. The seventeenth-century divine, Thomas Adams, expounded: "This miraculous preservation . . . serves for the Instruction and consolation of the militant Church unto the world's end."[23] Hooker writes: "Now the priuilege of the visible Church of God . . . is to bee herein like the Arke of Noah, that, for anything we know to the contrarie, all without it are lost sheepe."[24] Here is the rock-solid, bone-dry directive toward which "For February 14th" moves. Abrupt deflection from the series of questions followed by the final assertion with its end-stopped silence offers a sense of *fiat* which is that of *terminus ad quem*. If "For February 14th" itself functions as gift, then the heart of that giving is coming to an understanding by which one might, in the world, stay afloat. Thus the poet reasserts her stable ground, her commitment to the vocational nature of her writing, and its consolatory force. The poem becomes a vessel of grace, affirming that consolation which is salvation, and offering a means whereby, within the context of right thinking, creativity is ensured: a poetics of grace. Both Moore's mother and her brother would have affirmed this trajectory which the countervoice establishes against the questioning tone. The poem as object of exchange, then, remains a "sweet Valentine," but one directed now with singular focus at the miracle of the unsinkable ark, and hence at God; a familiar trope, lover to beloved, both ways round. As blandishment offered to the other and as figure for a life also construed as offered, in chastity and service, the "poem's cause" is still, after all, love.[25]

Yet the calm of this carefully constructed thought-through text, which finds its rationale and resolution in the articulation of poetry as a thing in which grace might inhere, is troubled by thought itself, the moment signalled by the sharp-toned counterassertion that "questioning is the mark of a pest," and linked to the dismissive final question,

> Why think
> only of animals in connection
> with the ark or the wine Noah drank?

(CPo 198)

Here is the unstable moment to which the speaker's questioning leads, where thought speaking firmly against itself is precipitately deflected from "animals" and "the wine Noah drank." We see the deflection, but we in turn are chastened, diverted; silenced as much by the crisp, self-critical tone as by the momentum of the conversation. The tonal shift of this sudden interjection mirrors the dynamic of the "Conversation Notebooks," and of those poems where Moore collages her mother's voice. That process is now evident as part of the dialectical movement within a single poem. If we do stop to think, however, to question beyond the critical interjection which seeks to contest, even to prevent, such questioning, what does the text establish as thought to be thought beyond?

It is a commonplace of the ark narrative that it overflows with pairing and coupling. The small gestures of desire displayed on Valentine's Day seem tame by comparison, yet generative force informs both occasions. Two kinds of making then: God's precise detailing as Architect of the vessel that will not founder, and Noah's, of the peoples of the earth. The moment of deflection to which the text leads only to turn away is what Moore termed in an earlier draft, "that matter of the wine";[26] Noah as husbandman and Noah's drunkenness, the consequence of his role as first vintner:

> Noah was the first tiller of the soil. He planted a vineyard; and he drank of the wine, and became drunk, and lay uncovered in his tent. And Ham, the father of Canaan, saw the nakedness of his father, and told his two brothers outside. Then Shem and Japheth took a garment, laid it upon both their shoulders, and walked backward and covered the nakedness of their father; their faces were turned away, and they did not see their father's nakedness. When Noah awoke from his wine and knew what his youngest son had done to him, he said, "Cursed be Canaan; a slave of slaves shall he be to his brothers."[27]

Noah's curse of Canaan completes the narrative of the jewel brought to the earth's surface by De Beers workers and strengthens the case for its rejection as gift. Biblical convention asserts that from Canaan are descended the tribes of Africa, while Noah's curse provides justification for slavery; the sins of the fathers visited upon the children for generations to come.[28] Moore contests such exegesis and so establishes the poem's other "cause"; not causal—occasional poem for Valentine's Day—but ideological. Social injustice, colonization, and slavery itself taint all the gifts, a point Miller, who sees the gifts as being "a memorial to colonization in some form," ar-

gues for, though the poem "leaves all critique of colonization, commodifi-
cation, and militarism unspoken."[29]

The critique of slavery is a constant in Moore's writing. It is evident in
"The Jerboa" in 1932:

> Africanus meant
> the conqueror sent
> from Rome. It should mean the
> untouched.

(CPo 13)

Touch is configured here as conquest rather than sensate delight. Yet Scipio, whose name became synonymous with Africa through his conquest of
it, also recalls "the continence of Scipio"—signifying the enslaved women,
spoils of conquest, whose virtue Scipio leaves intact. A parallel narrative
sees Alexander similarly configured. Despite their militaristic investments,
both figures also represent the preservation of chastity through continence.
In "The Jerboa," as in "For February 14th," to be untouched is to sustain
the condition of continence in the face of an equally forceful imperative to
be possessed. These overlapping tales of conquest and continence themselves come within the purview of Mary Warner's comments: "How ignorant the world is of that choice race," and "You ought to be ashamed to have
anyone know you had as much time as it would take to write that."[30]

"For February 14th," then, continues Moore's long-established agenda
of social and economic critique while arguing from a theological position
consistent with her mother and brother's sense of her writing as a vocational act of service. Yet conjuring Noah and his nakedness into the text
signals a volatile moment where narratives vie for attention. Only disci-
plining the text, deflection, and the endgame *fiat* of statement and silence
return the poem to its overt intent. If chastity is to be reaffirmed as "gift"
and, as vocation's concomitant, a choice well made, then Noah's nakedness is the sight from which one's eyes must necessarily be averted. The
injunction not to look upon, alien in Moore's oeuvre to her "observer's"
stance, operates here upon the poem itself. The rhetorical swerve in "For
February 14th" is the textual equivalent of averting one's eyes a moment
too late from the phallus. In that momentary aversion is both the defense
of chastity and its challenge. The "poem's cause" shifts again in a sleight
of hand gesture of silent aplomb in full view of an audience who allows its
attention to be diverted, forgetful a moment later when the poem's final
flourish claims attention.

Such deflection, however, always calls to account the thing from which
one is deflected, just as the question, "might you have liked," always raises
the possibility of unanswered desire. "For February 14th" patently debates

topics that in the Moore household were always contentious—marriage and sexuality. Moore's lightly evoked and even witty reason for disliking diamonds, "sour grapes," certainly remains at odds with the speaker in the "Conversation Notebooks": "Anyone who has enough animal passion to wish to be married is . . . capable of the . . . gross[est] crimes of which people are guilty."[31]

The most disenfranchising reading of Moore's work is that which sees her writing becoming intellectually less viable as she aged, or less able to engage in stringent debate, while to assume that sexual awareness is absent from Moore's poetry is to court profound misreadings of her poetry, including the late poems so often overlooked in favor of the earlier ones. "For February 14th," which echoes both the tonal complexities of the archive and the veiled contestations of poems which reframe Mary Warner's voice and values, demonstrates that following her mother's death, Moore revisited her life's arc, questioning its shape in order to renegotiate its certitudes.

Saint Valentine appears in another, eponymous poem linked to "For February 14th" by its invocation of a "permission to assist," though it is now the poet assisting Valentine rather that Valentine assisting the poet.

Saint Valentine,

permitted to assist you, let me see . . .
   If those remembered by you
are to think of you and not me,
   it seems to me that the memento
   or compliment you bestow
should have a name beginning with "V,"

such as Vera, El Greco's only
   daughter (though it has never been
proved that he had one), her starchy
   veil, inside chiffon; the stone in her
   ring, like her eyes; one hand on
her snow-leopard wrap, the fur widely

dotted with black. It could be a vignette—
   a replica, framed oval—
bordered by a vine or vinelet.
   Or give a mere flower, said to mean the
   love of truth or truth of
love—in other words, a violet.

> Verse—unabashedly bold—is appropriate;
>   and always it should be as neat
> as the most careful writer's "8."
>   Any valentine that is *written*
> Is as the *vendage* to the vine.
>   Might verse not best confuse itself with fate?

(CPo 233)

The debate in "Saint Valentine" also circulates around the appropriateness and function of gifts, "memento / or compliment." Only tokens beginning with "V" are considered: vignette, violet, verse. A distinction is made between object-token and written-token, while play with the letter "v" intermingles with a vintner's vocabulary: vine, vinelet, *vendage*. Moore etymologically aligns verse and writing, the "careful writer" set against verse's capacity to be—as befits a Valentine's token—"unabashedly bold." In contrast with gifts not the result of writing's "bold care," a written Valentine is the harvest, fruit of the vine, *vendage*. The poem's final shift conflates the written with the spoken: "Might verse not best confuse itself with fate?"[32] The image of the *vendage,* where wines are poured together, is sustained in the last line's "confuse," where it is proposed that "verse," the writing or turning of one poetic line into the next, might be mingled, "confused," with "fate," that which is spoken.[33]

"Saint Valentine," like "For February 14th" with its authoritative ending, asserts writing as that practice "fated" to be the focus of Moore's life. It also practices a textual sleight of hand so elegant it might be termed dissemblance. "Saint Valentine," evoking the Pauline verity of love undying,[34] plays with ideas of truth and love, or more precisely the moebic, palindromic, "love of truth or truth of love." But the love-of-truth / truth-of-love interchange is rendered problematic by a lie, a fiction Moore sustains only to undermine. The poem's first "v" gift is a "framed oval" vignetted "replica" of "Vera, El Greco's only / daughter." Moore provides further detail:

> one hand on
> her snow-leopard wrap, the fur widely
>
> dotted with black.

(CPo 233)

Vera's existence, however, is immediately threatened by the strongly voiced parenthesis, "(though it has never been / proved that he had one)," a countercomment reminiscent of Moore's habit in the "Conversation Notebooks" of placing her own voice in parentheses. The parenthesis preempts the description that follows. Vera, her name notwithstanding, is imagined; El Greco is nowhere recorded as having a daughter.[35] Assertion and counterassertion again sit side by side, contesting each other, but where a love of truth intersects with the truth of love, the speaker will not let the lie pass unremarked.

Moore's description of Vera matches El Greco's *Lady with a Fur* (1577–78, Glasgow Museum), widely held to be a portrait of Jeronima de las Cuevas, El Greco's lifelong companion and mother of his son, the woman with whom, we are told, El Greco spent his days.[36] In the painting Jeronima is anything but daughter. Thus Moore's awarding the unsubstantiated daughter of El Greco the name Vera, elides fiction and fact at the very moment that the parenthesis interjects. In foregrounding the role of daughter, Moore knowingly sublimates the "other" that is erotic love figured by Jeronima. Daughter is "confused" with lover so that the image of Vera both asserts and unsettles the filial. As daughter, Vera is neither lover nor indeed mother. El Greco's portrait records a narrative where, in his "life of the artist," there was no choosing between love's various aspects. Moore's poem must establish that verity which, in the first instance, is filial devotion, yet its dissimulation, like "For February 14th," both risks and requires scrutiny. Conversant with its own and love's complexities, the poem's self-aware voice contests itself in parenthetical countercomment, interrogating love, whose condition as gift is so often seen as relinquishment of self to other. "Saint Valentine" silently envisages in "verse" what is fated not to be spoken, the truth of love's other faces, confounding again Blackmur's myth of a self existing beyond awareness of the flesh, beyond conflict and debate. Love knowingly asserts its variant selves in Moore's work, and chastity remains a condition fraught with that knowing.

Vera, then, figures narratives of self that demonstrate an "unabashedly bold" stratagem of superimposition. The parenthetical aside which interrupts the text's dominant voice, inserts a loop in its logic and keeps open the play between statement and counterstatement with all the neatness of the "most careful writer's '8,'" constituting a "double circuit, one aspect of which is known while the other can never be," and suggesting again that Mary Warner may well have been a reader "who decides to read . . . univocally."[37] The narrative play in "Saint Valentine" distracts attention to establish that which the poet, beyond conjuring an ideal daughter, "truly" desires to be known: the complexity, in the life of the artist, of choices made, lived and, through what Schulman terms "an aesthetics of inquiry," always questioned. While interrogation within a context of gift giving may be deemed inappropriate, the "mark of a pest," a gift given without cost or consideration might equally be thought no gift at all.[38]

"Saint Valentine," like "For February 14th," reaffirms Moore's vocational commitment to her "lay" status. The poet aspires to that which she acknowledges in El Greco's work, his capacity to record without compromise the ecstatic, visionary moment. El Greco signifies the potential of the artist to achieve that ideal for which art strives:

> the rock
> crystal thing to see—the startling El Greco
> brimming with inner light—that
> covets nothing that it has let go. This then you may know
> as the hero.

(*CPo* 9)

If we are to conceive of the poetic voice as "daughter," we conceive of her here, as the "Saint Valentine" narrative directs, as El Greco's daughter.

Vera as valentine, then, figures a truth explicitly female, conjured to debate love and to conflate erotic and filial love with the love of God: "O true valeyntyne is oure lord to me."[39] So the portrait of Jeronima veils one truth as it offers at face value another. And if verse and *vendage* are to be aligned, then poetry, as both harvest and the vintage which follows, makes the poet always vintner, and writing, like the planting of vines, is a planting of the flag in otherwise unmarked ground.

> There is much ground that hath no owner; our globe can tell us of a great part of the world, that hath no name but Incognita . . . ; but a Vineyard was never without a Possessor; till Noah the true Ianus planted one, there was no newes of any.[40]

Thus the act of averting her eyes from Noah's generative force in "For February 14th" becomes aligned in "Saint Valentine" with Moore's appropriation as poet of that force, her possession of its authority. The poet, a Janus/Noah figure, looks back to the old order and forward, in knowledge, to the new, owning that which is laid down. Noah's vines encapsulated his relationship with God; Moore's texts, repeatedly interrogating the problematic of ownership and collection, of possession and possessiveness, debating both *vendage* and bitter wine, (La Fontaine's "embittered whine") do likewise.[41]

"And therefore, it is," said Bacon, "a good, shrewd Prouerb of the Spaniard; *Tell a lye, and find a Troth.*"[42] Living with family, Moore surely learnt from Bacon, "[p]enetration of Iudgment . . . what Things are to be laid open, and what to be secretted, and what to be shewed at Halfelights, and to whom, and when."[43] Indeed not family but Moore's implied reader, envisaged as having access to the animadversions of the archival altertexts, makes good Moore's claim that her verse has the capacity to be "unabashedly bold" and that "enigmas are not poetry" (*BMM* 207). Traversing coexistent readings that act as if to haunt each other, Moore's scholar/student is a doppelganger, another variety of hero, "patient / of neglect and of reproach" (*CPo* 102) who works where "the attention is enticed" (*CPr* 200), where public and private realms coalesce, and where fictions of family intersect with other compelling narratives.

Moore's two Valentine texts, construed as tokens offered ostensibly in exchange for "love undying," operate performatively to enact complex narratives of self: sustained filial devotion, vocational commitment to one's art, and, "bent over work, anxious, content, alone," the "heroics" of both.[44] The Valentine texts conjure and contest the dream of "stable ground": that geography of the mind where, "nothing is coveted that has been let go." The heroic cannot be vaunted, however, without an audience who knows, notes and considers the cost. "For February 14th" and "Saint Valentine" suggest that, for Moore, neither her brother nor her mother embodied ideal attention to her "vermin-proof and pilfer-proof" poems (*CPo* 147). Instead, the Valentine texts proffer the artist fated to find in writing her most careful consolation, offered to and embracing an ideal audience, Moore's scholar/student, toward whose existence Moore's archives, so patiently constructed, patently gesture.

NOTES

Maurice Blanchot, *The Space of Literature,* trans. Ann Smock (Lincoln: University of Nebraska Press, 1989), 27.

1. R. P. Blackmur, *Language as Gesture: Essays in Poetry* (London: George Allen & Unwin, 1954), 284.

2. William Carlos Williams, *The Autobiography of William Carlos Williams* (New York: Random House, 1957), 146.

3. Donald Hall, "The Art of Poetry: Marianne Moore: An Interview with Donald Hall," in *Marianne Moore: A Collection of Critical Essays,* ed. Charles Tomlinson (Englewood Cliffs, NJ: Prentice-Hall, 1969), 26.

4. See Jeredith Merrin, *An Enabling Humility: Marianne Moore, Elizabeth Bishop, and the Uses of Tradition* (New Brunswick, NJ: Rutgers University Press, 1990), 7.

5. I am indebted to Evelyn Feldman, Elizabeth Fuller, Greg Giuliano, and the staff of the Rosenbach Museum and Library who have supported me unstintingly during my visits.

6. Roland Barthes, *The Pleasure of the Text,* trans. Richard Miller (New York: Hill and Wang, 1999), 36.

7. Marianne Moore, conversation notebook, 1914–1921, 1250/24, folder VII:10:07, *RML,* 12.

8. Ibid., 66.

9. Ibid., 40.

10. See Victoria Bazin, "Marianne Moore, Kenneth Burke and the Poetics of Literary Labour," *Journal of American Studies* 35, no. 3 (2001): 439. Bazin discusses Moore's "masked or disguised resistance to the efficiency of a linguistic system that passively reflects the experience of the 'real' rather than disrupting it."

11. Moore, conversation notebook, 1250/24, *RML* 12.

12. Ibid., 34, 35.

13. See Grace Schulman, *Marianne Moore: The Poetry of Engagement* (Urbana: Uni-

versity of Illinois Press, 1986), 1. Schulman describes Moore's rhetorical strategies in terms of "simple conversations," "dialectical arguments," and "complex inner arguments."

14. Barthes, *The Pleasure of the Text,* 36.

15. Responding to Eliot's introduction to the *Selected Poems* (London: Faber and Faber, 1935), Moore comments: "my mother acknowledges being converted from what for years has been an aggrieved sense of the family gone astray." Eliot's response: "As for mothers, whenever I am disposed to be vainglorious, I should remind myself of a remark my mother once made to Sally Bruce Kinsolving of Baltimore. 'Mrs Kinsolving, I like your poetry, because I can understand it, and I don't understand my son's.'" See Marianne Moore to T. S. Eliot, 23 October 1934, and T. S. Eliot to Marianne Moore, 31 October 1934, *RML.*

16. Craig Abbott, *Marianne Moore: A Descriptive Bibliography* (Pittsburgh, PA: University of Pittsburgh Press, 1977), 70.

17. Cristanne Miller, *Marianne Moore: Questions of Authority* (Cambridge, MA: Harvard University Press, 1995), 194. In 1944, Joseph Cornell sent Moore books, asking that she "excuse the belatedness of the Valentine package," and "in the hope that it will give you that kind of feeling." Moore responded: "these books—these inspired by-paths of romance—are your own—especially this lady . . . with . . . shade-hat with long limber feather." See Marianne Moore to Joseph Cornell, April 11, 1944, in *Joseph Cornell's Theatre of the Mind: Selected Diaries, Letters and Files,* ed. Mary Ann Caws (New York: Thames and Hudson, 1993), 102–3.

18. See Patricia Willis, *Marianne Moore: Vision into Verse* (Philadelphia: The Rosenbach Museum and Library, 1987), 64.

19. *The Exploding Dictionary,* s.v. "Rhamnac," http://www.projects.ghostwheel.com/dictionary (accessed July 10, 2004); for the scriptural "vineyard of the sluggard," see Proverbs 24:30.

20. *The Compact Edition of the Oxford English Dictionary,* s.v. "Mimosa," A1.

21. See for example: ". . . this well-composed mynd; forestal'd / With heauenly riches: which had wholy call'd / His thoughtes from earth, to liue aboue In th' air / A very bird of paradice." Richard Crashaw, *Carmen Deo Nostro* (Paris: Peter Targa, 1652), fol. page ii verso.

22. Genesis 6:13–16 (Revised Standard Version).

23. Thomas Adams, *A Commentary or, Exposition upon the Divine Second Epistle Generall, Written by the Blessed Apostle St. Peter* (London: Printed by Richard Badger for Iacob Bloome, 1633), 589.

24. Richard Hooker, *The Laws of Ecclesiastical Politie* (London: John Windet, 1604), bk. 5, par. 68, p. 185.

25. See Miller's discussion of "Moore's repeated choice of love as a topic in her later poetry" in *Questions of Authority,* 195.

26. Marianne Moore, poetry drafts, "For February 14th," folder I:02:07, *RML.*

27. Genesis 9:20–25.

28. Moore again resists, conversationally, the "injustice" of biblical exegesis in "Propriety"; polite demurral precedes a theologically disputatious counterstatement in favor of "birth without taint": "blackened / because born that way" (*CPo* 150).

29. Miller, *Questions of Authority,* 201.

30. Marianne Moore, conversation notebook, 1920–1933, 1250/25, folder VII:11:01, *RML* 59.

31. Ibid., 1250/24, 37.

32. "Verse" from Latin *versus* from *vertere* = to turn; "fate" from Latin *fatum* = that which is spoken.

33. From Latin *con* + *fundere* = to pour together.

34. See Willis, *Vision into Verse,* 64.

35. From Latin *vera* = truth (feminine) or truths.

36. Moore's clippings include a reproduction of the painting from the *London Illustrated News,* December 19, 1959. See Marianne Moore, unpublished poetry drafts, "Saint Valentine," folder I:04:12, *RML.*

37. Maurice Blanchot, "The Clarity of Fiction," in *The Sirens' Song; Selected Essays by Maurice Blanchot,* ed. Gabriel Josipovici, trans. Sacha Rabinovitch (Brighton, UK: Harvester Press, 1982), 208; Barthes, *The Pleasure of the Text,* 36.

38. Schulman, *Poetry of Engagement,* 27.

39. *OED,* valentine, 2b.

40. Joseph Hall, "One of the Sermons Preacht at Westminister, on the day of the Publicke Fast (April 5, 1628)" (1634), in *The Works of Joseph Hall* (London: Printed for Nathaniel Butter, 1634), 309.

41. See Moore's translation of La Fontaine's "The Fox and the Grapes." She writes, "'These grapes are sour; I'll leave them for some knave.'// Better, I think, than an embittered whine" (*CPo* 251).

42. Francis Bacon, *The Essayes or Counsels, Civill and Morall* (London: Hanna Barret, 1625), 30.

43. Ibid., 26.

44. Wallace Stevens, "Notes toward a Supreme Fiction," in *The Collected Poems of Wallace Steven* (New York: Knopf, 1954), 406.

"Combat Cultural":
Marianne Moore and the Mixed Brow

Elizabeth Gregory

MARIANNE MOORE'S WRITING CAREER SPANNED MORE THAN FIFTY YEARS, and over that time her methods evolved to engage the changing world and to chart her unfolding responses to it. One often-noticed shift, sometimes described as a movement away from modernist edginess and toward a sentimental poetry of celebration, can be elucidated as a switch in brow level, from highbrow to middlebrow—from elevated to popular positioning. This essay explores this switch and its roots in Moore's early work, looking at Moore's readers' perceptions of her and her work and at the ways in which she addressed questions of brow, including explicit poetic argument, formal choices, and her public self-presentation.

When Moore began publishing in 1915, she entered a world fully engaged in the "Battle of the Brows," which, as Lawrence Levine demonstrates, has been ongoing in America since the mid-nineteenth century, in diverse configurations.[1] The brow terminology describes a social division based not directly on birth or wealth but on *culturedness,* a category that evades firm definition. The terms were tools of the effort to establish cultural order and hierarchy in the immigrant-thronged American scene, and their connotations mutated steadily. Highbrow, lowbrow and (later) middlebrow were employed to characterize both individuals and the texts and activities they consumed. Such characterization of individuals suggested the possibility of stable culture positions—that one might *be* one or another kind of consumer (the source of the brow terminology in racial theory is most obvious here).[2] Then as now, however, while fixed-brow terms might indicate an individual's or an author's intention, a mixed-brow experience was the norm for many, in a world of myriad media and countless cultural encounters. Clear determination of the brow level of a text was also dubious, both because the level of reflection with which one addressed a given text affected the experience and because the wider culture's ranking of the brow status of cultural productions often changed over time.

The cultural landscape of the early twentieth century was reshaped by development of the concept of the middlebrow. As Joan Shelley Rubin shows, in the twenties, thirties, and forties, middlebrow culture burgeoned: "Americans created an unprecedented range of activities aimed at making literature and other forms of 'high' culture available to a wide reading public."[3] Proponents specifically sought to bridge the brow gap, in a manner that was often seen as a watering down rather than a combination of diverse experiences. Virginia Woolf (1942) offers a lively characterization of the field: the highbrow is "the man or woman of thoroughbred intelligence who rides his mind at a gallop across country in pursuit of an idea" and the lowbrow "the man or woman of thoroughbred vitality who rides his body in pursuit of a living at a gallop across life." She champions both high- and lowbrows, as essential to one another and to life, and sets them against middlebrows, whom she derogates as "the man, or woman, of middlebred intelligence who ambles and saunters now on this side of the hedge, now on that, in pursuit of no single object, neither art itself nor life itself, but both mixed indistinguishably, and rather nastily, with money, fame, power, or prestige." But while the first two seem initially to differ from the third in being pure, Woolf insists that, while she counts herself a highbrow, her "imperfections in that line are well known to [her]."[4] Highbrow status is in this definition something to be labored toward, but Woolf does not account for the status one holds when one fails or succeeds imperfectly. She hints, however, at an interstitial option, wherein someone may occupy an unstable *mixed-brow* position, markedly distinguished from the middlebrow.

A similar instability is hinted at, but again not articulated, in Clement Greenberg's influential essay "Avant Garde and Kitsch" (1939). Greenberg defines the high/low divide in relation not to individuals but to the art they choose to view or read. The distinguishing factors are profit and reflection: kitsch is commercial and calls for no reflection where avant-garde work is done (largely) for its own sake and requires it. Reflection, for Greenberg, involves the work of thinking things through for oneself, rather than receiving a predigested meaning from the author, and is linked to class. The leisure enjoyed by the upper classes allows them the luxury of reflection, while the extended drudgery of the lives of industrial workers both reduces their opportunities for reflection and makes the effort reflection requires undesirable.[5]

The period in which the middlebrow developed coincides (not coincidentally) with the modernist period, wherein the upper reaches of the cultural hierarchy came to be fenced off from the crowds by difficulty of interpretation and obscure rules of approach. When modernist writers broke with conventional literary modes, they participated in the cultural ranking process, gaining highbrow authority through a complexity that excluded many. But at the same time, their work often challenged such categorizations and emphasized ambiguity over hierarchy. The work of Marianne Moore inhabits and explores this paradox.

Upon entering the field, Moore found quick acceptance among the modernist elite. Her highbrow status was well established by 1925, when Richard Aldington, reviewing *Observations,* declared that "[w]ithin the bounds of my feeble knowledge, Miss Moore is indeed the most high-brow poet in the world."[6] The height of her brow, he indicates, is demonstrated by her sophisticated irony, which

> gives her a most menacing superiority; one is conscious of a clear piercing gaze and an unfavourable judgment of oneself somehow emanating from the pages. Instinctively one straightens one's tie and tries hard to rub up a claim to something more than insignificance. I always feel I ought to apologise for having the presumption to read Miss Moore's poems; and at the thought that I am actually trying to review them the pen trembles in my hand.[7]

Aldington's comic trembling has several valences, one of which involves mimicking the ironic element that he includes among her highbrow qualities. He concludes saying, "with perfect sincerity that I think Miss Moore the best poet now living in America."[8]

Nine years earlier, H.D. took a more sober attitude, introducing Moore to the audience of the *Egoist* as an elite, ironic warrior, terms that also convey her superiority:

> And if Miss Moore is laughing at us, it is laughter that catches us, that holds, fascinates and half-paralyses us, as light flashed from a very fine steel blade, wielded playfully, ironically, with all the fine shades of thrust and counter-thrust, with absolute surety and with absolute disdain. . . .
>
> Miss Moore helps us. She is fighting in her country a battle against squalor and commercialism. We are all fighting the same battle. And we must strengthen each other in this one absolute bond—our devotion to the beautiful English language.[9]

Moore's humor is portrayed as a cauterizing protection against "squalor and commercialism," synonyms for the lowbrow here. Highbrow realms, H.D. implies by contrast, have more refined concerns of aesthetics and morality.[10]

But the equation of commerce with the lowbrow is not so clear-cut, since highbrow art also has a commercial side. This side was displayed in 1925, when a remarkable series of articles appeared in the *Dial,* two in January and one in each of the succeeding five months. They concerned Moore, the fourth winner of the $2,000 *Dial* prize for distinguished service to American letters, who had published ten poems in the *Dial* previous to her award, but was, as editor Scofield Thayer noted in his announcement of her honor, "among the unfortunate American public, so meagrely relished and so signally unacclaimed."[11] Yet, Thayer asserted, "those qualified to judge" held

Moore in universal high esteem. And it was his aim in honoring her both to acknowledge Moore's greatness as "America's most distinguished poetess" and to "flare" her work. This "flaring" he did not for Moore's sake—"([s]he does not go in for personal flaring)"—but for the sake of those who read the *Dial*.[12]

We flare not in glorification; we flare in practical service. Service not to that Juggernaut, the Reading Public,—that Juggernaut which is well served in being served badly. Service rather to the Imaginative Individual, to him who is in our world always the Marooned Individual. The towns, the villages, the prairies and the sandbars, of this North American Continent support many such. For since neither by the public pictures nor by the family radios are the hungerings of imagination appeased, therefore have these their being for ever in isolation, for ever shut and cut off. Therefore have these sharp eyes, the sharper for long fasting, eyes which, I have been encouraged to believe, are wont to pick out and to follow our own irregular and unchartered sailings. And it is for these important eyes that we run up, as one does a gala pennon, this blithe and gala name, this meadow-lark and white-heeled name, this name of Marianne Moore. . . . And it is to the hearts of these—being neither gross nor lax—that I do hereby commend the admonitory asceticisms of Miss Marianne Moore.[13]

Here Thayer directly engages in the maneuvering essential to the editors of little magazines, the effort to educate their public into interest in the material the magazines purvey through appeal to their sense of exclusivity. The Imaginative Individual for whom Thayer labors will find a soulmate in the Imaginative and Individual Moore and solace in subscribing to the *Dial*. In being thus "flared," Moore is both advertised and advertisement.[14] And the blending of commercial and aesthetic concerns is continued, as Robin Schulze shows, in Thayer's synchronizing of the *Dial* award with his own Dial Press's publication of Moore's *Observations*. Correspondence documents that he was simultaneously concerned with furthering Moore's career and in boosting sales of the magazine and the book (*BMM* 30–31). The $2,000 prize money emblematizes the commercial element in even this most erudite of awards.

But though Moore's early admirers insisted upon her high brow, her work points to the instabilities in such claims, challenging both this assignment and the brow division itself. Many critics have pointed to the destabilizing quality of Moore's frequent inclusion in her poems of quotations from non-literary, generally middlebrow sources (*The National Parks Portfolio, Vogue*, the *Illustrated London News*, etc.).[15] Her poem "England," first published in 1920, addresses the hierarchy of brows within a critique of hierarchy in general. In "England," the highbrow accomplishments of Europe and the Far East (older, thought-through cultures, "from which the grossness has been extracted") are contrasted with an apparently lowbrow America,

> where there
> is the little old ramshackle victoria in the south,
> where cigars are smoked on the street in the north;
> where there are no proof-readers, no silkworms, no digressions;
>
>
> the wild man's land; grassless, linksless, languageless country in which
>   letters are written
> not in Spanish, not in Greek, not in Latin, not in shorthand,
> but in plain American which cats and dogs can read!
>
> (*CPo* 46)

How much lower than the beasts can we go? Readers of Moore's animal-centric work will recognize the turnabout embedded in the logic here. The poem then goes on to make an explicit case for America as a place that does indeed manifest a valuable culture and an aesthetic sophistication, in spite of appearances:

> the flower and fruit of all that noted superiority—
> if not stumbled upon in America,
> must one imagine that it is not there?
> It has never been confined to one locality.
>
> (*CPo* 47)

The poem itself offers evidence of sophistication—skillful as it is, for instance, at turning its praise of Europe into, mitigated, censure, when it describes France as

> the "chrysalis of the nocturnal butterfly,"[16]
> in whose products mystery of construction
> diverts one from what was originally one's object—
> substance at the core:
>
> (*CPo* 46)

Old world and new world, highbrow and low, it is suggested, have each their own satisfactions. A substanceless sophistication can offer only limited gratification, and likewise with unsophisticated substance. But Moore's poem emphasizes and embodies a third alternative: one where high and low interpenetrate to create a thicker version of reality than either can provide alone, one that admits the complexity of individual enjoyment of daily life. As in common experience, Moore's poems move from elite subjects to mundane, from erudition to commerce. And these movements suggest the embeddedness of the terms in each pair.

Returning to the poem, in the line about cats and dogs, Moore plays with diction to demonstrate this thicker reality and names the special language that she employs in this project "American"—a language pointedly distinguished from English. The term "plain American" sounds like what it says, echoing the plain language of the plain man or woman on the street in its nationalism and in its colloquialism. But the plain American speaker of this phrase has a sophisticated point, put home through the artful manipulation of diction and the exuberant homespun metaphor. The plain American language (operative in spite of the earlier exaggerated claim that America is a "languageless country") functions differently from other languages (like English). It is extremely democratic—extending its offices even to animals, and, by implication, crossing many other dividing lines as well.

The animal reference gestures toward the canny wisdom of folk tales, camouflaged in apparent simplicity. The poem's title gives a related structural lesson in looking beyond initial impressions, since the title ("England") turns out not to indicate the subject of the poem overall, but rather to serve only as the subject of its first five lines. The expected hierarchy of cultures (England over America) is overturned along with expectations about the poem's focus. The poem gives a lesson about the inadequacy of familiar hierarchies to account for what matters—including the hierarchy of the brows. Apart from its brief descent into "American" the poem as a whole employs a markedly refined diction, but one that is destabilized by its own claims as its quotable maxims and humorous moments carry the poem into the realm of broad audience accessibility.

Though the poem in this reading critiques cultural hierarchies, that was not the impression received by Wilbert Snow, reviewing *Observations* in the insistently middlebrow *New York Herald Tribune* in 1925.[17] Snow echoes Aldington, but he reads the highbrow claims of Moore's work negatively as signs of an "aesthetic snobbishness" that seeks to exclude ordinary readers and to be read "'by little cliques only.'" He even cites, as evidence of Moore's failure to reach a wide audience, a portion of her antihierarchical claim that "[t]he letter *a* in psalm and calm when / pronounced with the sound of *a* in candle, is very noticeable," leaving off the mitigating "but // why should continents of misapprehension / have to be accounted for by the fact?" (*CPo* 46). Clearly, misapprehension did not disappear upon request. Snow's review both allows that Moore's work does, "beneath all the lumber and nonsense[,] . . . [have] a real poetic quality," and chafes at its difficulty.[18] The missed signals here suggest both the extent to which no author controls how readers will receive a text and the multiplicity of ways that each text may be received upon any reading. This uncontrollability in itself challenges the notion of static brow positionings and supports Moore's challenge to received ideas of brow and of hierarchy in the poem.

Around the time that Moore wrote "England," Alfred Kreymborg took her to a baseball game, doing so to "give myself the pleasure at least once of hearing her stumped about something." Recounting the episode in his memoir *Troubadour* (1925), he continues:

> Certain that only an experience completely strange to her would be the thing, I invited her to a ball game at the Polo Grounds. This descent into the world of the low-brow started beautifully. It was a Saturday afternoon and the Cubs and Giants were scheduled for one of their ancient frays. The 'L' was jammed with fans and we had to stand all the way uptown and hang on to straps. Marianne was totally oblivious to the discomfiture anyone else would have felt and, in answer to a question of mine, paraded whole battalions of perfectly marshalled ideas in long columns of balanced periods which no lurching on the part of the train or pushing on the part of the crowd disturbed. . . .

But Moore wasn't stumped:

> "Well, I got her safely to her seat and sat down beside her. Without so much as a glance toward the players at practice grabbing grounders and chasing fungos, she went on giving me her impression of the respective technical achievements of Mr. Pound and Mr. Aldington without missing a turn in the rhythm of her speech, until I, a little impatient, touched her arm and, indicating a man in the pitcher's box winding up with the movement Matty's so famous for, interrupted: 'But Marianne, wait a moment, the game's about to begin. Don't you want to watch the first ball?' 'Yes indeed,' she said, stopped, blushed and leaned forward. The old blond boy delivered a tantalizing fadeaway which hovered in the air and then, just as it reached the batter, Shorty Slagle, shot from his shoulders to his knees and across the plate. 'Strike!' bawled Umpire Emslie. 'Excellent,' said Marianne.
>
> "Delighted, I quickly turned to her with: 'Do you happen to know the gentleman who threw that strike?'
>
> "'I've never seen him before,' she admitted, 'but I take it it must be Mr. Mathewson.'
>
> "I could only gasp, 'Why?'
>
> "'I've read his instructive book on the art of pitching—'
>
> "'Strike two!' interrupted Bob Emslie.
>
> "'And it's a pleasure,' she continued imperturbably, 'to note how unerringly his execution supports his theories—'
>
> "'Strike three, batter's out!' concluded the umpire and, as Shorty Slagle slunk away, glared toward the Chicago bench for the next victim. . . ."[19]

While some of what Kreymborg "remembers" in his autobiography may be apocryphal, the story fits Moore's profile, and it certainly conveys Kreymborg's sense of Moore as consummate highbrow. In presenting Moore thus, Kreymborg, founder of the avant-garde magazine *Others,* and not without his own intellectual credentials, marks her as an intellectual's intellectual. But this story, like "England," complicates its claims, pointing as well to something problematic in the characterization of Moore as unswervingly highbrow. Not that it isn't true that she and her work fit that category, but it isn't sufficient.

We can return to Greenberg's terminology and note that Moore's work certainly calls for reflection on the part of the reader, but, as we've seen, it also challenges the divide between high and low. In the Kreymborg story this challenge occurs again, not only from the "high" side (where borrowings from the world of the "low" might arguably be seen as a kind of slumming) but from the other direction too: Moore portrays Mathewson (exactly the sort of writer her notes tell us she might read) as an author, like Moore and Kreymborg, and a theoretician. A man of the mind as well as of the body. In Kreymborg's description, we might recognize in both Moore and Mathewson a shared narrative principle: If a pitch can be defined in literary terms (and the game certainly unfolds like a narrative), Mathewson's fadeaway pitch would be a modernist pitch, with its self-conscious interruption of expected form (the sudden drop from shoulder-level to knee-level). Moore, or Kreymborg channeling what he knew of Moore, challenges the view of the brows as a static binary of high vs. low (or static triad, when the middlebrow is included), and presents them instead as a set of interactive cultural positions, which each individual may occupy serially or even simultaneously. And in yet another line-crossing move, Kreymborg intervenes in the creation of a popular persona by publishing this story about an "elite" poet.

Recently there has been increased critical focus upon the mutual entwining of high culture with low. On the one hand, we can recognize that "high" culture incorporates some of the pleasures of "low" culture—which might include humor, sentimentality, and narrative coherence—not just as a foil to play against but as a part of its own story. Robert Scholes points to the satisfaction readers take in finding the "resolution" (and *which* "resolution" depends on the reader) to the story of Molly and Poldy Bloom—in spite of, or in addition to, the pleasures found in *Ulysses*'s lessons about the irresolvability of language's multiple levels of signification.[20] On the other hand, "low" art may be read as embodying a serious critique of the bad faith of the "high," which is based in pretension to higher absolute value when the real difference is leisure and the wealth that affords the time to be reflective, time that multiple-shift workers don't have. This kind of critique operates through metastructural effects, including not just the physical structures of any given work but also the web of invisible structures—of reference, context, and expectation—through which a full meaning is actualized. This is the realm of intertextuality, in which not just other literary works but the world at large *qua* text enters into dialogue with the work at hand.

This metastructural dynamic, which requires the reader's reflective participation, is essential to reading Moore's work as well. Through her unusual line breaks and rhymes, her peculiar syllabic verse, her use of quotation where "originality" is expected, the exceptional range of sources from which she quotes, and the interaction of all these elements with the argument of the text, Moore makes every poem, no matter what its apparent subject, a consideration of the operation of poetry. Brow claims play a major role in this operation, defining the kind of cultural authority sought for the work and the writer. From early on, Moore's work engaged issues of brow, in part through a playful mobile wit, displayed at all levels of the text. Cristanne Miller links the "singular associative leaps, puns, and word play that characterize Moore's verse," with an iconoclastic creativity that "opens a space beyond fixed truths, conventions, perfection."[21] This wit challenges fixed-brow positioning by, among other things, undercutting the high seriousness that supports such claims. Marie Borroff remarks upon Moore's "solemnity-retardant" mode, and Miller points to its contribution to Moore's consistently antihierarchic attitude.[22] Among other things, this playfulness allowed Moore to mock her own role as elite poet, or to open herself to mockery in a manner that encouraged critique of the position of the high by the low.

"I, too, dislike it," the opening line of Moore's 1919 poem "Poetry," epitomizes this self-deprecating mode. The line invites readers into an initial compact against Poetry with a highbrow capital P, a world in which Moore is implicated by the context in which the poem appears. From this point, the poem moves on to redefine its art in terms that admit ordinary material (the stuff of daily life) and ordinary readers:

> Reading it, however, with a perfect contempt for it, one discovers in
> it after all, a place for the genuine.
>> Hands that can grasp, eyes
>> that can dilate, hair that can rise
>>> if it must, these things are important not because a
>
> high-sounding interpretation can be put upon them but because they are
> useful.

(CPo 266–67)

In contrast to "high-sounding interpretation," usefulness has a common cast. The odd line breaks and indentations ironize any claim to ordinariness this poem might seem to make, but at the same time the funny effects they create align the poem with deflated pretension. The poem manages to stand firmly on both sides of the high/low line at once, and that balancing act further reinforces both the highness and the lowness—the poem is both complicated and a good joke, and the fact that it is both complicates it further and improves the joke.

From the start of her career, the metastructural dynamics of Moore's work extended to her public persona. Created as much by those who responded to her as by herself, this persona had many of the qualities of a performance piece—a projection from the poetry, embodying its playful dynamics. In the examples cited earlier, Kreymborg and Aldington, certainly no lowbrows themselves, feel pressed to ally themselves with the low position against her. But the situation Moore creates is so complex that the differentiation of brows is overthrown, even while Moore seeks to be accessible to readers of all brows—for example, through her humorously incongruous apposition of high (the Moore persona) and low (baseball) in response to Kreymborg.

Pre-Warhol, and pre-Greenberg, but not before the point at which the high/low binary that Greenberg describes came into currency, Moore recognizes that the kind of division that Greenberg describes, and on which much modernist criticism has built, is flawed, if sometimes useful: reflection may and does occur within all brow contexts (though it may not be activated in all readings); and the narrative satisfactions of low- and middlebrow writing often also occur in highbrow work. This interrelation has recently been noted by modernist interpreters, and is a lesson with which readers of Moore have long been familiar.

Moore's reflections upon the dynamics of the brows in the 1920s prefigure the more radical brow play in which she engaged in her later career. In the late 1940s Moore's poetry became much more accessible to all readers, requiring little of the effort at the initial level that her earlier poetry had done; it was full of overt sentiment, fond humor, and celebrations of excellence. Simultaneous with these changes in her poetry, Moore promulgated a public performance of the highbrow as charmingly absurd. She actively took the part of ambassador between brows that Woolf (and others) disapproved. Her baseball poem "Hometown Piece for Messrs. Alston and Reese" (1956) and her "For February 14th" (1959) both appeared on the front page of the same middlebrow *New York Herald Tribune* in which Snow had spurned her in 1925. And from 1958 to 1970 her poems appeared regularly in the *New Yorker*.[23] Although the *New Yorker* began publishing "serious" poetry after William Shawn became editor in 1952, its role as purveyor of urbanity to the rest of the nation gave it a middlebrow cast in the eyes of many. And whether or not other poets tailored their work to fit the *New Yorker* context (as fiction writers of all ranks were made to do), Moore was certainly perceived to do so: "There is no doubt that in [Moore's] later work the cosy element in the poet, the element acceptable to the *New Yorker*, is in greater evidence," wrote Roy B. Fuller in 1968.[24]

Moore's second *New Yorker* poem, "The Arctic Ox (or Goat)" (September 1958), invokes the (ostensibly lower brow) world of advertising. The poem's final stanza begins with an unabashed summary of its disquisition on the virtues of choosing *qiviut,* "the underwool of the arctic ox," over fur: "If you fear you are / reading an advertisement, / you are" (*CPo* 193, 195). An experienced worker in the culture mines, Moore neither fears nor feels embarrassed about crossing the line into commerce, though she acknowledges that others may. The poem points quietly to the process enacted through its publication in this new venue: a similar, almost physical, crossing of that brow line.

In making that passage, Moore aids both the *New Yorker* and herself. The relation of the *New Yorker* to its readers in the fifties altered, as the magazine came to appeal to a wider variety of audiences than formerly—for various but linked reasons. Like the little magazines of earlier decades, the fifties' *New Yorker* makes an appeal to exclusivity—something it had done before, but this time with an element of literary sophistication formerly absent. Moore serves as a kind of archeological relic of the little magazines whose status the *New Yorker* now emulates. In 1957 Moore was featured in a *New Yorker* Profile. This celebratory piece constitutes a parallel to the series of *Dial* articles from 1925, insofar as it too "flares" Moore in pursuit of authoritative claims for the magazine.

The Profile makes a pointed connection to the *Dial* in an extended passage of which I quote a small part:

> [Her 1924 Dial Award] led Miss Moore into a long association with the *Dial,* a magazine that in the twenties held a unique position in the van of the nation's progressive literary and artistic life. . . . Looking back, Miss Moore remembers the *Dial* as "an elysium for people who were really interested in quality," and, like many others who have memories of its beautifully printed pages, she cannot restrain a feeling of nostalgia for the era of intellectual exuberance that the magazine represented. The drab conformity of Marxist thought that later paralyzed the minds of so many writers in Europe and the United States had yet to make itself felt, and the great tide of mechanized mass communication and mass entertainment that has since threatened to swamp the minds of thinking individuals was still far off.[25]

The closing line sets itself in opposition to mass entertainment, and assumes a readership of thinking individuals who can still recognize the need to struggle against its threats. As a relic of this lost elysium, Moore's presence in the pages of the *New Yorker,* particularly the presence of her poetry, shores up the magazine's claims to a highbrow status similar to that here attributed to the *Dial.*

In the *New Yorker,* as she had in the *Dial,* Moore promotes highbrow claims, but in a manner suited to the magazine's rather compromised position. She spoofs her own highbrow role, and so fits the magazine's familiar humor mode (Moore becomes a kind of living cartoon: elderly woman at racetrack in tricorn). In the Profile, her poetry is barely mentioned, and when it is, we are reassured that she doesn't really take it seriously (a view that Moore encouraged), and that we shouldn't either.

Moore's poem "Combat Cultural," which appeared in the *New Yorker* in June 1959, suggests Moore's sense of her situation. The poem charts an associative path, moving from athletic animals to dancing Cossacks (imitating warfare) to "the quadrille of Old Russia," to the present (1958), where, according to Moore's note, the Moiseyev Dance Company performed a dance entitled "Two Boys in a Fight."

> Cold Russia
> this time: the prize bunnyhug
> platform-piece of experts in the
> trip-and-slug of wrestlers in a rug.
>
>
> "Sacked" and ready for bed apparently—
> with a jab, a kick, pinned to the wall,
> they work toward the edge and stick;
> stagger off, and one is victim of a
> flipflop—leg having circled leg as thick.
>
> (*CPo* 199)

Though the title might be taken at this point to describe a cultured version of combat, a balletic battle, the next stanza raises issues that point to the battle of the brows, and Moore's position in it:

> "Some art, because of high quality,
> is unlikely to command high sales";
> yes, yes; but here, oh no;
> not with the frozen North's Nan-ai-ans[26]
> of the sack in their tight touch-and-go.
>
> (*CPo* 199–200)

Here, Moore suggests, is high art that *will* find a big audience—in spite of the received knowledge that calls that impossible (the "yes, yes" marks the speaker's familiarity with that view).

The poem describes the same sort of mixed-brow phenomenon that it enacts: The Russian troupe presents lowbrow wrestling within a highbrow dance frame, and then crosses the line again into commercial success. Moore offers an artfully self-conscious reflection on the interplay of high and low art, that also makes itself accessible as a celebration of athleticism and beauty and a blague on the obscurity of elite poets. And this on the pages of the *New Yorker,* where it reaches a wider audience than Moore's books of poetry ever did. The poem too does "a flipflop," dancing for us a version of Moore's own history of wrestling with the high/low dynamic, a comment on the cultural combat she observed around her, participated in, and intervened to alter. As she did in "England," and "Poetry" four decades earlier, Moore plays on both sides of the line.

The final stanza tells us that "Two Boys in a Fight" was danced by one person dressed as two, and ends with a moral: "we must cement the parts of any / objective symbolic of *sagesse*" (*CPo* 200). This rather obliquely phrased dictum might be understood to suggest that wisdom is best represented through recognition of continuities between apparent opposites. Certainly this method was Moore's, in the realm of the brows as in others. I have argued elsewhere that rather than devolving into sentimentality, the later Moore activated critical and reflective elements within a middlebrow position.[27] But my point here is not to choose between available readings of the older Moore, for instance as sell-out, dupe, retiree, or critical undercover agent, readings which might interestingly be mapped against middle-, low-, and highbrow positions. Instead I want to consider her as a willing mixture of the set. A commercially alert, sentimental and ironically self-conscious poet. All at once. A mixed-brow poet, skillfully guiding her cultural float.

Throughout her career, Moore's mixed-brow references challenge clear divisions and engage readers in the work of thinking through their own assumptions about how the high/low divide operates. In so doing, Moore offers herself as model, through both the poems and the persona that attaches to them, of the complexity of each individual's brow position and of what the division into brows may mean, as well as of the pleasures associated with all brow levels and inherent in the free play between them. This pointed complexity challenges reigning definitions of the poem as discrete from the real. Rather than representing a diminished portrait of experience, Moore's poems offer an emphatically multilayered, mixed-brow version of experience that calls for similarly multiplex responses on the part of their readers.

NOTES

1. See Lawrence Levine, *Highbrow/Lowbrow: The Emergence of Cultural Hierarchy in America* (Cambridge, MA: Harvard University Press, 1988).

2. See Levine on the theoretical association of skull shape and brow height with intelligence in the nineteenth century. "Lowbrowed" people were non-Caucasians and Caucasians from southern and eastern Europe (221–23).

3. Joan Shelley Rubin, *The Making of Middlebrow Culture* (Chapel Hill: University of North Carolina Press, 1992), xi.

4. Virginia Woolf, "Middlebrow," in *The Death of the Moth and Other Essays* (San Diego, CA: Harcourt Brace Jovanovich, 1970), 177–80.

5. Clement Greenberg, "Avant Garde and Kitsch" (1939), in *Art and Culture: Critical Essays* (Boston: Beacon Press, 1961), 3–21.

6. Elizabeth Gregory, *The Critical Response to Marianne Moore* (Westport, CT: Praeger, 2003), 74.

7. Ibid., 75.

8. Ibid.

9. Ibid., 20–21.

10. Charles Van Doren (1921) and Glenway Wescott (1923) also characterize Moore as an elite poet. See Gregory, *Critical Response,* 33–34, 42–43. T. S. Eliot (1923) critiques Wescott's characterization. See Gregory, *Critical Response,* 44–46.

11. Gregory, *Critical Response,* 53.

12. Ibid.

13. Ibid., 53–54.

14. In flaring Moore, Thayer continues his relation to the other award winners, but the number of articles increases threefold.

15. Among these, see Bonnie Costello, *Marianne Moore: Imaginary Possessions* (Cambridge, MA: Harvard University Press, 1981); Elizabeth Gregory, *Quotation and Modern American Poetry: "Imaginary Gardens with Real Toads"* (Houston, TX: Rice University Press, 1996); Jeanne Heuving, *Omissions Are Not Accidents: Gender in the Art of Marianne Moore* (Detroit: Wayne State University Press, 1992); Margaret Holley, *The Poetry of Marianne Moore: A Study in Voice and Value* (Cambridge: Cambridge University Press, 1987); and Cristanne Miller, *Marianne Moore: Questions of Authority* (Cambridge, MA: Harvard University Press, 1995).

16. Moore's note to this line reads, "Line 9: *'Chrysalis of the nocturnal butterfly.'* Erté." See *CPo* 268.

17. See Rubin's *The Making of Middlebrow Culture* on the role of the *New York Herald Tribune,* 36–92.

18. Wilbert Snow, "A Literalist of the Imagination," *New York Herald Tribune,* May 17, 1925, 3.

19. Alfred Kreymborg, *Troubadour* (New York: Boni and Liveright, 1925), 244–45.

20. Robert Scholes, "Exploring the Great Divide: High and Low, Left and Right," *Narrative* 11, no. 3 (October 2003): 264.

21. Miller, *Questions of Authority,* 91.

22. Marie Boroff, *Language and the Poet: Verbal Artistry in Frost, Stevens, and Moore* (Chicago: University of Chicago Press, 1979), 88; Miller, *Questions of Authority,* 89–91, 205–6.

23. At least one Moore poem appeared annually.

24. Gregory, *Critical Response,* 229–30.

25. Winthrop Sargeant, "Profiles: Humility, Concentration, and Gusto," *New Yorker,* February 16, 1957, 64.

26. Moore's note reads, "Line 29: *Nan-ai-ans.* The Nanaians inhabit the frigid North of the Soviet Union." See *CPo* 294.

27. Elizabeth Gregory, "Stamps, Money, Pop Culture and Marianne Moore, *Discourse* 17, no. 1 (Fall 1994): 123–46 (excerpted in Gregory, *Critical Response*).

Marianne Moore Today

Benjamin Friedlander

I HAVE CHOSEN TO SET FORTH THE ESSAY BELOW AS A SERIES OF ASSERtions followed by elaborations, qualifications, and counterarguments. Interspersed throughout are a series of contrasting statements from nine poets who generously responded to a query regarding their own senses of Moore's legacy. My hope is that these testimonies will serve as a representation in miniature of the field within which I would want the polemical portion of my essay to register.

I begin with an assumption:

Marianne Moore is not a credible model for contemporary poets and remains uncited, if not unread, even by those who seem to have absorbed her influence.

This has the benefit of compression, but for that very reason requires unpacking. Let me begin with "contemporary." I put my assertion in the broadest terms possible, but my remarks are framed with a particular sector of the poetry world in mind. This is not to retract my broader claim. It is, instead, to acknowledge that a different argument would be needed to account for Moore's reception in a different sector.[1] Marianne Moore's work remains, I would argue, an unassimilated challenge to contemporary poetry, but not for any one reason. How could it be, when there is no one reason poets write today as they do? Let my larger claim stand, then, as a fixed point for embarking upon a number of different arguments. The essay I have written attempts to trace just one.

But what is the sector I have in mind? The simplest way to answer, I suppose, would be to insert the word "experimental" between "contemporary" and "poetry." Unfortunately, I find this word (and its various cognates: avant-garde, alternative, radical, formally innovative) not only inadequate, but presumptuous and misleading as well, especially when defined in relation to an equally inadequate construct such as "mainstream." A better, albeit clumsier, answer would be: the writers of the last twenty-five years (most notably the Language poets) who have operated within an intellectual horizon staked out by Modernism, the New American Poetry, and critical theory.[2]

A number of writers within this horizon give evidence of Moore's influence. I think in particular of Rae Armantrout, whose combinations of descriptive and declarative utterance serve, as Moore's do, a didactic purpose; or Lytle Shaw, who shares with Moore a fascination with science writing; or Lyn Hejinian, whose long poem *A Border Comedy* is a network of propositions generated out of reading. I think of Susan Howe and Juliana Spahr, for whom a citation is no less poetic than allusion; or Robert Grenier and Ron Silliman, for whom a numerical pattern is no less poetic than sound. Yet none of these writers, so far as I know, has ever cited Moore as a predecessor. Indeed, with rare exception—Steve Farmer, Rachel Blau DuPlessis—the poets who operate within this sector ignore Moore altogether, at least in print.[3]

The silence on Moore only becomes more pronounced when we consider the opportunities for reappraisal offered by the landmark journal *HOW(ever)* (1983–1992) and its ongoing sequel, *How2* (begun in 1999). Founded by Kathleen Fraser with the explicit aim of making "a bridge between scholars thinking about women's language issues, vis-à-vis the making of poetry, and the women making those poems," the journal took its name from the second line of Moore's "Poetry"; yet despite the appearance of two brief notes in 1988 (one by DuPlessis), Moore scholarship has only just begun to make it across the proposed bridge, and Moore herself has yet to become a point of reference for the poets.[4]

This missed opportunity for engagement is a local instance of a more general state of affairs. Although poets have written a greater proportion of Moore scholarship than is the case with any of Moore's Modernist peers, the gains of this research have yet to be adequately registered by poets at large. Indeed, the difference between the scholar's Moore and the Moore of popular poetic imagination remains vaster, I would argue, than is the case with any other major writer of her generation.[5]

Rachel Blau DuPlessis

My sense is that, today, Moore is a precursor without acknowledged followers. What are the terms that Moore presents? Here are some: discursive slides of major, comic, satiric, almost in-your-face proportions. Including a lapidary diction out of the seventeenth century. The rhetorical desire to write "a plain American that cats and dogs can read"—hello! has no one seen how great and odd that is as a poetics, both plain-folks and wacky-epistemology at the same time. The desire to invent a prose strategy for poetry so unusual (syllabics) that she is basically placing herself as marginal to the whole of Anglo-American prosody and thus makes a major critique of normal poetry and its normal blandishments, including mellifluousness, beauty, and the lyric. This involves a quondam gender critique of poetry and some of its institutional practices (and is most powerful in the Moore of the teens and twenties of the twentieth century, sort of 80–90 years ago now). As for her critique of poetry—I love that, and I think to some degree I understand it, and even follow it.

When I wrote "No Moore of the Same," published a while ago, but whose shards appear in a chapter of *Genders, Races, and Religious Cultures,* I fore-grounded Moore's gender critique, which involves, inter alia, a critique of beauty and a witty, brilliant pox on both the houses of both the stagy "sexes." She really was a tertium quid, casting a very cool and amused eye on men and women and their pretensions (because she thought she was neither, I think). I also was inter-ested that she may have invented the citation strategy, or at least was one of the first users of the citation strategy fundamental to American modernist poetry; this has implications for collage textures of poetry and discursive slides by which I def-initely feel influenced. I did not model my own citation strategy in *Drafts* after hers any more (or any less!) than after Pound's or Eliot's or Williams's, but her use gave me a sense of support: she too had traveled down that road. And further: some of her reception is about her choices, but some not. For example: her faded, later po-ems, her Upstanding Protestantism: BORING!—but T. S. Eliot's faded, later po-ems, his Upstanding Protestantism—CULTURALLY HEGEMONIC! What, as the kids say, was That About? Moore is not well anthologized ("The Fish"). She is one of the most icy, ethically astute users of language who exists, especially icy because she claimed she was "not writing poetry"! But she didn't write enough. She became her own backwater. She is no Dickinson. There was some kind of fail-ure of nerve—seems simple but true to say—after her mother died. She decided to become "Marianne Moore" but picked (in my view) the "wrong" "Marianne Moore" to become, overlooking the one from the twenties in favor of the one from the forties. In any event, I have strongly suggested, and will again suggest, that in-ability to read the production of a woman (because of difficulty reading her vari-ous self-presentation strategies) is a major problem of her reception, and thus she needs a feminist reception (one asking gender questions) to be fully understood.

The question is why. Why is Moore unread, unassimilated, or unac-knowledged?

The ventriloquized "credible" in my initial assertion points toward one answer. For many readers, Moore's authority as a poet is compromised by her public persona and moral didacticism. Thus, Barrett Watten, while re-jecting my notion that, "in general, 'we' don't consider her worth reading," nonetheless affirms, "I often strain to separate the decorous, *New Yorker* side of genteel reading practices from the hard-edged innovator in Moore." I take this to mean that when Moore's later stance as an artist ("decorous," "genteel") becomes fixed in the imagination, our ability to read her work atrophies. And that we must strain against this atrophy.

But precisely because it is an atrophy of the ability to read, this rejection of Moore in her guise as cultural figure is a pre-rejection of her work, hence a prejudice, and does not begin to account for her omission from discus-sions by those who *can* read. Presumably, where atrophy and prejudice are not at issue, a more substantial explanation is required.

Jordan Davis

I disagree. Kenneth Koch taught her work in the first classes I took in contemporary poetry and imaginative writing, so I experience her as fairly close to the center of contemporary poetry. In her roles as editor and critic she was a shaper of literary modernism in America; without her in my cosmology I'd have a much harder time yoking both Eliot and Williams—I'd feel a counterproductive need to exclude one or the other from the range of possible influences. Strands of contemporary poetry that don't view Moore as not only credible but essential are, uh, unviable.

She's the modernist I'll always go back to. As with WCW and TSE, I prefer the early-middle work to the later work (as opposed to Stevens and Pound, whose middle-later work I go back to more often). If my psychological craving for unpleasable authority figures somehow vanishes, I may reevaluate how much I need her work.

Work work work work work.

To account for Moore's omission in a more substantive way, let me offer a second assertion:

Poetry has two general orientations, distinct in theory if overlapping in practice: toward the sharing of meaning in language, and toward an experience of language meaningful in its own right.

The two orientations are necessarily interdependent. Indeed, the nature of this interdependence is what gives a poet's work its particular character. Yet however overlapping in practice, the two aims are distinct in theory, and with rare exceptions (Wallace Stevens would be the most prominent that comes to mind), poets tend to emphasize one or the other in their poetics. When Ezra Pound defines poetry as "news that stays news," he is telling us that our experience of a poem's sound, syntax, shape on the page, etc., is of less moment than the poem's interpretable content. And when Robert Frost defines poetry instead as "what gets lost in translation," he is telling us that a poem's sensual characteristics are of greater moment than its meaning. Never mind that for most readers Frost is the more committed communicator or that Pound is the more fixed in language as such. In their *orientations,* Pound and Frost were set on a "sharing of meaning" and "experience of language," respectively.

To name these two orientations, I would like to borrow the philosophical distinction between sensible and intelligible objects of knowledge. We find this distinction in Plato's *Republic,* in the parable of the cave. There, you will recall, human beings chained with their backs to the light remain mesmerized by shadows. Only those who are able to escape learn to know things as they truly are. This knowing, for Plato, is intellection; our senses are the cave. Trapped within the cave, we only know a portion of what truly is: the material portion ("shadow"). For ideas (*eidoi*) we must escape the cave into the "light" of reason. Thus, while we can see, hear, touch, taste, and smell material objects such as plants or animals, to apprehend the *concept* of "plant" or "animal"—not to say abstractions such as "justice" or "value"—we must exercise another kind of faculty altogether.[6]

For Plato, then, we pass *beyond* the sensible *to* the intelligible, a hierarchy preserved by Kant, who nonetheless gives to sensibility and intelligibility a more nuanced relation. For Kant, the senses are not a prison, but a point of origin for reason's trajectory. Drawing a distinction between understanding and reason, he argues for a unity of knowledge that achieves intelligibility precisely by way of the senses. Understanding, then, is not an escape from sensibility, but a faculty that operates within the world it reveals. "*Understanding* and *sensibility*," he writes, "can determine objects *only when they are employed in conjunction*. When we separate them, we have intuitions without concepts, or concepts without intuitions."[7] Reason in turn is a faculty that operates within the world of intuitions and concepts that the understanding reveals. With reason, to be sure, the senses themselves are no longer revelatory, but the world of intelligibility is not, as in Plato, a world beyond: "Whatever in an object of the senses is not itself appearance, I entitle *intelligible*."[8]

Applied to poetry, the distinction between sensibility and intelligibility allows us to distinguish between two different aspects of poetic language in terms of the ways that the mind apprehends them: the sensual quality of words, on the one hand (what we generally call "the materiality of language"); on the other hand, the intelligible meaning of a trope (rhetoric). In this scheme, a poetry in which the sharing of meaning takes precedence over the sensual characteristics of language would be oriented toward intelligibility; a poetry in which the perceptible qualities of language are primary would instead be oriented toward sensibility.[9]

Brian Kim Stefans

I think she's a very credible model, but there are so many models out there that are underrecognized—just starting with Scottish poets, MacDiarmid, Finlay and the great W. S. Graham—that I'm not sure I would go out of my way to say Look at Moore, but alas she writes with a stanza that was defeated by the New Formalists and never acknowledged by the Language people (for example) that she has something quite unique to offer. Her sobriety is her strength and weakness.

I think she "permits" Bernstein to use collage—unassimilable quotes especially—in a fashion that is not nearly as impenetrable and highbrow as, say, Zukofsky. And her urbanity and easy wit obviously set the stage for the New York School to some degree.

I've often turned to her writings on animals and such as very exacting, visual analogues of, say, Demuth's and Scheeler's paintings (of course I'm not original in making this link—they are I suppose called the "Precisionists") and I think she may be the strongest representative of a school of American "animal" poetry—I always gave Holmes some credit for founding it with "The Chambered Nautilus." (I like looking at animals myself but of course it's never been my thing to use them as analogues for anything or to describe them.)

I've always enjoyed and benefited from arbitrary constraints on my writing—I appreciate when the form forces me to rewrite and do something unintuitive. I like elaborate structures as stand-ins for my failures as a visual artist and/or computer programmer—Moore's stanzas were interesting to me in this way, and my earliest way of writing poems was to write one stanza, and then make the rest of them conform to this first one. Don't know if I got that from Moore.

I do find, though, when I've gone back to read her, that I'm a bit bored by the coolness of her writing; I guess I'm a bit of a romantic myself and need a little anguish and heat in my poems.

"Sensibility" is of course a venerable term in literary criticism, and my description of a poetry of sensibility owes as much to Northrop Frye as it does to Plato and Kant. When Frye named the eighteenth century an age of sensibility, he had in mind a poetry "in which words are linked by sound rather than sense," in which the overall effect is "hypnotically repetitive, oracular, incantatory, dreamlike and in the original sense of the word charming."[10] More recently, Jerome McGann has drawn a connection between this work and the modern and postmodern poetry I have in mind in the present essay. For McGann, sensibility is not simply a luxuriating in the physical, but a challenge to the hierarchy that places the intellectual beyond the body's ken. Thus, in sensibility, "the poem generates almost no statemental content, its 'idea' is an embodied and literal act" and "the physique of language . . . in itself [becomes] a cognitive field." As heirs to this tradition McGann cites, among others, John Ashbery and Lyn Hejinian, but, "[o]f the imposing modernist writers," he asserts, "only Gertrude Stein kept perfect faith with this line of work."[11]

If Gertrude Stein is the preeminent modern poet of sensibility, Marianne Moore is her counterpart in intelligibility. This, I would argue, is how Wallace Stevens saw her. His essay on Moore draws on Plato's notion of a higher reality "apprehended by thought and not sense" to argue that a poem like "He 'Digesteth Hard Yron'" "is a revelation of reality." Insofar as he distinguishes between Moore and Plato, he brings her work closer in outlook to Kant, for whom thought and sense were not antagonistic but collaborative faculties. She thus reveals for Stevens "a solid reality which does not wholly dissolve . . . into the conceptions of our own minds." She has, he writes, "the faculty of digesting the 'hard yron' of appearance," and in this way brings us closer into "contact" with "a particular reality or, better, a reality of her own particulars."[12]

Pound is equally apt in his view. His note on Moore in the *Little Review* describes her work, and Mina Loy's as well, as "neither simple, sensuous nor passionate," but intellectual. Reaching for a proper term of appreciation, he classifies their work as "logopoeia or poetry that is akin to nothing but language, which is a dance of the intelligence among words and ideas and modification of ideas and characters." "Logopoeia," I would recall, is the last of Pound's three categories of poetic language, and the only one wholly given to intelligibility. The first, "melopoeia" ("poetry which moves by its music"), is a pure instance of sensibility; the second, "imagism," employs intelligibility, but as a means to achieve sensibility's ends.[13]

Jena Osman

I have to say that Moore is not a poet I feel to be an influence; however, the more I think about her, the more I realize that there are elements to her process that I feel extremely interested in—for instance her use of footnotes/citations, her delight in and recycling of newspaper items, and her "research-based" writing strategies.

But what most interests me about her is her living room. Here in Philadelphia the Rosenbach Library actually houses Moore's living room exactly as it was in her home in Greenwich Village. She willed it to the library. In any case, the room is lined with thousands of her books which are alphabetized by title, leading to some amazing juxtapositions. Also, she put lots of inserts in each of the books she read. All of us do it—use newspaper clippings and junk mail to mark a place, etc.—but Moore took this everyday gesture to an extreme degree. The inserts appear casual— an image cut out from a magazine or from a postcard, a letter, an advertisement— all seem to have found their way between the books' pages by chance, but in fact these inserts are in dialogue with the books' contents. I'm pretty sure the Rosenbach has taken out all of the inserts and placed them in archival plastic bags so the full effect can no longer be achieved. But I love the idea of how she seemed to be using her books as a foundation for a material (as opposed to cyber) hypertext.

Her study also contains a big chest of drawers, apparently containing the exact items that were there when she died. But clearly each drawer has been arranged for future viewing by Moore. The drawers remind me of Joseph Cornell boxes. As with the book inserts, there's the first impression of a casual everyday activity that, when looked at closely, reveals remarkable intentions. All of this interests me.

Also at the Rosenbach, you can get a really good sense of Moore's poem-writing process. The resources behind each poem are available so you can see very clearly how her writing came very much out of her reading. She would take notes and then circle words and phrases and then combine and recombine according to sound.

So somewhat ironically, I feel that the "performative"/procedural Marianne Moore is much more related to my interests as a writer than the textual one.

With this in mind, I would offer a second explanation for Moore's neglect:

Over the past twenty-five years, the poetry of sensibility has become dominant, and Gertrude Stein is now considered the most significant

**of the Modernists. Marianne Moore, as a poet of intelligibility, has suf-
fered a corresponding decline in reputation over the same period.**

One problem with this explanation is that many other poets of intelligibility
have retained or even increased their standing during this period. Mina Loy,
linked with Moore in Pound's estimation, would be a case in point. Laura
(Riding) Jackson is another. Loy, of course, despite Pound's comments about
logopoeia, provides a more conflicted record than Moore. Her syntactic play
and verbal excess, a formal extension of her thematic engagement with excess and play in sexuality, brings her well within the purview of the poetry
of sensibility. (Riding) Jackson, however, is unequivocally a poet of intelligibility, and her present status among poets who are themselves oriented
toward sensibility suggests that a further explanation is required.

Juliana Spahr

I guess my difficulty in answering this question means I have to agree. I don't
think I've ever cited Moore. I've read her. But I'm not sure I've absorbed her influence. I've always felt she was over my head to be honest. I can hear the music
but I can't document it in her work. I'm always scared I've missed some formal
part of it. I've never taught her work. I've never even thought of putting her on a
syllabus which is probably a sign of something.

Marianne Moore lived down the street from where Douglas Rothschild lived
for many years. And it was a few blocks away from where I live when I live in
Brooklyn. She had a pet crow and she played, perhaps taught, tennis in Fort Greene
Park or so the neighborhood publicity says. I think that is my relation to her work.
Perhaps I am saying she is a neighbor and I walk by her apartment frequently but
I don't stop in.

Why do poets oriented toward the experience of language read Pound's
Cantos for their linguistic textures and bric-a-brac quality, but not Moore's
"Camellia Sabina" or "An Octopus"? Why do they accept George Oppen's
"Of Being Numerous" for its affirmation of community, but not Moore's
"Steeple-Jack" or "New York"? Why is Laura (Riding) Jackson—who conceived of language as an unmediated sharing of truth—acknowledged as a
predecessor, but not Moore, whose emphasis on mediation fits more com-
fortably with present-day poetics? Clearly, Moore's dedication to a poetry
of intelligibility is not, in itself, a sufficient cause for her decline in reputation among poets with alternate commitments. The recuperation of other
poets who share Moore's general orientation shows this. The particularity
of her status is especially evident in comparison to that of (Riding) Jackson, whose Platonic rejection of sensibility is much more stringent than
Moore's Kantian subordination of sensibility to reason.

With this disparity in mind, I would like to offer a third and final explanation for Moore's neglect, one that takes into account the relationship *be-*

tween the poetries of sensibility and intelligibility. For if Moore's work differs from that of other poets who emphasize the sharing of meaning, it is in the way her work conceptualizes this meaning. Unlike (Riding) Jackson, whose rejection of sensibility is easily dismissed; and unlike Pound or Loy, whose extravagant uses of sensibility are easily assimilated; Moore's rigorous subordination of sensibility to intelligibility poses a challenge to the basic terms, borrowed from critical theory, with which the poetry of sensibility now explains itself.

This "now" is important. The distinction I am drawing between Moore's work and Stein's is much more pronounced today than it was when the two writers were alive. Moore herself was an admirer of Stein. She reviewed *The Making of Americans* in 1926 for the *Dial* and *The Geographical History of America* for the *Nation* in 1936, and the two books impressed her enough to include twenty years later as items 104 and 105 in a list of 112 titles for Raymond Queneau's *Pour une Bibliothèque Idéale.*[14] Moore's poetry, in other words, is not a challenge to that of Stein, but to the terms in which Stein's poetry is now upheld as superior.

Joshua Clover

Okay, you asked for it.

My first response to your assumption is, more or less, sure. I think that describes Shelley. And for that matter, Millay.

Influence quickly becomes invisible. Let's say my poetics are influenced by Guy Debord's political writings, which I suppose they are; already I have no idea how much I am influenced by his influences Bossuet and Gracian, having read neither in any great degree. Everyone influenced by Ashbery is influenced by Bishop (he once wrote that "Over 2,000 Illustrations and A Complete Concordance" was a favorite poem), and Bishop by Moore, and there you have it.

The other term you offer is that of credibility, a contingent historical category. So I guess I take your overall question to be as much about contemporary poets as about Moore's poetics considered in some more continuing terms.

But already I see I've made a mistake in accepting the category "contemporary poets." I can trust that you don't mean all poets writing now. So I then have to wonder at the extent to which the group you're defining isn't in some part selected according to the terms: poets who might be influenced by Moore, but who wouldn't necessarily admit it. So one might ask instead, what are the historical circumstances that might produce such a condition?

Okay, now that I've reframed your project on my behalf, the short answer is "because an ideology of poetics which constitutes your group holds that autonomous and/or critical art and hard formalism are antipathetic." Or to put it another way, we all know (always the introduction to ideology) that Dana Gioia would put Marianne Moore in an anthology, and this thrusts her beyond a certain discursive horizon. Or to put it another way, the extent to which she's not Gertrude Stein is coextensive with her exclusion from the canon of all the poets who have spent three decades canonizing Stein.

However, there's another component to contemporary ideology which valorizes the periodic recuperating of supposedly "conservative" figures, dragging them over to this side of the horizon and claiming them as heritage figures. The essential function here is not to save poets once marked as conservative for the progressive or avantist tendency of contemporaria. It's to demonstrate that the progressive/avantist tendency, inasmuch as it is now "revealed" to have bases as well in the traditional/conservative canon, should be recognized as substantial and even central rather than marginal.

So, to return to your question in its original form: I think your chapter may be a marker that Moore is passing from one position to another, from having use-value as an exclusion to having use-value as an inclusion. This will result in more "contemporary poets" reading her for a little while, just as everyone read John Clare for a while after Ashbery wrote about him.

I'm not sure that I can separate out my own history with Moore from polemics about ideology. I enjoyed her canonical works considerably as an undergraduate before being chivvied along to Bishop, to whom at the time I felt more kinship. I haven't returned to Moore much since then, but on the other hand, about a quarter of the poems in my first book are composed in syllabics; quantitative, nonmetrical verse still strikes me as substantial response to the question, albeit now obsolete, of the difference between American English and English English verse.

Here, then, is my third and final explanation for Moore's neglect:

Marianne Moore's poetry challenges the assumptions currently held by poets who are oriented toward sensibility, and challenges them in ways that are not easily answered.

Ron Silliman

If Marianne Moore were a product, she would be accused of mixing messages in her marketing. Is she part of the modernist revolution, alongside fellow Philadelphia-educated modernists H.D., Pound and Williams? Bryher, H.D.'s lover, published her first book. Is she the antimodernist, the editor of the journal the *Dial?* The fact that her own publishing went through a hiatus while she was at the *Dial,* combined with that journal's relatively timorous presentation of the twentieth century, certainly wed her to the school of quietude, although her poetry itself would appear to be more properly positioned amid the modernists. In trying to broker these two tendencies, which is how I read her, she ultimately became a creature of neither. In one sense, her fate is the inverse of Hart Crane's. If he was the most adventurous of the school of quietude poets, she was the least adventurous of the modernists. Neither gets read nearly as much nor as deeply as should be the case. But the fault ultimately is their own.

Earlier I spoke of a sector of poetry set within a horizon of Modernism, the New American Poetry, and critical theory. Put more simply, the writers thus described have synthesized compositional methods historically associated with the avant-garde and conceptions of language derived from lin-

guistics and philosophy. Critical theory is of course as broad a field as poetry and no one conception of language holds sway there, but insofar as the
compositional methods taken up by the poets involve a manipulation of
language understood as "material" for art, it is the concept of "materiality
of language" that has the greatest impact. Space does not permit me to summarize the complex history of this concept; nor have I the space to elucidate the leap involved when one moves from a notion of language as the
poet's basic material to a notion of language as material object. Suffice it
to say that one can manipulate a word's sound, letters, or arrangement on
the page without distinguishing this manipulation conceptually from the
manipulation of a word's meaning or associations. Unfortunately, the discourse of materiality *requires* this distinction; for although meaning is a
material for art, it is not a material object.[15]

As a keyword in poetics, "materiality" draws on a number of different
critical discourses, each one of which arrives at the concept by a different
path, with a different claim to place upon its usage. For some, the materiality is formal and implicit: the sound of a word when spoken and its
arrangement on the page when printed. For others, the materiality is historical and explicit: the specificity of *this* recorded voice or printed text.
For some, the object of study is a constituent part of language independent
of meaning: letters and syllables, graphemes and phonemes. For others, the
object of study is a particular language practice in which the meaning may
be determinant, for instance, quotation, memorization, and letter writing.
What all of these interests in "the materiality of language" share, however,
is an emphasis on the mediating qualities of language. They also share a
suspicion of critical discourses in which mediation is ignored.

Poets have taken up these ideas and transformed them, fitting them to a
context in which questions of composition are primary. Thus, where critics *study* mediation, poets *produce* it; and where critics reserve their suspicion for those who ignore mediation in their analyses (rightly assuming
that mediation is always present), poets extend this suspicion to those who
simply conceive of their practice in other terms (whether their work makes
meaningful use of mediation or not). Transposed from critical theory to poetry, in other words, "the materiality of language" becomes a program as
well as a concept.

When poets theorize this program, they tend to propose it as a "critique
of representation." Representation, in this context, becomes a general term
for all forms of communicated meaning, for declarative statements as well
as descriptions. "Critique," however, is a misnomer: poetry that produces
mediation *disrupts* representation; the critique is in the theory, not the work.

The theory goes something like this:

Poets who conceive of their production in terms other than mediation are "representational" and thus aim for a "transparency" of language: aim, that is, for an unmediated "view" into a world distinct from the language used to describe it. Poets who produce mediation aim instead for an "opacity" of language. This opacity, impeding representation, would remind us that when we "see" the world in language, we are *seeing language*.[16]

In connection with Moore, one problem with this account is its distinction between transparency and opacity, a distinction that defines meaning from sensibility's perspective, as a visualization.[17] Moore, to be sure, relied on language to make the world sensible to her readers; her powers of description are extraordinary. But Moore's language also makes the world *intelligible* to her readers. Equally problematic in connection with Moore is the assumption that an emphasis on mediation will necessarily take the form of an "opaque" language, that is, will necessarily take the form of an "impeding." This is only true, obviously, if one conceives of meaning as representation. Starting as Moore did from a different premise, mediation becomes at once more complex and more pervasive: more complex because, as Moore's work shows, one can be aware of mediations while negotiating them with ease; more pervasive, because their introduction into a poem can be coordinated with the sharing of meaning rather than treated as antagonistic to it. Indeed, one might well argue that the poetry of sensibility, in its emphasis on opacity as a form of materiality, naively assumes that the reader can enjoy an *un*mediated experience of language. In Moore's work, by contrast, even the "material" aspects of a poem (words broken at line endings, found language) are mediated by the historically determined forms in which they appear (stanzas, quotations, footnotes).

In Moore, then, there is no antagonism to sensibility, but her subordination of sensibility to intelligibility follows from a conception of poetic language that *is* antagonistic to the reduction of meaning to representation and of representation to illusion employed by sensibility's current practitioners. For Moore, representation is only one kind of meaning, and its effectiveness need not be minimized by an attention to its construction in language. Indeed, Moore's most precise and informative descriptions are often those places where the mediation of representational language is highlighted. Her pervasive use of quotation, for example, interposes other writers between herself and her readers and summons to mind contexts for understanding other than those reproduced within the poem.

Moore's poetry also operates at a different scale than the poetry of sensibility; it operates *between* her sentences as well as *within* them. Thus, even when the constituent elements of her poetry seem transparent, the connections between them will inevitably communicate a meaning for which visualization alone is insufficient. The simplicity of the parts is belied by the complexity of the whole, and in simplistic terms this relationship is like that between "sensibility" and "intelligibility"—simplistic because the individual statements also communicate a meaning beyond the merely sensible, for instance in their susceptibility to allegorical interpretation or in the meanings that unfurl when we know their historical contexts.[18] There is thus a hierarchy of meaning effects in Moore's poetry, which, when taken together, link the crude materiality of language as a thing to be experienced to the imperceptibility of concepts attained by reason. Indeed, few poets marshal as many faculties as Moore did in her writing, or exercise their faculties in so extensive a field of knowledge.

This, then, is Moore's principal challenge to the poets of sensibility: though her epistemology can account for their practice, their theory of language cannot account for what she knows.

Roberto Tejada

I think your assumption viz Moore's reception is immensely suggestive, and it seems suspended for me on the phrase "credible model." Very broadly, I think this can be attributed to how taste was—wittingly or unwittingly—supervised and reproduced according to the radicality gauge of a prior generation. Cid Corman somewhere describes MM's poetics as "Quaker baroque," and though he was wrong about Moore's religion, I think he's on to something in that he identifies a rift between a negative and positive aesthetics—one based on lack, the other on abundance; and would it be wrong to claim there are, in U.S. American advanced poetries, ever residues of a puritanical distrust of the latter? I was very close to MM for a few years in the late 1990s, and found the rhapsodic manufacture of her work a vast resource to be studied.

In Moore, materiality and mediation are highlighted but made subservient to the aims of representational language, which renders the world sensible. At the same time, representational language is itself made subservient to forms of knowledge that occur in imperceptible registers of the mind. In this way, her work measures the limits of representation much more rigorously and radically than does the antirepresentational language of the poets of sensibility. With this in mind I will conclude with an assertion about reading that is far from original and yet necessary to state again and again when making the case for a poetry such as Moore's:

Reading in its most meaningful construction is not a perception of objects external to language, nor a sensitivity to words, but a process of understanding.

Robert Creeley

"Marianne Moore is not a credible model for contemporary poets and remains uncited, if not unread, even by those who seem to have absorbed her influence." Even as one might say that, the contemporary is fading to the past. Language poetry melds with Imagism, and like some aureate glow, there's Romanticism back of them all. Marianne Moore has become so embedded in the poetry following hers that whatever one might think of her own poems, she'd be in so much else it would be impossible, and altogether pointless, to weed her out. Elizabeth Bishop is the first defining disciple—but there are veritable myriads more. People using her had always to figure their own way. She was too particular to be used "generally." Williams, in that respect, was far simpler—as were Pound, Stevens, and Eliot.

"What is your own opinion of (and/or relation to) Moore's work?" For myself and friends, particularly Robert Duncan, Marianne Moore was one of the defining Moderns along with Williams and Pound. Her editing of the *Dial* shows how much her contemporaries valued her—Eliot among them. If remembering lines, like they say, has anything to do with it, hers come back to me again and again. "Spenser's Ireland" is, put simply, a masterpiece in so many ways—its exceptional use of rhythms, for example—who else so quietly makes a line "beat backward," call it? Too often discussion of her work has got stuck in proposed formulae for her prosody, syllabics, etc. All such may be true enough but it is in the particulars of her work that all comes to bear, to take and find place. That fact is most evident in her use of rhyme, but it is everywhere—her pacing, her quick shifts of word ("enchantment/enchanter's/enchanted"), her ability to suspend time in remarkably extended periods—and to think/to see as she goes. So one wants to say as ever, "What goes around comes around"—as will her work and its readers.

But actually, why wait? Just now checking the Amazon sales rank of her *Collected Poems*, one finds it at 72,568—which seems to me entirely respectable? Stevens is 46,448—Williams, 80,437 (for the first volume, paper)—Cummings, 13,838 (hardcover!)—Eliot, 22,159 (also hardcover)—Yeats, 7,941—with Tennyson (*Selected Poems*) it fades, alas: 886,083 . . .

> On either side the river lie
> Long fields of barley and of rye,
> That clothe the word and meet the sky;
> And thro' the field the road runs by
> To many-tower'd Camelot . . .

But with Robert Lowell's recent *Collected Poems* (1,995!!), one's back in the race. So what else is new, eh?

In "The Mind Is an Enchanting Thing," we learn that the mind enchants and is enchanted by its affections. We also learn that the mind knows these affections by way of the senses, and knows itself *as if* with the senses. In this way, the mind assimilates a knowledge gained by the eye and ear to "memory's eye" and "memory's ear." Yet the mind is more than this assimilation of knowledge, and its poetry—picking and choosing between sense impressions and ideas, between certainties of orientation and inconsistencies of application—celebrates a higher order of intelligence: the ability to true, prove, and consciously change:

The Mind Is an Enchanting Thing

is an enchanted thing
    like the glaze on a
katydid-wing
      subdivided by sun
      till the nettings are legion.
Like Gieseking playing Scarlatti;

like the apteryx-awl
    as a beak, or the
kiwi's rain-shawl
      of haired feathers, the mind
      feeling its way as though blind,
walks along with its eyes on the ground.

It has memory's ear
    that can hear without
having to hear.
      Like the gyroscope's fall,
      truly unequivocal
because trued by regnant certainty,

it is a power of
    strong enchantment. It
is like the dove-
      neck animated by
      sun; it is memory's eye;
it's conscientious inconsistency.

It tears off the veil; tears
    the temptation, the
mist the heart wears,
      from its eyes—if the heart
      has a face; it takes apart
dejection. It's fire in the dove-neck's

iridescence; in the
    inconsistencies
of Scarlatti.
      Unconfusion submits
      its confusion to proof; it's
not a Herod's oath that cannot change.

                    (*CPo* 134–35)

I take this poem as a manifesto, with the interplay between its title and first line—between "enchanting" and "enchanted"—as a diagnosis of the mind's twofold nature. Creatures of sensibility and intelligibility, we both succumb to the sensual and exercise faculties to which the sensual must succumb. It is this doubleness that marks our lives in nature and in history, and that marks Moore's poetry as equal to that life.

She is, for me, the one irreplaceable Modernist.

ACKNOWLEDGMENTS

I am deeply indebted to all of the poets who took time to answer my query: Charles Bernstein, Joshua Clover, Robert Creeley, Jordan Davis, Rachel Blau DuPlessis, Lyn Hejinian, K. Silem Mohammad, Jena Osman, Lytle Shaw, Ron Silliman, Juliana Spahr, Brian Kim Stefans, Roberto Tejada, Barrett Watten, and Rebecca Wolff. Jessica Miller helped me to think about Plato and Kant; Carla Billitteri assisted in the composition; Linda Leavell, Cristanne Miller, and Robin Schulze provided guidance in revision. My thanks are also due to the many Moore scholars whose papers, informal talks, and conversation helped to shape this text, in particular Logan Esdale, Fiona Green, Jeanne Heuving, Stacy Hubbard, Elisabeth Joyce, Linda Leavell, Ellen Levy, Cristanne Miller, Robin Schulze, Heather White, and Jeff Wood.

NOTES

1. Regarding Moore's credibility in other sectors, I would cite, as partial confirmation of my thesis, Joseph Parisi's preface to *Marianne Moore: The Art of a Modernist* (Ann Arbor, MI: UMI Research Press, 1990), a collection of essays by Richard Howard, Robert Pinsky, Sandra M. Gilbert, Alicia Ostriker, David Bromwich, and John Hollander: "Despite the major achievements in her innovative poetry and her extensive contributions as a prose stylist, [Moore] also retains curious distinction as the most undervalued writer of [her] distinguished company. . . . [C]ompared with her peers, Marianne Moore has been misperceived and poorly attended" (xi). More pointedly, when Parisi's six poets consider Moore's influence on later practitioners (in their transcribed "Symposium," 121–23) they are hard pressed for examples and sketchy in their analyses.

2. Moore, I would note, appears in Jerome Rothenberg's 1974 anthology *Revolution of the Word: A New Gathering of American Avant Garde Poetry, 1914–1945* (New York: Seabury Press, 1974), which mapped out a possible canon at just the moment when critical theory began to reorient poetic attention. It is this subsequent moment that defines for me the contemporary.

3. Steve Farmer's "Marianne Moore" appeared in *Jimmy & Lucy's House of "K"*, no. 3 (January 1985): 15–22. DuPlessis writes about Moore in "No Moore of the Same," 6–32, and "'Corpses of Poesy': Some Modern Poets and Some Gender Ideologies of Lyric," in *Feminist Measures: Soundings in Poetry and Theory*, ed. Lynn Keller and Cristanne Miller (Ann Arbor: University of Michigan Press, 1994). Both essays are absorbed into her *Genders, Races and Religious Cultures in Modern American Poetry* (Cambridge: Cambridge University Press, 2001).

4. The most substantial attempt to integrate Moore so far is Cynthia Hogue's "Another Postmodernism: Towards an Ethical Poetics," *How2* 1, no. 7 (Spring 2002), http://www.scc.rutgers.edu/however/v1_7_200/current/in_conference/msa/hogue.shtm. Kathleen Fraser refers to the "bridge" in her inaugural editorial; she cites Moore as the source for the journal's name in *Translating the Unspeakable: Poetry and the Innovative Necessity* (Tuscaloosa: University of Alabama Press, 2000), 36.

5. For examples of scholarly work by poets, see, in addition to the works cited above, Donald Hall, *Marianne Moore: The Cage and the Animal* (New York: Pegasus, 1970); Pamela White Hadas, *Marianne Moore: Poet of Affection* (Syracuse, NY: Syracuse University Press, 1977); Taffy Martin, *Marianne Moore: Subversive Modernist* (Austin: University of Texas Press, 1986); Grace Schulman, *Marianne Moore: The Poetry of Engagement* (Urbana: University of Illinois Press, 1986); Lisa M. Steinman, *Made in America: Science, Technology, and American Modernist Poets* (New Haven, CT: Yale University Press, 1987); Jeredith Merrin, *An Enabling Humility: Marianne Moore, Elizabeth Bishop, and the Uses of Tradition* (New Brunswick, NJ: Rutgers University Press, 1990); and Jeanne Heuving, *Omissions Are Not Accidents: Gender in the Art of Marianne Moore* (Detroit: Wayne State University Press, 1992).

6. See Plato, *The Republic,* 514b–518b for the parable of the cave; Plato prepares the way for this parable at 509c–511d, in his discussion of *"eidoi"* (a word often translated as "forms").

7. Immanuel Kant, *Critique of Pure Reason,* trans. Norman Kemp Smith (Boston and New York: Bedford/St. Martin's Press, 1965), 274.

8. Kant, *Critique of Pure Reason,* 467.

9. The scheme is complicated but not vitiated by the fact that poetry of the first sort is often focused in its meaning on sense perception, while poetry of the second sort is often written for reasons that are less materialist than conceptual.

10. Northrop Frye, *Fables of Identity: Studies in Poetic Mythology* (New York: Harcourt, Brace & World, 1963), 133.

11. Jerome McGann, *The Poetics of Sensibility: A Revolution in Poetic Language* (Oxford: Clarenden Press, 1998), 1, 23, 134.

12. Wallace Stevens, *Collected Poetry and Prose* (New York: Library of America, 1997), 700, 701, 706.

13. See Ezra Pound, "Others," *Little Review* 4 (March 1918): 56–58. A shorter version of this note appears under the title "Marianne Moore and Mina Loy" in Pound's *Selected Prose 1909–1965* (New York: New Directions Press, 1973).

14. See *CPr* 128–31, 339–41, 668–90.

15. I say unfortunately because the end result has often been a misconstrual of meaning as immaterial.

16. The sketch I have just given is a drastic simplification of complex arguments and, more importantly, of varied practices that imply or produce variations of the basic theory. I have no doubt, therefore, that poets who recognized some semblance of their projects in this sketch would question its veracity. As a representation, it affirms the ineffectiveness of representation. But my aim here is not to provide a "thick description" of the poetry of sensibility. Rather, I want to provide an account of the assumptions, or some of them, with which this poetry explains itself.

17. The distinction between transparency and opacity was familiar to Moore, but she did not consider the qualities that these terms name as intrinsic to texts. Rather, she considered them as readerly experiences, that is, as markers of our ability or inability to negotiate a text. Thus, of Gertrude Stein, Moore wrote, "one is abashed not to have understood instantly; as water may not seem transparent to the observer but has a perspicuous opacity in which the fish swims with ease." Transparency is here a metaphor for understanding: one

can swim through language that impedes the eyes, for there is more than one way to understand, and sometimes "fish" are better suited to the task than "observers" (*CPr* 340).

18. What I am saying here is of course a platitude: that the meaning of the poem is the whole poem, not its separate parts. But the necessity for insisting on this only makes more pointed the fact that contemporary conceptions of poetic language fail to take account of the qualitative difference between the way one understands a "part" and the way one understands a "whole." This is partly because few poets push the issue of this difference as far as Moore.

Poems by Jeanne Heuving

Fortunate Torsos

Something like me. Dirty water in the quart jar we tried to keep clean. Slosh with boats of bark, slur into currents. Three plastic daisies on astroturf. Nothing strikes like a hawk, a crouching hare. She sings her rose petal body home. To rinse until the clear whitens. Angle eyes. Sweetheart.

Fine Reticule

To say any such thing that will make us glad. Rub a dub dub three men in a tub. Three plastic daisies on astroturf. Entangling strands of dirty water. To clean until the clear whitens. Pitches salt. Sheep roam in the gloaming.

Brows

Mouth around mouth around words. Mouthing words. Soft Shoe. Shoeing it. Schussing down the mountain. Sluice run off. Such unnatural preternatural clarity. Rough brown roads visible from this far distance. Lofty. Rafter. Browse.

Grays

A lemon snow cone. Sluice run off. Fine screen catching stones, some pretty. Tiny craniums, blackened skulls. Black netting crawling over eyes. Beauty mark. A valve or gate to regulate the flow. To flood or drench with released water. To draw off. Sidelong. Graze.

Drowse

Berries. Black dot. Glistening. Piled to the rafters. Popping bird. Toppling trees. Twig in beak. Beaking it. B-eking it. Clattering capsules. Broken chamois. Bare branched mountain ash with clusters of orange-red. Smashed on sidewalk. Smeared yellow. Dowse.

Douse

Drenched weave. Reordering to get the snap of synapse. Lines on cerebral cortex. Lines inside fleshy creases creasing secreting lemony watery. Berry juice on lips. Berry flesh on tongue. Douse.

Furrow

How all is a fertile field ever threatening
Plowed too close like an ominous sky
Disappointment wanting to shut down
Earth ever opened the possibility of
Into the plowed furrowed lined earth
A fertile plow into the staid forestation
Into the silvered peat moss lined with
A jewelry box felted with diamonds

A heavy earth weeps in undulation
A long yellow swathing of the sky
Searing the dogs of Europe, hypocrite,
Lecteur, O keep the dogs far hence.
Travelling the horizon in great strides
Spills down from the sky, fissuring
Silver rivulets of earth-felled dawn
Etched mercury in blasted abutments
Gray mazy cells to pick from other
Culled, picked through, picked over

---

seeds with their hooded black jackets
carapace of insect left to wither in the wind
to mash with a mallet to get the insides out
harvested when a light brown will turn black
a round hole bored in the seed by a weevil
seeds of the penstemons and the mulleins
are easy to remove by the crushing method
to remove the seed heads the cones must be
split open washed inside minute stuffs

---

the possibility of light falling onto his face
the possibility of walking into a sunlit alcove
the sunlit alcove fitting rippling like a glove
the glove moving from finger tip to forearm
silky on flesh receptive to being touched

deadening hollow black seeds refusing
this morrow ever turning over onto itself

What does not go away this
Mascared eyes, Cleopatra
Charcoaled Marlene Dietrich
Wanting at the grave as it
Descend into pasturelands
Green rolling, swollen

SOURCES

Harry. R. Phillips, ed. *Growing and Propagating Wildflowers,* Chapel Hill: University of North Carolina Press, 1985.

Poem by Lisa M. Steinman

Marriage—

a state or action that's been called a form
of friendship recognized by the police,
blending tradition and modernity,

like the mix in the name of a local
store, "The Vinyl Bridal Shoppe." Or in the
names given by a neighborhood woman

to her three kids: Mannix, Starsky and Hutch,
and George. A singular institution
made of dreams and discussions of who'll do

dishes. Of learning it's small potatoes
if, while clearing the table, one of you
always leaves behind a solitary

fork or spoon "to appease the gods," or that
only one of you believes doors can be
left open . . . that one of you collects

kewpie dolls, while the other's passionate
about divestment. You need not expect
that you'll share absolutely everything:

old friends and tee-shirts and taste. So you make
do, make it up as you go along, wing
it to discover, near the unwashed socks,

piles of discarded words: *uxorious,*
husbandry, covenant, to bind, wedlock,
having or *taking,* although you can still

hold affection. Whatever marriage is,
it no longer appears to be simple.
It's certainly not "he said, she said," though

it may be "I said, we said." Of course, this
is a dialogue. "Hello," she says to
the winter sun each morning. "Hello, your-

self," he says back. It's an estate of peace—
"of liberty and union," as Webster's
statue says. Nuptials, like fields

of potatoes or grain, give sustenance.
As when, up late arguing, no one yields,
but each rises next morning converted.

Or when the leaver of cutlery clears
everything away, and, disconcerted,
the other misses stray forks on the table

after meals. The married speak in the first
person plural, the unfashionable
'we' without which there's no 'I' to speak of,

no 'you' to speak to, no people in places
held in common. At root, marriage hovers
between "good luck" and "congratulations,"

between the done and the beginning. We
still tie knots & say "I do," one on one
daily, in the first person, in the flesh,

which is why we still throw rice at weddings—
to show it's not against the grain, this two-
sided consensual negotiation.

Bibliography

A Celebration of H.D. and Marianne Moore. Special issue, *Poesis* 6, nos. 3–4 (1985).

Abbott, Craig S. *Marianne Moore: A Descriptive Bibliography.* Pittsburgh, PA: University of Pittsburgh Press, 1977.

Adams, Thomas. *A Commentary or, Exposition upon the Divine Second Epistle Generall, Written by the Blessed Apostle St. Peter.* London, Printed by Richard Badger for Iacob Bloome, 1633.

Adamson, Jane, Richard Freadman, and David Parker, eds. *Renegotiating Ethics in Literature, Philosophy, and Theory.* Cambridge: Cambridge University Press, 1998.

Altieri, Charles. *Painterly Abstraction in Modernist American Poetry: The Contemporaneity of Modernism.* Cambridge: Cambridge University Press, 1989.

———. "What Differences Can Contemporary Poetry Make in Our Moral Thinking?" In *Renegotiating Ethics in Literature, Philosophy, and Theory,* edited by Jane Adamson, Richard Freadman, and David Parker, 113–33. Cambridge: Cambridge University Press, 1998.

Ariès, Phillipe. *Centuries of Childhood: A Social History of Family Life.* New York: Knopf, 1962.

Ashbery, John. "The Impossible." *Poetry* 90, no. 4 (July 1957): 250–54.

———. "Straight Lines Over Rough Terrain." *New York Times Book Review,* November 26, 1967, 1.

Avedon, Richard. *Evidence, 1944–1994.* Edited by Mary Shanahan. New York: Random House, 1994.

Babcock, Robert. "Verses, Translations, and Reflections from 'The Anthology': H. D., Ezra Pound, and the Greek Anthology." *Sagetrieb* 14, nos. 1–2 (Spring/Fall 1995): 202–16.

Bacon, Francis. *The Essayes or Covnsels, Civill and Morall.* London, Hanna Barret, 1625.

Barthes, Roland. *Camera Lucida: Reflections on Photography.* Translated by Richard Howard. New York: Hill and Wang, 1981.

———. *The Pleasures of the Text.* Translated by Richard Miller. New York: Hill and Wang, 1999.

Baxter, Richard. *The Saints' Everlasting Rest.* 1650. Edited by William Young. London: Religious Tract Society, 1907.

Bazin, Victoria. "Marianne Moore, Kenneth Burke, and the Poetics of Literary Labour." *Journal of American Studies* 35, no. 3 (2001): 433–52.

Bhabha, Homi. *The Location of Culture.* London: Routledge, 1994.

Bishop, Elizabeth. "Efforts of Affection: A Memoir of Marianne Moore." *Vanity Fair,* May 1983. Reprinted in *The Collected Prose of Elizabeth Bishop,* edited by Robert Giroux, 121–56. New York: Farrar, Straus and Giroux, 1984. All page references are to the reprint.

Blackmur, R. P. *Language as Gesture: Essays in Poetry.* London: George Allen & Unwin, 1954.

———. "The Method of Marianne Moore." In *Marianne Moore: A Collection of Critical Essays,* edited by Charles Tomlinson, 66–86. Englewood Cliffs, NJ: Prentice-Hall, 1969.

———. "The Clarity of Fiction." In *The Sirens' Song: Selected Essays by Maurice Blanchot,* edited by Gabriel Josipovici. Translated by Sacha Rabinovitch. Brighton, UK: Harvester Press, 1982.

Blanchot, Maurice. *The Space of Literature.* Translated by Ann Smock. Lincoln: University of Nebraska Press, 1989.

Bloom, Harold, ed. *Marianne Moore.* Modern Critical Views Series. Broomall, PA: Chelsea House, 1987.

Bornstein, George. *Material Modernism: The Politics of the Page.* Cambridge: Cambridge University Press, 2001.

Boroff, Marie. *Language and the Poet: Verbal Artistry in Frost, Stevens, and Moore.* Chicago: University of Chicago Press, 1979.

Boswell, James. *The Life of Samuel Johnson.* 3rd ed. 4 vols. London: C. Dilly, 1799.

Brooke-Rose, Christine. "Palimpsest History." In Umberto Eco, *Interpretation and Overinterpretation,* with Richard Rorty, Jonathan Culler, and Christine Brooke-Rose. Edited by Stefan Collini. Cambridge: Cambridge University Press, 1992.

Brosterman, Norman. *Inventing Kindergarten.* New York: Harry N. Abrams, 1997.

Browne, Sir Thomas. *The Major Works.* Edited by C. A. Patrides. Harmondsworth, UK and New York: Penguin, 1977.

Browning, Robert, and Elizabeth Barrett. *The Letters of Robert Browning and Elizabeth Barrett, 1845–1846.* 2 vols. New York: Harper Brothers, 1899.

Bunyan, John. *The Pilgrim's Progress from This World to That Which is to Come; Delivered Under the Similitude of a Dream.* 1678. Buffalo, NY: Geo. H. Derby and Co., 1853.

———. *The Pilgrim's Progress.* 1678. Edited by N. H. Keeble. Oxford: Oxford University Press, 1998.

Byrne, Donn. "The Rock Whence I Was Hewn." *National Geographic Magazine,* March 1927, 257–316.

Cantrell, Caroll H. "'The Roar of Ice': Motion, Language, and Silence in Marianne Moore." In *New Essays in Eco-Feminist Literary Criticism,* edited by Glynis Carr, 157–74. Lewisburg, PA: Bucknell University Press, 2000.

Carey, M. C. "The Octopus in the Channel Islands." *Graphic,* August 25, 1923, 282.

Caws, Mary Ann. *The Eye in the Text: Essays on Perception, Mannerist to Modern.* Princeton, NJ: Princeton University Press, 1981.

Cleto, Fabio. *Camp: Queer Aesthetics and the Performing Subject: A Reader.* Ann Arbor: University of Michigan Press, 1999.

Colum, Padraic. *The Big Tree of Bunlahy: Stories of My Countryside.* New York: Macmillan, 1933.

Cooper, James Fenimore. "American and European Scenery Compared." In *The Home-Book of the Picturesque: or American scenery, art and literature.* 1852. A facsimile reproduction of the first edition with an introduction by Motley F. Deakin. Gainesville, FL: Scholars' Facsimiles & Reprints, 1967.

Cornell, Joseph. *Joseph Cornell's Theatre of the Mind: Selected Diaries, Letters and Files.* Edited by Mary Ann Caws. New York: Thames and Hudson, 1993.

Costello, Bonnie. *Marianne Moore: Imaginary Possessions.* Cambridge, MA: Harvard University Press, 1981.

————. *Shifting Ground: Reinventing Landscape in Modern American Poetry.* Cambridge, MA: Harvard University Press, 2003.

Cotton, John. *The Way of Life, Or, Gods Way and Course, in Bringing the Soule into, keeping it in, and carrying it on, in the wayes of life and peace. Laide downe in foure severall Treatises in foure Texts of Scripture.* 1641. In *Colonial and Federal American Writing,* edited by George F. Horner and Robin A. Bain, 92–98. New York: Odyssey, 1966.

Crashaw, Richard. *Carmen Deo Nostro.* Paris: Peter Targa, 1652.

Dahl, June Wilkinson. *A History of Kirkwood Missouri: 1851–65.* Kirkwood, MO: Kirkwood Historical Society, 1965.

Degler, Carl N. *In Search of Human Nature: The Decline and Revival of Darwinism in American Social Thought.* New York: Oxford University Press, 1991.

Deleuze, Gilles. *The Logic of Sense.* New York: Columbia University Press, 1990.

Dickey, James. "What the Angels Missed." Review of *Tell Me, Tell Me: Granite, Steel, and Other Topics* by Marianne Moore. *New York Times Book Review,* December 25, 1966, 1.

Diehl, Jeanne Feit. *Elizabeth Bishop and Marianne Moore: The Psychodynamics of Creativity.* Princeton, NJ: Princeton University Press, 1993.

————. "In the Twilight of the Gods: Women Poets and the American Sublime." In *The American Sublime,* edited by Mary Arensberg, 173–214. Albany: State University of New York Press, 1986.

DuPlessis, Rachel Blau. "'Corpses of Poesy': Some Modern Poets and Some Gender Ideologies of Lyric." In *Feminist Measures: Soundings in Poetry and Theory,* edited by Lynn Keller and Cristanne Miller, 69–95. Ann Arbor: University of Michigan Press, 1994.

————. *Genders, Races, and Religious Cultures in Modern American Poetry, 1908–1934.* Cambridge: Cambridge University Press, 2001.

————. "No Moore of the Same: The Feminist Poetic of Marianne Moore." *William Carlos Williams Review* 14, no. 1 (Spring 1988): 6–32.

Earls, Brian. "Bulls, Blunders, and Bloothers. An Examination of the Irish Bull." *Béaloideas* 56 (1988):1–92.

Eco, Umberto. *Interpretation and Overinterpretation.* In collaboration with Richard Rorty, Jonathan Culler, and Christine Brooke-Rose. Edited by Stefan Collini. Cambridge: Cambridge University Press, 1992.

Edgeworth, Maria. *The Absentee.* Edited by W. J. MacCormack and Kim Walker. New York: Oxford University Press, 1988.

————. *Castle Rackrent.* 1800. Edited by George Watson. New York: Oxford University Press, 1964.

————, and Richard Lovell Edgeworth. *Essay on Irish Bulls.* Philadelphia: William Duane, 1803.

Emerson, Ralph Waldo. *Selected Writings of Ralph Waldo Emerson.* Edited by Donald McQuade. New York: Modern Library, 1981.

English, Hugh. " 'By Being Outside of America': Gertrude Stein's 'Geographical History' of Gender, Self and Writing." In *Women, America, and Movement: Narratives of Relocation,* edited by Susan L. Roberson, 258–80. Columbia: University of Missouri Press, 1998.

Erasmus. *Collected Works of Erasmus.* Translated by Margaret Mann Phillips and R. A. B. Mynors. Toronto, Canada: University of Toronto Press, 1992.

Erickson, Darlene Williams. *Illusion Is More Precise than Precision: The Poetry of Marianne Moore.* Tuscaloosa: University of Alabama Press, 1992.

Erkkila, Betsy. *The Wicked Sisters: Women Poets, Literary History, and Discord.* New York: Oxford University Press, 1992.

Farmer, Steve. "Marianne Moore." *Jimmy & Lucy's House of "K",* no. 3 (January 1985): 15–22.

Feldman, Evelyn, and Michael Barsanti. "Paying Attention: The Rosenbach Museum's Marianne Moore Archive and the New York Moderns." *Journal of Modern Literature* 22, no. 2 (Fall 1998): 7–30.

Fenton, James. *The Strength of Poetry: Oxford Lectures.* New York: Farrar, Straus and Giroux, 2001.

Fraser, Kathleen. *Translating the Unspeakable: Poetry and the Innovative Necessity.* Tuscaloosa: University of Alabama Press, 2000.

Friedman, Susan Stanford. *Mappings: Feminism and the Cultural Geographies of Encounter.* Princeton, NJ: Princeton University Press, 1998.

Froebel, Friedrich. *The Education of Man.* Translated by W. N. Hailmann. New York: D. Appleton, 1895.

Frye, Northrop. *Fables of Identity: Studies in Poetic Mythology.* New York: Harcourt, Brace & World, 1963.

Gallagher, Tess. "Throwing the Scarecrows from the Garden." *Parnassus* 12, no. 2 / 13, no. 1 (1985): 45–60.

Garrigue, Jean. *Marianne Moore.* Minneapolis: University of Minnesota Press, 1965.

Gilbert, Sandra. "Marianne Moore as Female Female Impersonator." In *Marianne Moore: The Art of a Modernist,* edited by Joseph Parisi, 27–48. Ann Arbor, MI: UMI Research Press, 1990.

———, and Susan Gubar. *No Man's Land: The Place of the Woman Writer in the Twentieth Century.* Vol. 3: *Letters from the Front.* New Haven, CT: Yale University Press, 1994.

Goodridge, Celeste. *Hints and Disguises: Marianne Moore and Her Contemporaries.* Iowa City: University of Iowa Press, 1989.

———, ed. *Marianne Moore.* Special issue, *Sagetrieb* 6 (Winter 1987).

Graham, Theodora Rapp, ed. *Marianne Moore.* Special issue, *William Carlos Williams Review* 14 (Spring 1988).

Graphic. "The Laboratory of the S-Ray: Where Statistics Are Made Fascinating," August 25, 1923, 284.

———. "The Mystery of an Adjective, and of Evening Clothes." June 21, 1924, 1006.

Greenberg, Clement. "Avant Garde and Kitsch." 1939. In *Art and Culture: Critical Essays,* 3–21. Boston: Beacon Press, 1961.

Gregory, Elizabeth, ed. *The Critical Response to Marianne Moore.* Westport, CT: Praeger, 2003.

———. *Quotation and Modern American Poetry: "Imaginary Gardens with Real Toads."* Houston, TX: Rice University Press, 1996.

———. "Stamps, Money, Pop Culture, and Marianne Moore." *Discourse* 17, no. 1 (Fall 1994): 123–46.

Hadas, Pamela White. *Marianne Moore: Poet of Affection.* Syracuse, NY: Syracuse University Press, 1977.

Hall, Donald. "The Art of Poetry: Marianne Moore: An Interview with Donald Hall." In *Marianne Moore: A Collection of Critical Essays,* edited by Charles Tomlinson, 20–45. Englewood Cliffs, NJ: Prentice-Hall, 1969.

———. "Interview with Marianne Moore by Donald Hall." In *Poets at Work,* edited by George Plimpton, 75–100. New York: Penguin, 1989.

———. *Marianne Moore: The Cage and the Animal.* New York: Pegasus, 1970.

Hall, Joseph. "One of the Sermons Preacht at Westminster, on the day of the Publicke Fast (April 5, 1628)." In *The Works of Joseph Hall.* London, Printed for Nathaniel Butter, 1634.

Haller, Mark H. *Eugenics: Hereditarian Attitudes in American Thought.* New Brunswick, NJ: Rutgers University Press, 1963.

Hamill, Samuel. "Poets Against the War" project. http://www.poetsagainstthewar.org/ (accessed July 10, 2004).

Hartog, Francis. *The Mirror of Herodotus: The Representation of the Other in the Writing of History.* Translated by Janet Lloyd. Berkeley and Los Angeles: University of California Press, 1988.

Herodotus. *The History.* Edited by David Grene. Chicago: University of Chicago Press, 1987.

Heuving, Jeanne. *Omissions Are Not Accidents: Gender in the Art of Marianne Moore.* Detroit: Wayne State University Press, 1992.

Hickok, Gloria Vando, ed. *Marianne Moore.* Special issue, *Helicon Nine* (Summer 1988).

Hogue, Cynthia. "Another Postmodernism: Towards an Ethical Poetics." *How2* 1, no. 7 (Spring 2002) http://www.scc.rutgers.edu/however/v1_7_200/current/in_conference/msa/hogue.shtm (accessed July 9, 2004).

———. *Scheming Women: Poetry, Privilege, and the Politics of Subjectivity.* Albany: State University of New York Press, 1995.

Hollander, John. "Seeking Poetic Justice." *Los Angeles Times,* March 3, 2003, sec. A1, 10–11.

Holley, Margaret. *The Poetry of Marianne Moore: A Study in Voice and Value.* Cambridge: Cambridge University Press, 1987.

Honigsblum, Bonnie. "An Annotated Bibliography of Works about Marianne Moore, 1977–1990." In *Marianne Moore: Woman and Poet,* edited by Patricia C. Willis, 443–620. Orono, ME: National Poetry Foundation, 1990.

Hooker, Richard. *The Laws of Ecclesiastical Politie.* London: John Windet, 1604.

Horner, George F., and Robin A. Bain, eds. *Colonial and Federal American Writing.* New York: Odyssey, 1966.

Hotelling, Kristin. " 'The I of each is to the I of each, a kind of fretful speech which sets a limit on itself': Marianne Moore's Strategic Selfhood." *Modernism/Modernity* 5, no. 1 (1998): 75–96.

Howard, Richard. "The Monkey Business of Modernism." In *Marianne Moore: The Art of a Modernist,* edited by Joseph Parisi, 1–12. Ann Arbor, MI: UMI Research Press, 1990.

Hubbard, Stacy Carson. "The Many-Armed Embrace: Collection, Quotation and Mediation in Marianne Moore's Poetry." *Sagetrieb* 12, no. 2 (Fall 1993): 7–32.

Illustrated London News. "Everest the Merciless and Still Unconquered: A Climbing Tragedy," June 28, 1924, 1231.

Jarrell, Randall. "Her Shield." In *Marianne Moore: A Collection of Critical Essays,* edited by Charles Tomlinson, 114–24. Englewood Cliffs, NJ: Prentice-Hall, 1969.

Johnson, Samuel. *The History of Rasselas, Prince of Abyssinia.* 1759. Edited by Gwin J. Kolb. New York: Appleton Century Crofts, 1962.

Joyce, Elisabeth W. *Cultural Critique and Abstraction: Marianne Moore and the Avant-garde.* Lewisburg, PA: Bucknell University Press, 1998.

Juhasz, Suzanne. *Naked and Fiery Forms: Modern American Poetry by Women, A New Tradition.* New York: Harper Colophon, 1976.

Kadlec, David. "Marianne Moore, Immigration, and Eugenics." *Modernism/Modernity* 1, no. 2 (April 1994): 21–49.

———. *Mosaic Modernism: Anarchism, Pragmatism, Culture.* Baltimore: Johns Hopkins University Press, 2000.

Kant, Immanuel. *Critique of Pure Reason.* Translated by Norman Kemp Smith. Boston and New York: Bedford/St. Martin's Press, 1965.

Kappel, Andrew J., ed. *Marianne Moore Issue.* Special issue, *Twentieth-Century Literature* 30 (Summer/Fall 1984).

———. "Notes on the Presbyterian Poetry of Marianne Moore." In *Marianne Moore: Woman and Poet,* edited by Patricia Willis, 39–51. Orono, ME: National Poetry Foundation, 1990.

———. "The *Verba Ardentia* of Richard Baxter in the Poems of Marianne Moore." *Christianity and Literature* 41 (Summer 1992): 421–44.

Keller, Lynn. "'For inferior who is free?': Liberating the Woman Writer in Marianne Moore's 'Marriage.'" In *Influence and Intertextuality in Literary History,* edited by Jay Clayton and Eric Rothstein, 219–44. Madison: University of Wisconsin Press, 1991.

Kenner, Hugh. *A Homemade World: The American Modernist Writers.* Baltimore: Johns Hopkins University Press, 1975.

Kent, Kathryn R. *Making Girls into Women: American Women's Writing and the Rise of Lesbian Identity.* Durham, NC: Duke University Press, 2003.

Kline, Stephen. "The Making of Children's Culture." In *The Children's Culture Reader,* edited by Henry Jenkins, 95–109. New York: New York University Press, 1998.

Knight, Christopher J. *The Patient Particulars: American Modernism and the Technique of Originality.* Lewisburg, PA: Bucknell University Press, 1995.

Kreymborg, Alfred. *Troubadour.* New York: Boni and Liveright, 1925.

Lakritz, Andrew M. *Modernism and the Other in Stevens, Frost, and Moore.* Gainesville: University Press of Florida, 1996.

Lane, Gary. *A Concordance to the Poems of Marianne Moore.* New York: Haskell House, 1972.

Lears, Jackson. *No Place of Grace: Antimodernism and the Transformation of American Culture 1880–1920.* New York: Pantheon Books, 1981.

Leavell, Linda. *Marianne Moore and the Visual Arts: Prismatic Color.* Baton Rouge: Louisiana State University Press, 1995.

———. "Marianne Moore, Her Family, and Their Language." *Proceedings of the American Philosophical Society* 147, no. 2 (2003): 141–43.

———. "Marianne Moore, the James Family, and the Politics of Celibacy." *Twentieth-Century Literature* 49, no. 2 (summer 2003): 219–45.

Levine, Lawrence. *Highbrow/Lowbrow: The Emergence of Cultural Hierarchy in America.* Cambridge, MA: Harvard University Press, 1988.

Lindenbusch, John. *Four Walking Tours of Kirkwood Missouri* (1981). Kirkwood Cham-

ber of Commerce, Kirkwood, MO. http://www.kirkwoodarea.com/tourism/walking_
tours.htm (accessed July 24, 2003).

Los Angeles Times. "Seeking Poetic Justice," A1, March 3, 2003.

Malamud, Randy. *Poetic Animals and Animal Souls.* New York: Palgrave, 2003.

Marek, Jayne E. *Women Editing Modernism: "Little" Magazines and Literary History.* Lexington: University Press of Kentucky, 1995.

Martin, Taffy. *Marianne Moore: Subversive Modernist.* Austin: University of Texas Press, 1986.

McGann, Jerome. *The Poetics of Sensibility: A Revolution in Poetic Language.* Oxford: Clarenden Press, 1998.

Merrin, Jeredith. *An Enabling Humility: Marianne Moore, Elizabeth Bishop, and the Uses of Tradition.* New Brunswick, NJ: Rutgers University Press, 1990.

———. "Sites of Struggle: Marianne Moore and American Calvinism." In *The Calvanist Roots of the Modern Era,* edited by Aliki Barnstone et al., 91–106. Hanover, NH: University Press of New England, 1997.

Miller, Cristanne. "Marianne Moore and a Poetry of Hebrew (Protestant) Prophecy." In *Twentieth-Century American Women's Poetics of Engagement,* edited by Cristina Giorcelli, Cristanne Miller and Shira Wolosky. Special issue, *Sources: Revue d'etudes Anglophones* 12 (Spring 2002): 9–47.

———. *Marianne Moore: Questions of Authority.* Cambridge, MA: Harvard University Press, 1995.

———. "Sexology, Style, and the Poet's Body." In *Cultures of Modernism: Marianne Moore, Mina Loy, and Else Lasker-Schüler.* Ann Arbor: University of Michigan Press, 2005.

Miller, Perry. *The New England Mind in the Seventeenth Century.* Cambridge, MA: Harvard University Press, 1939.

Milton, John. *John Milton: Complete Poems and Major Prose.* Edited by Merritt Y. Hughes. New York: Macmillan, 1985.

Mirollo, James V. *Mannerism and Renaissance Poetry: Concept, Mode, Inner Design.* New Haven, CT: Yale University Press, 1984.

Molesworth, Charles. *Marianne Moore: A Literary Life.* New York: Atheneum, 1990.

Monroe, Harriet. "A Symposium on Marianne Moore." *Poetry* 19, no. 4 (January 1922): 208–16.

Moore, Marianne. *Becoming Marianne Moore: The Early Poems, 1907–1924.* Edited by Robin G. Schulze. Berkeley and Los Angeles: University of California Press, 2002.

———. *The Collected Poems of Marianne Moore.* New York: Macmillan, 1951.

———. "Coming About." Unfinished, unpublished memoir. Moore Family Collection, West Hartford, CT.

———. The *Complete Poems of Marianne Moore.* New York: Macmillan/Viking Penguin, 1967. Revised edition, New York: Macmillan/Viking, 1981. Page references are to the revised edition.

———. *The Complete Prose of Marianne Moore.* Edited and with an introduction by Patricia Willis. New York: Viking Penguin, 1986; issued in paperback by Penguin, 1987.

———. Moore Family Collection. West Hartford, CT.

———. Marianne Moore Collection. Rosenbach Museum & Library, Philadelphia, PA.

———. *Observations.* New York: Dial Press, 1924.

———. *The Pangolin and Other Verse.* London: The Brendin Publishing Co., 1936.

————. *Poems.* London: The Egoist Press, 1921.

————. *The Poems of Marianne Moore.* Edited by Grace Schulman. New York: Viking, 2003.

————. *The Selected Letters of Marianne Moore.* Edited by Bonnie Costello, Celeste Goodridge, and Cristanne Miller. New York: Knopf, 1997.

————. *Selected Poems.* Introduction by T. S. Eliot. London: Faber and Faber, 1935.

Morris, Timothy. *Becoming Canonical in American Poetry.* Urbana: University of Illinois Press, 1995.

Muir, John. *Our National Parks.* Boston: Houghton Mifflin, 1901.

————. "The Wild Parks and Forest Reservations of the West." *Atlantic Monthly* 81 (January 1898): 15–28.

Nash, Roderick. *Wilderness and the American Mind,* 3rd ed. New Haven, CT: Yale University Press, 1982.

New, Elisa. *The Line's Eye: Poetic Experience, American Sight.* Cambridge, MA: Harvard University Press, 1999.

New York Center for Visual History. *Marianne Moore: In Her Own Image.* Voices & Visions Television Series, Program 8. Directed by Jeffrey Schon. Santa Barbara, CA: Intellimation [distributor], 1988. Video recording.

Ó'hÓgáin, Dáithí. "*An é an t-am fós é?*" *Béaloideas* vol. 42–44 (1974–76): 213–308.

Ostriker, Alicia. *Dancing at the Devil's Party: Essays on Poetry, Politics, and the Erotic.* Ann Arbor, MI: University of Michigan Press, 2000.

————. *Stealing the Language: The Emergence of Women's Poetry in America.* Boston: Beacon Press, 1986.

Parisi, Joseph, ed. *Marianne Moore: The Art of a Modernist.* Ann Arbor: UMI Research Press, 1990.

Parker, David. Introduction to *Renegotiating Ethics in Literature, Philosophy, and Theory.* Edited by Jane Adamson, Richard Freadman, and David Parker, 1–20. Cambridge: Cambridge University Press, 1998.

Paul, Catherine. *Poetry in the Museums of Modernism: Yeats, Pound, Moore, Stein.* Ann Arbor: University of Michigan Press, 2002.

Phelps, William Lyon. *Robert Browning: How to Know Him.* Indianapolis, IN: Bobbs-Merrill Company, 1915.

Pinsky, Robert. "Compiled by Robert Pinsky." http://www.alumni.rutgers.edu/attack/poems/ (accessed July 10, 2004).

————. "Poetic Response: Robert Pinsky Responds to the Tragedy Through Poetry." *A NewsHour with Jim Lehrer Transcript,* Online NewsHour, PBS, September 18, 2001. http://www.pbs.org/newshour/bb/terrorism/july-dec01/poem_9–18.html (accessed July 10, 2004).

Poirier, Richard. *Trying It Out in America: Literary and Other Performances.* New York: Farrar, Straus and Giroux, 1999.

Pound, Ezra. "Others." *Little Review* 4 (March 1918): 56–58.

————. *Selected Prose, 1909–1965.* New York: New Directions Press, 1973.

Pycraft, W. P. "The World of Science: Good News for the Gourmet." *Illustrated London News,* June 28, 1924, 1218.

Rich, Adrienne. "When We Dead Awaken: Writing as Re-Vision." In *On Lies, Secrets, and Silence: Selected Prose 1966–78,* 33–49. New York: Norton, 1979.

Rosenberg, Rosalind. *Beyond Separate Spheres: Intellectual Roots of Modern Feminism.* New Haven, CT: Yale University Press, 1982.

Rotella, Guy L. *Reading and Writing Nature: The Poetry of Robert Frost, Wallace Stevens, Marianne Moore, and Elizabeth Bishop.* Boston: Northeastern University Press, 1997.

Rothenberg, Jerome, ed. *Revolution of the Word: A New Gathering of American Avant Garde Poetry, 1914–1945.* New York: Seabury Press, 1974.

Rubin, Joan Shelley. *The Making of Middlebrow Culture.* Chapel Hill: University of North Carolina Press, 1992.

Runte, Alfred. *National Parks: The American Experience.* 2nd ed. Lincoln: University of Nebraska Press, 1987.

Ruskin, John. *The Works of John Ruskin.* Edited by E. T. Cook and Alexander Wedderburn. 39 vols. London: George Allen, 1903–12.

Russet, Cynthia E. *Sexual Science: The Victorian Construction of Womanhood.* Cambridge, MA: Harvard University Press, 1989.

Sargeant, Winthrop. "Profiles: Humility, Concentration, and Gusto." *New Yorker,* February 16, 1957, 38–77.

Scholes, Robert. "Exploring the Great Divide: High and Low, Left and Right." *Narrative* 11, no. 3 (October 2003): 245–69.

Schulman, Grace. *Marianne Moore: The Poetry of Engagement.* Urbana: University of Illinois Press, 1986.

———. "Marianne Moore: The Poetry of Engagement." Ph.D. diss., New York University, 1971.

Schultz, Susan. "Gertrude Stein's Self-Advertisement." *Raritan* 12, no. 2 (Fall 1992): 71–87.

Schulze, Robin G. "Marianne Moore's 'Imperious Ox, Imperial Peach' and the Poetry of the Natural World." *Twentieth Century Literature* 44, no. 1 (Spring 1998): 1–33.

———. *The Web of Friendship: Marianne Moore and Wallace Stevens.* Ann Arbor: University of Michigan Press, 1995.

Sekiguchi, Chiaki. "In Touch with the World: Marianne Moore, Objects, Fantasy, and Fashion." Ph.D. diss., State University of New York at Buffalo, 2003.

Shearman, John. *Mannerism.* Harmondsworth, UK: Penguin Books, 1964.

Shelley, Percy Bysshe. *Shelley's Poetry and Prose: Authoritative Texts, Criticism.* Edited by Neil Fraistat and Donald H. Reiman. New York: Norton, 2002.

Shoemaker, Mary Craig. *Five Typical Scotch-Irish Families of the Cumberland Valley.* Albany, New York, 1922.

Siebers, Tobin. *The Ethics of Criticism.* Ithaca, NY: Cornell University Press, 1988.

Sielke, Sabine. *Fashioning the Female Subject: The Intertextual Networking of Dickinson, Moore, and Rich.* Ann Arbor: University of Michigan Press, 1997.

Slatin, John M. *The Savage's Romance: The Poetry of Marianne Moore.* University Park: Pennsylvania State University Press, 1986.

Smith, George A. *The Book of the Twelve Prophets Commonly Called the Minor* 2 vols. New York: Doubleday, Doran & Company, 1896.

———. *Modern Criticism and the Preaching of the Old Testament.* London: Hoder and Stoughton, 1901.

Smith-Rosenberg, Carroll. *Disorderly Conduct: Visions of Gender in Victorian America.* Oxford: Oxford University Press, 1986.

Snow, Wilbert. "A Literalist of the Imagination." *New York Herald Tribune,* May 17, 1925, 3.

Sollors, Werner. *Beyond Ethnicity: Consent and Descent in American Culture,* New York: Oxford University Press, 1986.

Sontag, Susan. "Notes on Camp." In *Camp: Queer Aesthetics and the Performing Subject: A Reader,* edited by Fabio Cleto, 57–58. Ann Arbor: University of Michigan Press, 1999.

———. *On Photography.* New York: Farrar, Straus and Giroux, 1977.

Spenser, Edmund. *A View to the Present State of Ireland.* 1596. Edited by W. L. Renwick. London: Eric Partridge, 1934.

Spivak, Gayatri. *A Critique of Postcolonial Reason: Toward a Vanishing Present.* Cambridge, MA: Harvard University Press, 1999.

Stallybrass, Peter, and Ann Rosalind Jones. "Dismantling Irena: The Sexualizing of Ireland in Early Modern England." In *Nationalisms and Sexualities,* edited by Andrew Parker et al. New York: Routledge, 1992.

———. "Fetishizing the Glove in Renaissance Europe." *Critical Inquiry* 28, no. 1 (Autumn 2001): 114–32.

———. *Renaissance Clothing and the Materials of Memory.* Cambridge: Cambridge University Press, 2000.

Stamy, Cynthia. *Marianne Moore and China: Orientalism and a Writing of America.* Oxford: Oxford University Press, 2000.

Stapleton, Laurence. *Marianne Moore: The Poet's Advance.* Princeton, NJ: Princeton University Press, 1978.

Stein, Gertrude. "Composition as Explanation." 1926. Reprinted in *Gertrude Stein: Writings 1903–1932,* edited by Catharine R. Stimpson and Harriet Chessman, 520–29. New York: Library of America, 1998. Page references are to the reprint edition.

———. *Four in America.* New Haven, CT: Yale University Press, 1947.

———. *How to Write.* Paris: Plains Editions, 1931. Reprinted with preface and notes by Patricia Meyerowitz. Toronto, Canada: Dover, 1975. Page references are to the 1975 edition.

———. *The Geographical History of America or the Relation of Human Nature to the Human Mind.* New York: Random House, 1936. Reprinted with an introduction by William H. Gass. Baltimore: Johns Hopkins University Press, 1995. Page references are to the 1995 edition.

———. *Lectures in America.* Boston: Beacon Press, 1957.

———. *Stanzas In Meditation.* In *The Yale Edition of the Unpublished Writings of Gertrude Stein,* edited by Carl Van Vechten, 1–152. New Haven, CT: Yale University Press, 1956. Reprinted, Freeport, NY: Books for Libraries Press, 1969. Page references are to the 1969 edition.

———. *Tender Buttons: Objects, Food, Rooms.* New York: Claire Mary, 1914. Reprinted, Los Angeles: Sun and Moon Press, 1990. Page references are to the 1990 edition.

Steinman, Lisa M. *Made in America: Science, Technology, and American Modernist Poets.* New Haven, CT: Yale University Press, 1987.

Stevens, Wallace. "A Poet That Matters." Review of *Selected Poems* by Marianne Moore. In *Opus Posthumous.* Rev. ed. Edited by Milton J. Bates, 217–22. New York: Knopf, 1989.

———. *The Collected Poems of Wallace Stevens.* New York: Knopf, 1954.

———. *Collected Poetry and Prose.* New York: Library of America, 1997.

Tambimuttu, ed. *Festschrift for Marianne Moore's Seventy Seventh Birthday.* New York: Tambimuttu and Mass, 1964.

Tomlinson, Charles, ed. *Marianne Moore: A Collection of Critical Essays.* Englewood Cliffs, NJ: Prentice-Hall, 1969.

Vaisse, Pierre. "Portrait of Society: The Anonymous and the Famous." In *A New History of Photography,* edited by Michel Frizot. Translated by Helen Atkins, Susan Bennett, Liz Clegg, John Crook, and Caroline Higgitt, 495–513. Köln, Germany: Konemann, 1998.

Villa, José Garcia, ed. *Marianne Moore Issue.* Special issue, *Quarterly Review of Literature* 4, no. 2 (1948).

Vincent, John Emil. *Queer Lyrics: Difficulty and Closure in American Poetry.* New York: Palgrave, 2002.

Warner, John Riddle. *Sermons of the Rev. John R. Warner, D.D., with a Sketch of his Life.* Edited by Mary Warner Moore. Philadelphia: J. B. Lippincott, 1895.

Watson, Hildegarde. *The Edge of the Woods: A Memoir.* Rochester, NY: 1979.

Wheeler, Lesley. *The Poetics of Enclosure: American Women Poets from Dickinson to Dove.* Knoxville: University of Tennessee Press, 2002.

White, Heather Cass. "Morals, Manners and 'Marriage': Marianne Moore's Art of Conversation." *Twentieth-Century Literature* 45, no. 4 (1999): 488–510.

Wilcox, W. D. *Rockies of Canada.* New York: Putnam's, 1901.

Williams, Talcott. "The Kindergarten Movement." *Century Magazine,* January 1893, 69–79.

Williams, William Carlos. *The Autobiography of William Carlos Williams.* New York: Random House, 1957.

———. "Marianne Moore (1925)." In *Marianne Moore: A Collection of Critical Essays,* edited by Charles Tomlinson, 52–59. Englewood Cliffs, NJ: Prentice-Hall, 1969.

———. "Spring and All." In *Imaginations: William Carlos Williams,* edited by Webster Schott. New York: New Directions, 1970.

Willis, Patricia C. "Images of Marianne." *Marianne Moore Newsletter* 3 (1979): 20–24.

———, ed. *Marianne Moore Newsletter* 1–7 (1977–1983).

———. *Marianne Moore: Vision into Verse.* Philadelphia: The Rosenbach Museum and Library, 1987.

———, ed. *Marianne Moore: Woman and Poet.* Orono, ME: National Poetry Foundation, 1990.

———. "The Notes to 'Spenser's Ireland.'" *Marianne Moore Newsletter* 4, no. 2 (1980): 2–9.

———. "The Road to Paradise: First Notes on Marianne Moore's 'An Octopus.'" *Twentieth-Century Literature* 30, nos. 2–3 (Autumn 1984): 242–66.

Woolf, Virginia. "Middlebrow." In *The Death of the Moth and Other Essays,* 177–80. San Diego, CA: Harcourt Brace Jovanovich, 1970.

Worster, Donald. *Nature's Economy: A History of Ecological Ideas.* San Francisco: Sierra Club Books, 1977. Reprinted Cambridge: Cambridge University Press, 1985. Page references are to the 1985 edition.

Yeats, W. B. *The Autobiography of William Butler Yeats, Consisting of Reveries Over Childhood and Youth, The Trembling of the Veil, and Dramatis Personae.* Garden City, NY: Doubleday & Company, 1958.

Young, Robert J. C. *Colonial Desire: Hybridity in Theory, Culture, and Race.* New York: Routledge, 1995.

Zona, Kirstin Hotelling. *Marianne Moore, Elizabeth Bishop, and May Swenson: The Feminist Poetics of Self-Restraint.* Ann Arbor: University of Michigan Press, 2002.

Notes on Contributors

CHARLES BERGER is Professor of English at Southern Illinois University. He is the author of *Forms of Farewell: The Late Poetry of Wallace Stevens*, and has written essays and reviews on modern and contemporary American poetry. His current project, *Advancing Modernism: The Progressive Poetry of Modernity*, has chapters on Stevens, Moore, Crane, Auden, and Bishop. He also plans a book on John Ashbery and James Merrill. He has been the recipient of a Guggenheim Fellowship.

BENJAMIN FRIEDLANDER is Assistant Professor of English at the University of Maine. His books include *Simulcast: Four Experiments in Criticism* (2004) and *A Knot Is Not a Tangle* (2000), a collection of poems. He is also the coeditor of *The Collected Prose of Charles Olson* (1997).

FIONA GREEN is a lecturer in the Faculty of English, University of Cambridge and a Fellow of Jesus College.

ELIZABETH GREGORY is Associate Professor of English and Director of the Women's Studies Program at the University of Houston. She is the author of *Quotation and Modern American Poetry: "'Imaginary Gardens with Real Toads'"* and editor of *The Critical Response to Marianne Moore*. She is currently at work on a book on confessional poetry and another on the trend to "late-onset motherhood" (first child at or after age 35, by birth or adoption) and its effects on individuals, families, and society.

JEANNE HEUVING is the author of *Omissions Are Not Accidents: Gender in the Art of Marianne Moore* and multiple articles on twentieth-century innovative poetry and avant-garde texts. She recently published the experimental, cross genre work, *Incapacity*, and is working on a book-length critical manuscript, *The Transmutation of Love in Twentieth Century Poetry*. She is a recipient of grants from the National Endowment for the Humanities, Fulbright Foundation, Simpson Center for the Humanities, and Beinecke Library. She is on the faculty of the University of Washington, Bothell and on the graduate faculty of the University of Washington, Seattle.

CYNTHIA HOGUE has published five collections of poetry, most recently *Flux* and *The Incognito Body*, and has coedited the anthology, *We Who Love To Be Astonished: Experimental Women's Writing and Performance Poetics*. For her work, she has been awarded National Endowment for the Arts, National Endowment for the Humanities (Summer Seminar), and Fulbright Fellowships. She is the Maxine and Jonathan Marshall Chair in Modern and Contemporary Poetry in the Department of English at Arizona State University.

STACY CARSON HUBBARD is Associate Professor of English and Adjunct Associate Professor of Comparative Literature at SUNY at Buffalo, where she teaches courses in nineteenth- and twentieth-century American literature, women's writing, visual culture, and poetry and poetics. She has published essays on Thomas De Quincey, Gwendolyn Brooks, Edna St. Vincent Millay, Marianne Moore, Marilynne Robinson, and Jane Addams and Frank Lloyd Wright, and is a recipient of the Florence Howe Award for Feminist Criticism from the Women's Caucus of the Modern Language Association. She is currently at work on a study of feminism and the Emersonian tradition in America.

LINDA LEAVELL, Associate Professor of English at Oklahoma State University, is the author of *Marianne Moore and the Visual Arts: Prismatic Color* (1995), which won the South Central Modern Language Association Book Prize. She has received fellowships from the American Philosophical Society and the National Endowment for the Humanities to support work on her current project, a biography of Marianne Moore.

JOANIE MACKOWSKI'S *The Zoo* (2002) was awarded the Associated Writing Program's Poetry Prize for 2000, and the book was subsequently selected for the Kate Tufts Discovery Prize in 2003. Mackowski has received fellowships from the Wallace Stegner Program at Stanford University and the Rona Jaffe Foundation. She has studied at Wesleyan University, the University of Washington, and at the University of Missouri-Columbia, where she received her doctorate in English. She is currently Assistant Professor at the University of Cincinnati.

JEREDITH MERRIN, author of two collections of poetry—*Shift* (1996) and *Bat Ode* (2001)—published a book of criticism, *An Enabling Humility: Marianne Moore, Elizabeth Bishop and the Uses of Tradition* (1990). Her essays and reviews on Moore, Bishop, Randall Jarrell, Billy Collins, John Clare and others have appeared in the *Southern Review* and elsewhere, and her poems may be found in the *Hudson Review, Ploughshares*, the Paris Review, *Slate*, the *Southern Review*, the *Yale Review*, and many other journals.

Two books are in the offing: a new poetry collection, *Mon Age*; and a collection of essays, *Of Two Minds*.

CRISTANNE MILLER is W. M. Keck Distinguished Service Professor at Pomona College. On Moore, she has published *Marianne Moore: Questions of Authority* (1995), *The Selected Letters of Marianne Moore* (coedited with Bonnie Costello and Celeste Goodridge, 1997), and *Cultures of Modernism: Marianne Moore, Mina Loy, and Else Lasker-Schüler. Gender and Literary Community in New York and Berlin* (2005). Other published work includes *Emily Dickinson: A Poet's Grammar* (1987), *Feminist Measures: Soundings in Poetry and Theory* (coedited with Lynn Keller, 1994), and *Words for the Hour: A New Anthology of American Civil War Poetry* (coedited with Faith Barrett, 2005).

LAURA O'CONNOR is an assistant professor at the University of California, Irvine, where she teaches poetry, Irish literature and culture, and Anglophone literature. She is the author of *Haunted English: the Celtic Fringe, the British Empire, and de-Anglicization*, which is forthcoming. Her current book project, "Minority Voice," reads Gaelic poet Nuala Ní Dhomhnaill's work in relation to a constellation of contemporary Irish poets writing in English and Gaelic, with an emphasis on her poet-translators.

GRACE SCHULMAN'S latest poetry collections are *The Paintings of Our Lives* (2001) and *Days of Wonder: New and Selected Poems* (2002). Recent awards include a Guggenheim Fellowship for the writing of poems (2004-05); the Aiken Taylor Award for Poetry (2002); and the Distinguished Alumna Award, New York University (2003). She is editor of *The Poems of Marianne Moore* (Viking 2003) and Distinguished Professor of English, Baruch College, CUNY.

ROBIN G. SCHULZE is a Professor of English at Penn State University. She is the author of *Marianne Moore and Wallace Stevens: The Web of Friendship* (1995) and editor of *Becoming Marianne Moore: The Early Poems 1907-1924* (2002). She has published articles on modernist poetry, textual studies and editorial theory, and literature and nature.

LISA M. STEINMAN, whose fifth volume of poetry is *Carslaw's Sequences* (2003) teaches at Reed College and coedits the poetry magazine, *Hubbub*. She has received National Endowment for the Arts and Rockefeller fellowships and has also published two books about poetry (*Made in America* and *Masters of Repetition*). Her poems have been published in the *Massachusetts Review, Prairie Schooner, Notre Dame Review*, the *Women's Review of Books*, and elsewhere.

HEATHER CASS WHITE is an assistant professor of English at the University of Alabama. She has published essays on Gertrude Stein, Marianne Moore, Lorine Niedecker, and Elizabeth Bishop. She is currently working on a book about lyric address in twentieth-century American poetry.

PATRICIA C. WILLIS is the Elizabeth Wakeman Dwight Curator of American Literature at the Beinecke Library, Yale University. She discovered the newly arrived Moore archive at the Rosenbach Museum and Library in Philadelphia while looking for a dissertation topic and later served as its curator for twelve years. Her publications include *Marianne Moore and the Pipes of Pan: Mt. Rainier and Mt. Olympus* and editions of *The Complete Prose of Marianne Moore* (1986) and *Marianne Moore: Woman and Poet* (1990).

ELIZABETH WILSON is with the Department of English at the University of Auckland, New Zealand, where she teaches twentieth-century and contemporary literature, poetics, American poetry, and Modernism. Her current research focuses on Marianne Moore.

Index